'Eminently readable and thoroughly engaging, [...] useful guide for anyone interested in exploring how and why stories presented on the musical stage affect us so strongly.' — *William Everett, Professor of Musicology, University of Missouri-Kansas City, USA.*

'A refreshing new approach to the study of musical theatre that demystifies and clarifies the genre.' — *Tim Stephenson, Senior Lecturer, University of Leeds, UK.*

The ideal accompaniment to any study of musical theatre, this lively textbook provides a comprehensive overview of the history, theory and practice of this popular theatre form. Bringing critical theory and musical theatre together, Millie Taylor and Dominic Symonds explore the musical stage from a broad range of theoretical perspectives, including narrative theory, orientalism, gender theory and globalization.

Focusing on opera as well as musical theatre, *Studying Musical Theatre* considers dozens of diverse shows from 1607 to the present day. From Monteverdi to *Mamma Mia*, and from *HMS Pinafore* to *Hedwig*, this book offers an accessible and up-to-date guide to musical theatre for students, aficionados and enthusiasts alike.

Millie Taylor is Professor of Musical Theatre at the University of Winchester, UK. She is author of *Musical Theatre, Realism and Entertainment*, among other titles.

Dominic Symonds is Reader in Drama at the University of Lincoln, UK. He is co-editor of the *Studies in Musical Theatre* journal, and author of the forthcoming *We'll Have Manhattan: The Early Work of Rodgers and Hart*, among other titles.

Studying Musical Theatre

Theory and Practice

Millie Taylor
and
Dominic Symonds

 macmillan education · palgrave

First published 2014 by
PALGRAVE

Palgrave in the UK is an imprint of Macmillan Publishers Limited, registered in England, company number 785998, 4 Crinan Street, London N1 9XW

Palgrave Macmillan in the US is a division of St Martin's Press LLC, 175 Fifth Avenue, New York, NY 10010.

Palgrave is the global imprint of the above companies and is represented throughout the world.

Palgrave® and Macmillan® are registered trademarks in the United States, the United Kingdom, Europe and other countries

ISBN: 978–1–137–27095–5 hardback
ISBN: 978–1–137–27094–8 paperback

This book is printed on paper suitable for recycling and made from fully managed and sustained forest sources. Logging, pulping and manufacturing processes are expected to conform to the environmental regulations of the country of origin.

A catalogue record for this book is available from the British Library.

Library of Congress Cataloging-in-Publication Data
Taylor, Millie, author.
    Studying musical theatre : theory and practice / Millie Taylor and Dominic Symonds.
        pages cm
    ISBN 978–1–137–27094–8 (paperback)
    1. Musicals – History and criticism. 2. Musical theater – History. I. Symonds, Dominic, author. II. Title.
ML2054.T393 2014
792.609—dc23   2014030377

Printed in China

Contents

PART IV   Rethinking Relationships

List of Illustrations

Acknowledgements

We are grateful to Jenni Burnell, Felicity Noble and Lucinda Knight at Palgrave Macmillan, whose steady support in putting together this manuscript has been invaluable. We would also like to thank Charlie Smith and Rosalyn Casbard, whose help in sourcing images and permissions has been unceasing. We are also grateful to the anonymous reviewers of our manuscript, whose enthusiasm and encouragement was complemented by generous advice and very useful suggestions. Without the support of our institutions, it would have been far more difficult to find the time and resources to write this book. The University of Winchester generously funded a period of leave for early work on the research for the book, and colleagues and students at the Universities of Winchester, Portsmouth and Lincoln have offered support, insight and feedback on the material in various chapters. Likewise, our colleagues internationally have been a continuing source of inspiration and support, not least delegates at several Song, Stage and Screen conferences, participants of music theatre working group sessions with the International Federation for Theatre Research and members of the US-based Musical Theatre Forum and the UK-based British Musical Theatre Research Institute. But perhaps our biggest thanks goes to several cohorts of undergraduates with whom we have shared seminars. All of this material has been road-tested on students, whose own passion for musical theatre has been inspirational and whose intelligent insights have informed our work enormously.

Introduction

It can be difficult to know where to start exploring musical theatre. 'Start at the very beginning', someone once said – very sensibly, no doubt. But Maria didn't really give any of us a proper handbook for getting to grips with the wonderful world of the musical. She sang at us a lot – thrilling us with infectious energy and charming us with her voice; and she taught us that you can banish the demons of the world just by coming together as a community, joining together in song and thinking of a few of your favourite things. But even though we might want to believe that musical theatre can banish demons – dealing with serious issues like 'proper' drama; gaining respect in society like literature, classical music or ballet – that's really all fantasy, isn't it? Musicals are flossy and flimsy; wonderful but lightweight. They don't really *matter*, we are told; and if we show more than a passing interest we become *one of them* – a character from *Glee* who must be a misfit or an emotional wreck or who must keep to himself/ herself the fact that he/she likes musicals. Yet when no one is watching we still sing those songs out loud, diving into that fantasy world just for a moment, until the fear that we might get caught makes us stop being Little Orphan Annie or Tracy Turnblad, or the sweet transvestite Frank 'n' Furter in front of the mirror.

Perhaps starting with our favourite things is the right idea – shows we have grown up with, been involved in, or seen on life-changing trips to the big city. Perhaps learning how to talk about them intelligently, know-ledgeably and critically is a way to make them less flimsy, a way to make them matter.

If this nervousness about musical theatre makes our involvement with it rather self-conscious, that's a trope that is familiar from the shows them-selves. Like *Glee,* many of the stories of musical theatre are reflexive (they tell stories about musical theatre itself) or contain diegetic songs or dances (songs or dances that are performances within the story of the show). *Show Boat* (1927) contains scenes from shows on the boat; the leading ladies in *Chicago* (1975) are both performers imprisoned for murder; *Kiss Me, Kate* (1948) concerns the onstage and backstage antics of a company performing *The Taming of the Shrew*; and *The Producers* (2001) focuses on the economic difficulties experienced by mounting a supposed sure-fire flop on Broadway.

Throughout its history musical theatre's stories have created plausible opportunities for performers to sing and dance. In the long-running hit *A Chorus Line* (1975), Cassie tells us of her passion for the musical. The show is a real-time audition to sing and dance in the chorus of a new Broadway musical. 'All I ever needed was the music and the mirror and the chance to dance for you,' she sings, giving voice to the dream to which many of us may aspire.

But it's not just on stage that characters sing and dance; one of the most important features of musical theatre is that characters also sing and dance *away from* the stage – expressing emotions, narrating events, discussing, debating and deliberating life's enigmas. Like those deliberations, musical theatre questions and explores the dynamics of our lives – and it does this in song and dance, excessive expressive gestures of the body and voice that excite, stimulate and beguile us. Studying the narratives or plots of musical theatre is not sufficient to understand the form. We also need to know when and where characters sing and dance, why they do so, and how singing and dancing contributes to the performance.

These considerations, about the very dynamics that make up the aesthetic (or rather, aesthetics) of the musical stage, bring complexities to our study but deeply enrich our relationship with the musical. Why, for example, do the violent gang members of *West Side Story* (1957) dance with such unexpected grace? Why is Fantine's dream expressed in the music of a 1980s power ballad rather than a mid-nineteenth-century street song? Is it really plausible that the lifelong gambler and cool cat Sky in *Guys and Dolls* (1950) should end up banging a drum for the Salvation Army, all because of love?

These questions cause us to reflect about the musical more seriously. In its wonderfully evocative worlds, its enchanting music and its dynamic physicality, it excites all sorts of passions within us. But those worlds have relationships with the real world, and like all art, the reflection of the real world that is revealed in 'the music and the mirror and the chance to dance' can teach us a great deal about our relationships, our attitudes and our ideologies in real life. As such it is fascinating to consider the assumptions that are expressed in the stories of musical theatre – the fact that every boy falls in love with a girl and in the end gets wed; or the fact that any wannabe performer can find his/her way to fame and fortune. What about those that don't fulfil their dreams? What about boys that don't fall in love with girls? What about audiences that don't see their real world reflected on stage? What about communities that aren't represented at all?

Since musical theatre is a commercial form that is extremely popular, the reach of its ideologies is also large, but perhaps the way audiences respond to musical theatre varies from time to time and place to place. How can we begin to account for how audiences might understand or read a work – or the performance of a work? How is the audience affected by singing and dancing? Is that affect the result of the story being told, or the character doing the singing and dancing, or simply a physiological response to the song and dance? The complexity of musical theatre's combination of elements (singing, dancing, acting, orchestration, design, production, global marketing) requires that students focus on particular aspects separately and with considerable clarity. Is it the story that you're talking about? Or the song lyrics? The orchestration? Or the performance by a particular star? And what dramaturgies are revealed when all these elements come together, as ultimately in performance they must?

From this preamble it is clear that musical theatre is an enormously complex theatre form, and it can be very difficult to know how or where to begin to study it. Clearly, one part of that study must include an understanding of the significant developments of opera and musical theatre history. Some musical theatre histories begin by documenting the development of the commercial form of musical comedy on Broadway in the early twentieth century – the Princess Theatre shows in New York; the 'Girl' shows of George Edwardes in London; and the musical revues that thrived on both sides of the Atlantic. Others begin by identifying the genesis of the musical play with *Show Boat* in 1927. Still others identify a starting point by discussing the idea of 'integration' and *Oklahoma!* (1943). But there were influences on musical comedy from Europe, especially the work of Gilbert and Sullivan, Offenbach and Lehár and later the European-styled shows of the Americanized Rudolf Friml and Sigmund Romberg. In turn, their work developed in the context of European opera, which we can't ignore. So that takes us back about 400 years and covers a wide geographical area. What any study of musical theatre's histories reveals is that there is not a single linear development of musical theatre and opera across Europe and the United States that can tell the whole story of all the diverse lines of development and relationships that impact on musical theatre.

But what is the difference between musical theatre and opera, not to mention opera comique, opera buffa, opera seria and grand opera, music drama and dramma per musica, musical plays, music hall, vaudeville, variety and burlesque? Perhaps, rather than thinking about the differences between these forms and their terminology, or the ways they have influenced one another historically we might focus on their similarities. How might we articulate what is important about works of music theatre across the whole spectrum while developing effective strategies and tools for reading them?

While it is important to place works in their historical and geographical contexts, this book has a different strategy that complements and challenges the usual historical study of musical theatre. Rather than presenting a historical survey of works, significant developments and identification of differences, we discuss musical theatre by introducing a number of critical perspectives. This will enable you to conceptualize works of musical theatre and opera and their performance texts within an academic and theoretical framework. It will allow you to discover the similarities between different types of musical theatre works and to critique or analyse seemingly diverse performance texts.

In order to explode the canon of musical theatre and operatic texts that are usually kept in discrete boxes, we take examples from both popular and operatic Western forms from throughout the past 400 years. Within this very wide historical and geographical area, we focus predominantly on musical theatre as a twentieth- and early-twenty-first-century form most commonly represented by the commercial output of Broadway (New York) and the West End (London). Specific examples are drawn from works as diverse as *HMS Pinafore* (1878) and *Here Lies Love* (2013). These are set alongside examples from the operatic repertoire from Monteverdi's *L'Orfeo* (1607) to Orlando Gough and Stephen Plaice's community opera *Imago* (2013). This is not an inclusive strategy – we're not attempting to demonstrate continuity – it is a provocation to view diverse works through the prism of a particular theoretical perspective that casts them in new light and simultaneously gives you the tools or methods for analysing, understanding or critiquing other works.

Part I begins our story with a focus on the way we understand the musicals as texts. We introduce you to some widely used structural devices for thinking about the politics revealed in stories and the ways academics theorize audience understanding. Part II focuses on how musical theatre negotiates its position in the wider world both in its stories and in its production. Here we look at the global expansion of culture in the nineteenth and twentieth centuries and consider how contact with other cultures has influenced musical theatre, broadening its reach, but at times leading to exploitative or marginalizing dynamics in its production. Part III turns to individuals, recognizing the affiliation of various communities with the musical stage. We explore ways in which particular identities are constructed within the stories of musical theatre and notice how in various guises the musical has appealed to different ages, ethnicities, sexualities and genders. Finally, Part IV becomes more philosophical by discovering the web of relationships from which interpretations emerge. We consider features of performance such as the voice, and interesting relationships the musical has with time and space, intertextuality and entertainment.

Each chapter contains a discussion centred on a particular critical theory illustrated with case studies from musical theatre and opera. Suggestions for further reading at the end of each chapter offer ideas on how to broaden your exploration into the area. We hope you use the case studies to understand the theoretical concepts and then apply those concepts yourself to other musical theatre works. You might begin at the beginning of this book and work your way through – the chapters and the discussions they contain become increasingly complex as they progress – or you might use the book to dip into as a reminder of theoretical ideas or as a provocation to your understanding of a particular work. Just as there is no single way to understand musical theatre history and no simple way of analysing any musical theatre work, there are many ways to use this book. The most important thing for us is that your study of musical theatre is enhanced by the provocations we offer here and that you enjoy and appreciate the complexity of musical theatre and all that it can tell you about the world in which we live.

PART I
Reading Texts

I   'A Tale as Old as Time': Narrative Theory

'Once upon a time, in a faraway land, a young Prince lived in a shining castle. Although he had everything his heart desired, the Prince was spoiled, selfish and unkind.' So the fairytale *Beauty and the Beast* (1994) begins, as if conjured up on stage by those familiar words. It is, as Mrs. Potts later sings, a 'tale as old as time', and the framing device of the Narrator at the beginning of the show seems to reinforce that the story is somehow set apart from the world we inhabit and takes on the magical quality of a fairytale. In just two lines of narration, a whole host of narrative details are given: introducing a hero who is tragically flawed and destined to live his life as an ugly beast, until... Ah, but that would be telling!

Far away in another land, another narrative begins: 'Once upon a time...', barks the Narrator, at which point we cut directly into the scenario he is narrating; 'I wish!' sings Cinderella, expressing her greatest desire, 'More than anything!' Stephen Sondheim's *Into the Woods* (1986) introduces not just one but a handful of familiar fairytales, cleverly interwoven and overseen by the *all*-seeing eye of the Narrator.

The Narrator is not a character who appears very regularly in musical theatre: there is a Narrator in *Joseph* (1968) ('Way, way back, many centuries ago...') and another in *The Rocky Horror Show* (1973) ('I would like – if I may – to take you on a strange journey...'); there's a Leading Player in *Pippin* (1972) ('Join us! Come and waste an hour or two'); and characters called the Emcee in *Cabaret* (1966) and the Reciter in *Pacific Overtures* (1976) welcome us, respectively, into the worlds of the cabaret club in Berlin and the islands of Japan. In other shows there are named characters who provide the narration, positioning the narrative as their own point of view: it's through the eyes of Tevye in *Fiddler on the Roof* (1964), for example, that we see the world of Anatevka; and through the camera lens of Mark in *Rent* (1996) that we are introduced to Alphabet City. Elsewhere, the job is often left to the chorus – think of the many opening numbers in which the ensemble sets the scene: 'Morning in Paris, the city awakes to the bells of Notre Dame!' (*The Hunchback of Notre Dame*, 1996); 'One night in Bangkok and the world's your oyster' (*Chess*, 1986); 'New York, New York, it's a helluva town!' (*On the Town*, 1944). Whether or not an explicit *Narrator* is used, the idea of the *narrative* is fundamental and has been central to many art forms for thousands of years.

In their simplest forms, narratives tell stories about characters and events that happen to them, and they usually tell these stories in a logical way: *chrono*logically. This idea seems to make sense – after all, this is a familiar pattern in our own lives, which unfold chronologically, involve a central character and feature significant events from time to time. When we are relating an anecdote to friends about something that has happened to us, we construct a narrative, and we are often instinctively good at doing this. Even though this ability seems instinctive, the techniques we use are complex. For example, we don't detail every single moment of the story; we selectively identify significant points and shorten the tale considerably. We tell the story from a particular point of view – our point of view – which may differ from the perspective of someone else involved. We leave things out, to focus on the important elements or to avoid overwhelming our lis-tener with redundant information. And we exaggerate elements to give our story impact, drama or excitement. All of these techniques show our under-standing of how narratives work, a skill that seems innate but which has been learned through experience, trial and error and familiarity with how great stories have been told. Some people tell stories better than others, of course; they probably go on to be the storytellers.

This chapter explores how narratives are structured, considering ideas first expressed by the Greek philosopher Aristotle. We discuss some of the features of a story and the way it is told: what is being told, how it is being told, who is doing the telling and who is being told. We look at some classic narrative models and how they feature in musicals, and we also see how Aristotle's theories offer ways to understand the DNA of the narrative, and specifically the integrated narratives that have become conventional in musical theatre.

Narrative form

Aristotle was writing during the fourth century BC, a generation or two after a prodigious theatrical period featuring the plays of Aeschylus, Aristophanes, Sophocles and Euripides. He wrote about many things, but his collected thoughts about drama in the *Poetics* have provided some of his most influential ideas. Although it is thought that Aristotle also wrote a book about Comedy, it is his work on Tragedy that survives, offering a blueprint for subsequent dramatic writing and influencing the whole of

The integrated musical

The idea of 'integration' dominates historiographies of the musical, with Richard Rodgers and Oscar Hammerstein II credited as the most consistent writers of integrated shows. This type of musical tells a story using song and scene in a way that makes dramatic sense, with musical numbers appearing as apparently naturalistic extensions of spoken scenes. The first show they wrote together – the example cited most regularly as exemplifying integration – was *Oklahoma!* (1943). Many shows from the 1940s to the early 1960s – the period most associated with integration – form a 'canon' of classic work. Writing in 1967, Lehman Engel compiled a list of representative integrated musicals: *Pal Joey* (1940), *Oklahoma!* (1943), *Carousel* (1945), *Annie Get Your Gun* (1946), *Brigadoon* (1947), *Kiss Me, Kate* (1948), *South Pacific* (1949), *Guys and Dolls* (1950), *The King and I* (1951), *My Fair Lady* (1956) and *West Side Story* (1957). He subsequently added *Gypsy* (1959), *Fiddler on the Roof* (1964), *Company* (1970) and *A Little Night Music* (1973) to the list. Engel offers a basic blueprint for integrated structure, built around a 'trajectory of desire'. The protagonist expresses a need in an 'I Want' song near the beginning ('I'll know when my love comes along', sings Sarah in *Guys and Dolls*), and the rest of the show plays out the fulfilment of that need, through a series of obstacles (two different lifestyles that seem completely mismatched) which are eventually resolved (when the couple marries).

Oklahoma! (1943)

Music by Richard Rodgers
Book and lyrics by Oscar Hammerstein II

Adapted from Lynn Riggs's play *Green Grow the Lilacs* (1931)

Synopsis: Curly and Laurey are in love, though they won't admit it – he is a cowboy used to life on the open prairie, she is a farm-girl used to cultivating the land (Figure 1.1). They are clearly smitten with one another, though they lead each other on a flirtatious chase, feigning disinterest and playing with each other's emotions. Stakes are raised when the violent and dislikable farmhand Jud Fry takes Laurey to the ball (in this case, the 'box social') and makes a forceful attempt to win her picnic hamper in a tense auction scene, a sort of sparring match between him and Curly. Things don't go Jud's way, and he turns to violence to get his own back and win the girl. The audience is kept on tenterhooks until Curly at last kills Jud in a fight, and he and Laurey are able to get together.

Figure 1.1   Boy meets girl: Gordon Macrae and Shirley Jones in the 1955 film of *Oklahoma!*

Western literary practice. In brief, he suggests that Tragedy involves action, not merely narration (Book III); that there should be agents – or characters – who drive the action (Book VI); that Tragedy should have a beginning, a middle and an end (Book VII); and that the audience should be able to relate to it through its handling of universal themes (Book IX). Finally, through relating to the Tragedy, the audience should benefit from *catharsis*, the purging of the emotions (Book VI).

This basic narrative structure is relatively simple: a hero is introduced who is generally 'good' but who has a tragic flaw (the *hamartia*) that will be his undoing (Curly and Laurey in *Oklahoma!* are too proud to admit they love one another). Some event occurs (the *peripeteia*), a catalyst to which the character reacts, succumbing to the influence of the tragic flaw (Laurey allows herself to be taken to the box social by Jud, and Curly doesn't intervene). In a moment of revelation (*anagnorisis*), the protagonist realizes the true nature of the situation (Curly admits he loves Laurey and outbids Jud at the auction), and the ensuing events lead to a tragic ending in which everyone (in this case, just Jud) dies (the *catastrophe*). Thus there is a beginning, a middle and an end to the story, a sympathetic central character to whom we can relate and a storyline that shows us the consequence of human actions, causing us to reflect and experience a cathartic release. In this formula, Aristotle neatly explains why we engage with tragic theatre and establishes the principles of dramatic structure.

Aristotle's theories were certainly influential: most subsequent drama, at least until the twentieth century, embraced this framework. Of course, not all theatre is seen as tragic in *content* – and certainly it is unusual in twentieth-century theatre, particularly musical comedy, for all the characters to die. However, Aristotle's vision of drama through his writing on Tragedy is something that has contributed to the *form* of a great many dramatic narratives.

In musical theatre, Aristotle's basic structure has been accepted and moderated to fit the form. The narrative could be conceptualized as a sort of arc that is launched at the beginning of the story, develops through the action and resolves itself towards the end. Typically, this narrative articulates a 'Trajectory of Desire' – the protagonist voices his or her desire at the beginning, either overtly or implicitly in what is called the 'I Want' song: Dorothy in *The Wizard of Oz* (1939) desperately wants to find something and imagines 'Somewhere over the rainbow'; Tony in *West Side Story* (1957) senses something 'only just out of reach' in 'Something's Coming'; the five daughters of Tevye in *Fiddler on the Roof* (1964) imagine their lives improving once they find their soulmates ('Matchmaker'); while Ariel in *The Little Mermaid* (1989) dreams of a better life on land in 'Part of your world'. Each of these 'I Want' numbers establishes the main thrust of the storyline and prepares us to expect a resolution by the end of the show. *The Magic Flute* (1791) is another example: Tamino sees the picture of Pamina and falls in love with her in his 'I Want' song 'Das Bildnis ist bezaubernd schön' (This picture is enchantingly lovely); a trajectory of desire is launched and arcs through the complexities of finding her and bringing her back; finally, they conquer fire and water together and are married in the temple to the resolution number 'Heil sei euch geweihten' (To you who are blessed). Here the story ends 'happily ever after', though resolutions do not always bring whatever is desired – Dorothy and Ariel find that the grass is not any greener in the lands of their dreams; Tevye's daughters find that married life issues far more complex challenges than they had ever imagined; and Tony finds that his dreams lead only to violence, hatred and death. Nevertheless, these are all resolutions that somehow respond to the 'want' and answer it to bring their narratives to a close.

The eternal narrative: boy-meets-girl – *Oklahoma!*

In clichéd terms, the trajectory of desire is very often a boy-meets-girl, boy-loses-girl, boy-wins-girl-back storyline (*Brigadoon*, 1947; *Guys and Dolls*, 1950; *Avenue Q*, 2003), and musical theatre conventionally adheres to this formula or – in more recent examples – deliberately turns against it. The boy-meets-girl narrative trades on a simple but effective trajectory, and the audience's interest and excitement are sustained by the tension of the dramatic journey. We know the couple will end up together, which reassures us, but we also know that they will have to undergo certain tests before their love can be confirmed, which gives us the excitement and tension we expect from drama. Each of the shows we are discussing involves a plot of this sort – though they treat the boy-meets-girl narrative with varying degrees of sincerity (*The Magic Flute*) or tongue-in-cheek (*The Pirates of Penzance*). No better example represents the boy-meets-girl narrative than *Oklahoma!*.

As it happens – and this is a common feature of narratives of this sort – an additional narrative of boy-meets-girl offers a comic parallel to the main event: Will Parker and Ado Annie, who are well-suited, and who we know will finally be united, encounter their own obstacle in the character of Ali Hakim. This parallel storyline is more light-hearted than the Curly-Laurey-Jud drama and serves to lighten the audience's concern at darker points of the show. As expected, Will and Ado Annie, like Curly and Laurey, overcome their problems and are united by the end of the narrative. Our expectations are satisfied, and any tension in the trajectory of the musical is finally resolved.

You'll notice that this notion of integration doesn't yet feature the idea that songs form a part of the storyline, though of course musical theatre wouldn't be musical theatre without some use of song. In fact, the use of the word 'integration' points to the way in which song is 'integrated' into that dramatic narrative – the way that the narrative (the telling of the tale) uses the language of song at moments of emotional intensity to enhance and develop the drama and the characters. Indeed, music plays an integral part in the characterizations of Curly and Laurey, and frequently throughout their story the characters express themselves in song. Curly opens the musical with the pastoral 'Oh, What a Beautiful Mornin'', which Laurey picks up in her idle humming moments later: here music is used to show them 'speaking' the same language, revealing their compatibility and establishing them as viable partners. Before long, he woos Laurey with his tall tale of the wonderful 'Surrey with the Fringe on the Top' in which he will take her to the box social. This is their 'I Want' song, expressing their desires for each other not in explicit terms but through coy flirtation and a vision of what could be in their idyllic romance. The music cleverly defines the relationship of the couple, offering a romantic 'pretend-space' (a bit like a dream world) that sets the trajectory for the rest of the narrative (see Figure 1.1). Later, the song 'People Will Say We're in Love' expresses the tension between them, operating both as a love song and as a statement of rejection – what has been called a 'conditional love song' (Lahr,

2002, p. 155), a type of song Rodgers and Hammerstein used regularly to create complexities between characters (think of *Carousel*'s 'If I Loved You'). Here, despite the fact that the couple deny romantic feelings, it is clear that they are in love; they protest just to prevent themselves from getting hurt. In its most stylistic use of music, *Oklahoma!* introduces a celebrated 'dream ballet' just before the interval, in which the dramatic stakes are raised, restating the tension of the narrative in the theatrical languages of music and dance.

Morphologies and character types

In *Oklahoma!*, music – song, instrumental underscore, orchestrated ballet accompaniment – magnifies the dramatic narrative and offers nuance and texture to the clearly defined characters. This is one of the reasons *Oklahoma!* has been seen as the first real 'integrated' musical. But the music works only in relation to the dramatic structure of the narrative. We like things to be structured, and our understanding of the world is made clear through the building blocks of structure and form that create for us intelligible patterns (like cause and effect; or beginning, middle and end). Not surprisingly, our study of the fact that we do this has been called 'Structuralism', and this recognizes that we tend to perceive the world in rather simplistic, patterned ways. For example, we often think in opposites (or *binaries*), as song titles like 'Night and Day', 'Black or White' and 'When a Man Loves a Woman' reveal. Building on these, we often tend to impose assumptions of linearity and development on our reading of the world, telling histories about our progress from the primitive 'Dark Ages' to the more recent 'Enlightenment' ('The Sun Will Come Out Tomorrow'). Seeing the world in simple paradigms like this has been at the heart of our understanding, and following in Aristotle's footsteps (there's another example of structurizing expression: *following in the footsteps*), other thinkers have sought to identify, classify and detail the structures that guide our thoughts.

One type of structuralism was known as 'Formalism' – the study of the shape or form of a piece of work. This drew on the classical idea that 'natural' beauty (or rather, the beauty bestowed on us by the Gods as a reward for our duty) was in balance and proportion: the beautiful face has symmetry; the perfect body is in balance. In art we sought to replicate this sort of perfection by finding the most perfect forms in which to construct our compositions; and where that form could not be instantly perceived (as it often can be, e.g., in pottery, portraiture or architecture), scholars sought to unearth it from the complexities of the expressions that we make.

This was the project of one Russian Formalist named Vladimir Propp, who in 1907 analysed thousands of Russian folktales. He found that there was a surprising degree of consistency both in terms of the events that occurred and the characters who appeared in these tales. So he put together a *Morphology of the Folktale* detailing the formula to which they all subscribed; this included 31 stages to the narrative and 7 key character types who feature in most.

The quest narrative: *The Magic Flute*

In broad terms, it is fairly simple to identify these building blocks in a piece of musical theatre. In *The Magic Flute*, for instance, there are some obvious plot points:

- Tamino and the Queen of the Night meet;
- she sends him on a quest;
- he finds what he is seeking;
- he has to undergo certain challenges; and
- he succeeds and returns home.

This very basic outline of the story – a typical quest narrative – clearly leaves out nuances and details and doesn't touch on the trajectory of desire suggested earlier, which runs parallel to the quest; however, the bare bones of the story are present. Likewise, there are evident character types: a hero (Tamino), a heroine (Pamina), a villain (Queen of the Night), a parental figure (Sarastro) and a magical helper (the boys).

    The Magic Flute sets itself up as a quest narrative from the very beginning. In the opening aria, Tamino hurtles into the story fleeing a ravenous monster. 'Help me! Help me!' he cries. Immediately, this establishes him as an action hero in a dire situation. If it weren't for the sudden arrival of three beguiling ladies brandishing magical powers, Tamino's story would be short. But they slay the monster and leave Tamino unconscious; he is found by a local peasant, the bird-catcher Papageno.

    Straightaway the narrative is one of adventure, and the hero and his companion have been introduced – one princely and one lowly, a combination replicated in other quests as well (Frodo and Sam Gangee in *The Lord of the Rings*, Don Quixote and Sancho Panza in *Don Quixote*). The magical ladies return, and this time they bring a mission from the Queen of the Night: Tamino is to seek the kidnapped princess Pamina and bring her safely back from the clutches of the evil sorcerer Sarastro. Tamino – smitten

---

The Magic Flute (1791)

Music by Wolfgang Amadeus Mozart

Libretto by Emanuel Schikaneder

Mozart's final work reflects his desire to write an opera for the everyday people rather than for the court. This steps down from the style of Italian *opera seria*, and it not only speaks to its audience in their own language, German, but also introduces dialogue scenes between its arias, rather than the conventional recitative. It's the equivalent of an action movie – fast paced, accessible and exciting; and it continues to be popular over two centuries later.

Synopsis: Tamino, prince of a mythical land, is sent by the Queen of the Night to rescue her daughter Pamina, who has been kidnapped by the evil sorcerer Sarastro. Tamino and his companion Papageno set off, armed only with a magic flute, some magic bells and three small boys as guides. They soon find where Pamina is being kept, and Tamino falls in love with her. However, they discover that in fact Sarastro is not evil, and that they have been misled by the Queen of the Night, who is. In order to convince Sarastro that they have Pamina's best intentions at heart, Tamino and Papageno undergo a series of trials. First, they must go without speaking (which Papageno finds terribly hard); then, they must walk through fire and water to escape. Tamino plays his magic flute, and the music is so powerful that it allows them to pass through the flames and the water to safety. In the end, Papageno meets the girl of his dreams, so the romantic couple are balanced by the comedy couple Papageno and Papagena. The Queen of the Night is banished, and Tamino and Pamina end the opera together.

---

by his first glance at the princess's picture – agrees to embark on the quest, and to help in his journey he is given a series of magical aids: a magic flute, some magical bells for Papageno and the guidance of three small boys.

This is a classic quest, then, in which a goal is identified, a fellowship of companions is gathered and a dangerous journey is started. The action proceeds in turns, alternating between life-threatening dangers and points of reflection. In the course of the narrative, the hero falls in love with the damsel in distress, is torn between ambiguous forces of good and evil and must undergo a number of challenges before the quest is completed. Overcoming the forces of evil requires a little bit of magic, to be sure, but more importantly, it requires many of the moralistic virtues that condition Western thinking: honesty, integrity, goodness, courage and love.

The fact that this quest is located in a mythical world of magic and superstition is no surprise: such unfamiliar terrain is a substitute for the classic deep, dark forest (found in so many fairytale quests), or the underworld (found in many of the Greek narratives). Here the conventions of society are overshadowed by the supernatural, magic and confusion. In this in-between space – the liminal space of the journey – expectations are turned on their head, and for a time, order is threatened by chaos. Shakespeare excelled at this sort of narrative, moving many of his greatest plots into a wood outside the town (*A Midsummer Night's Dream*, *As You Like It*, *King Lear*). The musical stage has likewise explored this idea: one of the very first operas, Monteverdi's *L'Orfeo* (1607), recounted the quest of Orpheus to rescue his beloved Euridice from the clutches of Pluto in the underworld. Here, as elsewhere, the 'middle' of the beginning-middle-end narrative arc is a place of confusion and soul-searching, which is metaphorically represented by the characters' relocation to supernatural or unsettling places like forests or underground tunnels.

One of the wonderful features of musical theatre's engagement with the quest is that music plays a prominent role in enabling the drama to unfold. Orfeo is characterized by his extraordinary musical ability, and it is his song 'Possente spirto' (Powerful spirit) that beguiles the ferryman Charon and allows him to gain access to the underworld. In *The Magic Flute* it is the mesmerizing sounds of Tamino playing his flute that first beguile the animals of the forest (commanding nature, overcoming the unfettered power of the natural world) and then assist his passage through fire and water; Papageno too finds musical expression through his bells, which summon up his perfect partner, Papagena. Of course, the characters also sing – and it is their voices in song that express their most important characteristics: the panic of Tamino fleeing the monster in the opening ('Zu hilfe!' [Help!]); his wonder at the beauty of Pamina when he sees her portrait ('Das Bildnis ist bezaubernd schön' [This picture is enchantingly lovely]); her desperation when Tamino is wrested away ('Ach, ich fühl's, es ist verschwunden' [Ah, I feel it, it has gone]); the wrath of the Queen of the Night when she is found out ('Der Hölle Rache kocht in meinem Herzen' [Hell's vengeance boils in my heart]); and the steadfastness of Sarastro holding power over his empire ('In diesen heil'gen Hallen' [In these holy halls]). Interestingly, a significant amount of Papageno's language is given 'musical' expression, initially when he is 'muted' by the magical ladies, forced only to hum through the obstacle of a mouth-clamp; later when challenged not to speak as one of the trials of his quest; and finally, when he meets Papagena with whom he finds a common expression, the bird-like song of 'Pa pa pa'. As such, music is interwoven into the aesthetic of the quest narrative and comes to represent one of the virtues that accompanies the hero and 'conquers' the challenges of the quest.

The tale and the telling: the rags-to-riches narrative – *42nd Street*

42nd Street (Warner Bros., 1933)

Music by Harry Warren, lyrics by Al Dubin

Screenplay by Rian James and James Seymour

Directed by Lloyd Bacon with choreography by Busby Berkeley

Starring Ruby Keeler

Adapted from the novel *42nd Street* by Bradford Ropes

Hollywood had only recently developed the ability to record sound, but once perfected, it led to a boom in movie musicals in the 1930s – Fred Astaire and Ginger Rogers at RKO, the first cartoon musicals by Disney and the Busby Berkeley films at Warner Bros. *42nd Street* was adapted into a stage musical in the 1980s, though it is the film version that has achieved classic status. It is a quintessential example of a 'backstage musical', set in the world of the Broadway theatre, where song and dance are 'natural' ways for the characters to express themselves.

Synopsis: Young wannabe Peggy Sawyer comes to New York to seek fame and fortune on Broadway. She auditions with numerous other hopefuls, but her prospects seem hope*less* until she meets the show's juvenile lead, Billy Lawler. He befriends her, and when female lead Dorothy Brock sprains her ankle just before opening night, Peggy is given the chance to shine. Opening night comes, Peggy takes to the stage and wins over everybody with her wonderful performance. The film features three main musical numbers showcasing Berkeley's famous patterns of chorus girls and Keeler's impressive tap dancing: 'Shuffle Off to Buffalo', 'Young and Healthy' and '42nd Street'.

The mythical dimension of most quest narratives sites the action of the diegesis in a far-removed world that resonates with ours in terms of allegory. One of the ways we relate to such a narrative is in seeing parallels between the stages of the quest and the stages of our lives. Given this, it is not surprising that narratives play a prominent role in educating us, offering risk-free examples of trajectories that our own lives may take, and introducing us to codes, expectations and aspirations that will help us to face trials. To some extent all narratives work on this basis: some are more explicit in their pedagogical intentions; some offer us stark warnings about immoral or unethical behaviour; some give us inspirational models to guide us as we develop.

Diegesis and mimesis

The way we encounter stories varies depending on the form or medium in which they are presented. A book *tells* a story, recounting events in a report, whereas a piece of theatre *shows* us a story, representing (re-presenting) the fiction in front of our eyes. Two Greek words describing this difference are useful and are often used in discussions of Narrative Theory. For the Greeks, the term *mimesis* refers to the representation of the world, and from this root come familiar words like 'mime' and 'mimic' – the idea of presenting the story through *show*. The word *diegesis*, on the other hand, refers to *telling* the story, and it stems from a Greek word meaning 'to guide', or 'to lead'. A related word, which has become widely used in musical theatre, is borrowed from film studies. This word – *diegetic* – refers to the world shown in the film, but *literally* just that which is shown. Anything outside the boundaries of the frame is referred to as 'non-diegetic', or 'extra-diegetic'. The word 'diegetic' has found currency in musical theatre particularly because of the contribution of voices and instruments from outside the stage space; the pit orchestra, for example, contributes to the telling of the tale by providing atmospheric but non-diegetic music.

The rags-to-riches narrative is one such affirming example, showing us that even the lowliest can succeed, and is most obviously represented by the fairytale of Cinderella. But the story of Cinderella is just one example of this formula, reminding us that each narrative 'type' can be told in different ways, that there is a sort of 'ur-text' and then a wealth of discrete, specific tellings (for more on this, see Jones, 2004, pp. 57–61). This distinction forms a central part of narrative theory, which recognizes, on the one hand, the 'Histoire' (the original 'mythic' tale) and, on the other, the 'Discours' (the current telling of the story).

In musical theatre's rags-to-riches narratives (*42nd Street*, 1933; *Babes in Arms*, 1937; *A Chorus Line*, 1975; *Copacabana*, 1994) the root story is nearly always the same: a young protagonist comes to a big city, perhaps escaping impoverished life in the country, and stumbles into work in the uncertain and dangerous world of the stage. Here she is the lowliest of the low – a faceless chorus girl, maybe even just a wannabe auditioning for a show, as in *42nd Street*. She has hopes and dreams of finding love, happiness and success, though the world she is faced with gives the impression that these things are unreachable goals, impossible dreams. Once again, though, the audience anticipates that this heroine's dreams will come true, and in showing important virtues, the heroine wins over significant helpers

Figure 1.2   Ruby Keeler in *42nd Street* (1933): a narrative of success on the Great White Way

who already have a foot up the ladder. Together they tackle the impediments – often unsavoury people – and in a final turn of events, the heroine is plucked from obscurity to become the star, winning fame, fortune and love (see Figure 1.2). Once again, there are significant elements of the quest narrative here, key formulaic plot points and key character types.

42nd Street's story is a particularly poignant narrative for young audiences; the central character is often – and in this case – young and vulnerable, and the narrative therefore serves as a coming-of-age allegory. This allows a young audience to process the rite of passage into adulthood into a story that resonates with their anxieties (the daunting city; the hostile adult characters) and aspirations (ultimate success; fame, fortune and love). It also tracks onto a dominant ideological narrative in American society – the American Dream – which suggests that even 'the commonest citizen can rise by pluck, luck and talent into the aristocracy of success' (Lahr, 1996, p. 243).

It is easy to see how this idea maps onto the narratives of other shows even if they are not situated within the world of the theatre (*The Wizard of Oz*, 1939; *The Sound of Music*, 1959). By locating many of these narratives in the world of musical theatre, however, the staging of singing and dancing becomes fundamental to the plot. Moreover, the key nodes in the journey of the main protagonist – the important milestones – are very often situated at moments of performance (the audition; the rehearsal; the first night). Thus music and song are used to voice the character's emotional development from vulnerability through confidence to success. That 'success' is very often articulated in the most impressive virtuoso examples of song and dance in the show: in this case, the *only* musical numbers in the film, which are given the Busby Berkeley treatment culminating in the exhilarating finale, '42nd Street'. In this respect, song and dance serve a particular function in concluding the narratives of musical theatre, providing a climactic energy (a high) to what is dramatically a return to stability or normality (a low).

The *deus ex machina*: The Pirates of Penzance

The Pirates of Penzance (1879)

Music by Arthur Sullivan
Book and lyrics by William Schwenk Gilbert

Synopsis: The pirates of Penzance are a jolly lot with an apprentice, Frederic, who aged 21 is being released from his apprenticeship. He is put ashore, where he sets eyes on the plain Mabel. Having never seen a woman, he is smitten and pledges to marry her. However, since he is leaving the pirates, he warns them that he must now become an honourable citizen and therefore hunt down and catch any pirates he sees. The pirates in any case are not very successful, since as orphans, they sympathize with other orphans on the high seas; as everyone knows this, rival gangs always claim to be orphans and thereby escape from the clutches of the Penzance crew. When the pirates too fall for a bevy of beauties, the daughters of a Major General, he prevents them from kidnapping his offspring by claiming to be an orphan; they take pity on him and make him an honorary member of their gang. The police are summoned to arrest the pirates, but Frederic realizes that, having been born on 29 February, he is not 21, but only 5. He feels honour-bound to complete his apprenticeship and rejoins the pirates for the next 60 or so years. He informs them that the Major General lied about being an orphan, and they swear revenge. They steal ashore, meet the police lying in wait and swiftly overcome them. The story looks like it would turn gruesome until the Major General pleads for a cease-fire 'in Queen Victoria's name'. The pirates accept, all is forgiven, Frederic and Mabel are reunited and the Major General gives his daughters' hands in marriage to the pirates.

The narratives of the musical stage very often conclude rather suddenly, their dramatic substance falling a bit flat but being compensated by a stirring finale. One of the reasons for this is that musicals are pressed for time: since singing takes up more time than speaking, a musical covers less ground than a play (and certainly less than a novel). Thus the writers are left with little time to tie up loose ends. Indeed, in many musicals and operas, the ending is artificially engineered by what is known as the *deus ex machina* (which translates as something like the 'hand of god'). This device goes back to the very birth of opera, when Monteverdi and Striggio decided (in the end) to conclude *L'Orfeo* by having the god Apollo descend from the heavens to rescue Orfeo and accompany him to heaven ('Perché a lo sdegno ed al dolor in preda così ti doni, o figlio?' [Why do you so freely give yourself to anger and grief, oh son?]). This unexpected happy ending (modifying the Aristotelian tragic form) allows the chorus to conclude the opera with a show-stopping song and dance ('Vanne Orfeo, felice appieno' [Go, Orfeo, happy at last]). This looks a little bit like cheating, but although it might rankle dramatically, it satisfies us musically. *Oklahoma!* has a similar unlikely reversal at the end, when the community court overlooks the fact that Curly is implicated in Jud's death; *42nd Street* trades on the unlikely catapulting of chorus girl to star; and *Pirates of Penzance* concludes with an ending that is ludicrous – though extremely efficient – in finishing off the story.

It's clear from the synopsis of *Pirates of Penzance* that the plot is rather ridiculous. First of all, it hinges on the conceit that Frederic is only 5 years old when everyone thinks he is 21; it features comically unlikely characters, such as the benevolent pirates with their sympathy for orphans; it involves numerous unexpected plot points; and it ends with a bolt from the blue – in this case, the use of Queen Victoria's name to end the feud between the pirates and the police. The same is true of other Gilbert and Sullivan shows, which feature mistaken identity, twins swapped at birth and all manner of magical artefacts that enable a bit of hocus-pocus to save the day. The point here is that the story being told, however *naturalistic*, does not have to be *realistic*; it simply has to operate within the 'rules' of the fictitious world. Penzance for Gilbert and Sullivan is not the *real* Penzance; it is a world – almost like a fairytale world – in which characters have unlikely qualities, in which magic can happen and into which we venture as part of the charm of the narrative experience.

The reason that this is particularly important for musical theatre is because the musical expects its audience to accept that people are going to burst into song and dance at the slightest provocation. Someone sees a picture of a beautiful girl and expresses how they feel in song (Tamino in

The Magic Flute); someone sniffs some smelling salts and gets catapulted into a dream ballet (Laurey in *Oklahoma!*); someone wants something badly enough and finds that events conspire to make it happen (Peggy in *42nd Street*); and someone considers the story done, so they find a device to get it over and done with (Gilbert and Sullivan with *Pirates*).

In many ways, then, the story *is* just a framework onto which the intriguing, entertaining and captivating elements of the production (the song, the dance, the virtuosity, the humour) are hung; and this is actually true of all narrative art forms – when we appreciate a novel it is because of the elegant writing, the poetry, the sensitive handling of the words or the imagery and rarely the plot. What *narrative* involves is a skilful working together of a workable plot (one that interests us, one that goes somewhere, one that involves interesting characters) with a skilful handling of the way in which it is told (a way that entertains us, that intrigues us, that stimulates us).

On its own, the plot of *Pirates* would render the whole piece forgettable and trite; however, in combination with the way the story is told – with beautiful music, memorable melodies, witty lyrics, pace and energy from the songs and larger-than-life characters – it becomes something that is more valuable. The same is true in reverse: wonderful music, great lyrics, interesting rhythms are all very well; but without characters and a dramatic story that *interest* us, they do not make a viable show.

By way of explaining or refining the concepts of Aristotle and Propp that we have explored in this chapter, subsequent thinkers such as Roland Barthes have tried to show even more clearly the structural underpinning from which our narratives are formed. His essay 'An Introduction to the Structural Analysis of Narratives' (1977, pp. 79–124) is just one of his many important contributions to structuralist and post-structuralist theory which attempts to understand how we make and interpret meaning in the world. To him, narratives involve three main elements: plot points, character types and ways of telling the story (which he refers to, respectively, as functions, actions and narratives). We might see them – even more simply – to comprise the story and the way it is told: for whom, by whom and in what way. However, as we go on to explore in subsequent chapters, narrative is not the only way meaning presents itself in musical theatre. To look into this in more detail, we have to turn to another field, the study of semiotics.

Further reading – theoretical

Booker, Christopher (2004) *The Seven Basic Plots: Why We Tell Stories* (London: Continuum).

Engel, Lehman (2006) *Words with Music: Creating the Broadway Musical Libretto* (updated and revised by Howard Kissel) (New York: Applause Theatre and Cinema Books).

McQuillan, Martin (ed.) (2000) *The Narrative Reader* (Abingdon and New York: Routledge).

Further reading – relating to the examples

Abbate, Claudia and Roger Parker (2012) *A History of Opera: The Last 400 Years* (London and New York: Allen Lane).

Carter, Tim (2007) *Oklahoma! The Making of an American Musical* (New Haven and London: Yale University Press).

Eden, David and Meinhard Saremba (2009) *The Cambridge Companion to Gilbert and Sullivan* (Cambridge Companions to Music) (Cambridge: Cambridge University Press).

Engel, Lehman (1967) *The American Musical Theatre: A Consideration* (New York: Macmillan).

Hoberman, J. (1993) *42nd Street* (BFI Film Classics) (London: British Film Institute).

2   'A Man Who Can Interpret Could Go Far': Semiotics and Semiology

The ability to follow a narrative is crucial for any engagement with storytelling, and we have seen how some fundamental strategies of narrative theory have been absorbed into the storytelling of the musical stage. However, following a story with its characters, plot points and beginning-middle-end trajectory is really only the most basic way of engaging with a text, particularly a performance text such as those of musical theatre. In this chapter, we are going to look in more detail at how these things called musicals make sense to us. We do this by considering *semiotics*, or the study of signs.

One of the most popular scenes in Tim Rice and Andrew Lloyd Webber's *Joseph and the Amazing Technicolor Dreamcoat* (1968) is the one in which Pharaoh remembers a strange dream and asks Joseph to interpret it. Pharaoh, the song has it, was wandering along the bank of the Nile one day when he saw seven healthy cows emerge from the water followed by seven skinny cows. The thin cows ate the healthy cows, though they stayed just as thin as before. Pharaoh is baffled: 'Hey, hey, hey Joseph, / Won't you tell poor old Pharaoh / What does this crazy dream mean?', he sings. Joseph responds, explaining that 'All these things you saw in your pyjamas / Are a long range forecast for your farmers': the cows represent harvests, with seven years of plenty being followed by seven years of drought. Joseph's ability to interpret the dream is celebrated across Egypt and leads to him becoming Pharaoh's right-hand man.

Joseph's understanding of the dream is based on far more than an ability to follow the narrative; that much Pharaoh could do, though since its beginning, middle and end did not follow a logical cause and effect, it was a narrative that made little sense. Instead, Joseph's success is thanks to a more sophisticated skill: being able to interpret elements of the dream as signs, symbolic allusions whereby one thing (a healthy cow) stands for another (a good harvest).

We encounter signs all the time, of course: road-signs or shop signs give us information or instructions; signs we make ourselves (waving, frowning) help us to communicate; and for some, superstitious signs in tea leaves, crystal balls or weather patterns foretell future events, impending disasters or lucky breaks. The meaning of a sign is not always obvious: even conscientious drivers can be baffled by unfamiliar road-signs, for example, and the ability to 'read' tea leaves is undoubtedly an acquired skill, but as we shall see, the ability to read *anything* is an acquired skill, even if we are sometimes not aware we are using it.

The terms 'semiotics' and 'semiology' are usually connected with two scholars who established useful principles about the ways we understand signs – the Swiss linguist Ferdinand de Saussure (1857–1913) and the American mathematician Charles Sanders Peirce (1839–1914). Their ideas stem from around the turn of the twentieth century (though we have been using and interpreting signs for far longer than that). Saussure focussed on language as a sign-system, whereas Peirce explored the way people understand and interpret signs. Our discussion, exploring some of the sign-systems we encounter in musical theatre, reveals not only how intrinsic the knowledge of language is, but also a host of other significant elements that generate meaning, from the musical to the theatrical, and from the cultural to the stylistic. Let's start by looking at two of the basic points in Saussure's *Course in General Linguistics*, published after his death, in 1916. The first of these introduces the terminology *langue* and *parole*; the second introduces the terms *signifier* and *signified*.

Saussure suggests that language – any language – is made up of a system (its alphabet, its grammar, its syntax, etc.) and individual utterances that use the system ('I closed my eyes'). In English, we use a particular alphabet with 26 letters, a particular set of symbols that signify those letters and certain grammatical rules to order combinations of those letters into words, phrases and sentences. A familiarity with the workings of this system (the *langue*) will allow us to understand what is meant by a particular utterance (the *parole*). Thus the sentence 'I closed my eyes' means something to you because you understand what each word means, and you recognize that their ordering in this sequence presents an idea that makes sense. Any other ordering of these words would not follow the logic of our sign-system and would therefore sound odd ('closed I my eyes'), archaic ('my eyes I closed') or nonsensical ('eyes closed I my').

One of the things we often forget, though, is that this system is itself a *learned* system; it has been artificially constructed in order to help communication, and we take time to learn its rules. Words, phrases and sentences *in themselves* do not mean anything, but because we have learned that the curly squiggle 'e' represents a letter, and that the set of curly squiggles 'e-y-e' represents something else, we can read and write expressions meaningfully. Language, then, is made up of *abstract* and *arbitrary* signs that could conceivably have different meanings. When the decision was made to represent an eye using those symbols 'e-y-e', a decision could have been made to use the symbols 'o-j-o'. Indeed, as you probably know, different people *did* decide to use those symbols (and others), and therefore different languages (*langues*) – in this case Spanish – developed.

Theatre theorists such as Patrice Pavis, Marco de Marinis and Keir Elam have built on the work of the early semioticians, analyzing how signs operate in relation to theatre. Patrice Pavis has even created a useful questionnaire for students to consider the various and diverse signs relating to performance (Pavis cited in Aston and Savona, pp. 110–111). Here, beyond the script, theatre becomes a dense, multifaceted text with many sign-systems at work in the staging, design and performance. Thus a musical theatre 'text' becomes more than just a script and score *on the page*; it becomes necessary to consider the dynamics of how theatre and music create meaning *on the stage*.

Joseph and the Amazing Technicolor Dreamcoat (1968)

Joseph and the Amazing Technicolor Dreamcoat

Music by Andrew Lloyd Webber
Lyrics by Tim Rice
Based on the story of Joseph from Genesis 37–50.

Synopsis: Way, way back, many centuries ago, Jacob and his family lived in Canaan. Jacob has 12 sons, but his favouritism for Joseph, to whom he gives a dazzling coat of many colours, makes the others jealous. They sell him as a slave to the Egyptian Potiphar, where he is seduced by Potiphar's wife and thrown into jail. Joseph has a remarkable ability to interpret people's dreams, and as word spreads, the Pharaoh of Egypt summons Joseph to his palace. Joseph interprets Pharaoh's dream, forecasting seven years of bumper harvests followed by seven years of drought. Thanks to this warning, the Egyptians can prepare for the drought, and Joseph becomes Pharaoh's right-hand man. Meanwhile, the drought hits hard in Canaan, and the brothers travel to Egypt to seek help. At the palace they do not recognize Joseph, but Joseph plants a golden cup in his youngest brother's sack, accusing him of stealing it and then threatening terrible punishment. The brothers are horrified and plead for mercy. Seeing their compassion, Joseph realizes they have changed and reveals his identity before being reunited with his father.

Let's look more closely at Pharaoh's song from *Joseph*. As we have seen, its actual theme is about interpreting signs, which makes it appropriate to discuss in this context; however, it is also constructed from signs. For now, let's leave aside its linguistic signs (the lyrics) – though we will come back to some of them in due course.

One of the meaningful signs of this song that would come across only in performance is that it is in a certain style. 'The Song of the King' is a pastiche of rock 'n' roll: a basic, three-chord rhythm and blues number like 'Hound Dog' (1956) or 'All Shook Up' (1957). It has a simple melody, a classic 'walking' bass-line and idiomatic 'doo-wop' backing vocals. It presents a very specific character: not just the King (Pharaoh) of Egypt, but also the King of rock 'n' roll, Elvis Presley. In performance, Pharaoh is typically played as an impersonation of Elvis, with a characteristic voice, quiffed hair, plenty of pelvis movement and a Las Vegas-period white jumpsuit (see Figure 2.1). In terms of semiotics, the significance of the song therefore extends beyond the immediate scenario of the storyline to reference something externally with which the audience is already familiar (Elvis and his performance). We'll explore the idea of this cross-referencing in a later chapter. The significant thing to note at this stage is that it is because of signs within the song (and its performance) that we recognize the pastiche.

Now let's return to the lyrics, since even some of the more innocuous words carry meaning. The opening line, for example, begins with the word 'Well', an extraneous preliminary to the actual meaning of the sentence. Yet this apparently irrelevant word sets up the Elvis pastiche, reminding us of characteristic phrases such as at the beginning of 'All Shook Up' ('Well

Figure 2.1   Pharaoh (Robert Torti) and Joseph (Donny Osmond) in *Joseph and the Amazing Technicolor Dreamcoat* (1999). Really Useful Films

bless my soul, what's wrong with me?'). Indeed, more than just mimicking the word, Rice and Lloyd Webber's use of this feature cleverly mimics the sort of performative aural gesture that Elvis gave his lyrics. At the beginning of 'All Shook Up', Elvis actually sings something like 'Ah-well-ah bless-ah my soul, ah-what's-ah wrong with me?', turning the opening word into a three-syllable ornament that rises and falls back to the starting note.[1] In 'The Song of the King', Rice and Lloyd Webber construct a similar effect over the words 'Well I was': this phrase also rises and falls back to the starting note, and uses alliteration to mimic Elvis's aural gesture. Elsewhere, the exclamatory remarks 'Uh-huh' in Pharaoh's song ('...out of the Nile, uh-huh', etc.), remind us of the way the verses in the same Elvis song end ('Mm mm oh oh yeah yeah').

Music and semiotics

While a letter combination like 'e-y-e' has a prescribed meaning that we would find in a dictionary, a musical combination, for example, 'A-F#-G', generally does not. Nevertheless, music is very definitely coded into a system with grammar and syntax, and what you might call its own alphabet. Moreover, just as certain countries have established a particular language as their default, Western music has established a particular system known as the 'diatonic' system, which uses a specific selection of notes within a standardized framework. In Western music – unlike that of some other cultures – there are only 12 notes, most easily understood if you picture a piano keyboard, which usually has just over 7 sets of these notes (88 keys in all). Each key on the piano – black and white – represents a different note, and if you start on what is called A and work up *chromatically*, you will encounter all 12: A, A#, B, C, C#, D, D#, E, F, F#, G and G#. After that, the sequence begins again, only higher in pitch. With the Western musical 'alphabet' limited to those notes, the number of possibilities for musical expression is clearly restricted, and just as in language there are phrases that will make sense, some that will sound odd or archaic and others (though very few) that will make no sense. Like the decision to use 26 letters in our language's alphabet, though, the decision to use a sequence of 12 notes in our music is entirely arbitrary, and further 'grammatical' decisions are equally artificial. According to the 'grammar' of Western music, for example, music *should* use just 7 of those 12 notes (a scale, or key), though composers can choose to select either major or minor collections of notes, and also choose to select which key to write in. The 7 notes have two sets of positional names – one from the Sol-Fah system, familiar from *The Sound of Music*'s 'Doh, a Deer'; the other a more formal set of terms including Tonic (for the first note of the scale), Subdominant (for the fourth) and Dominant (for the fifth). They are also given Roman numerals such that the Tonic is I and the Dominant is V and so on. Thus a composer writing in E major (and not breaking any of the rules) would write their piece using only the notes E (the Tonic), F#, G#, A (the Subdominant), B (Dominant), C# and D#; the notes played in that particular order represent the scale of E major (see Figure 2.2). By reordering the sequence of notes, by duplicating occurrences of each, by borrowing from higher and lower octaves and by colouring the character of each note through rhythmic and harmonic variation, the possibilities *seem* limitless, which is indeed testament to the brilliance of this diatonic system.

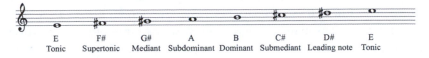

E	F#	G#	A	B	C#	D#	E
Tonic	Supertonic	Mediant	Subdominant	Dominant	Submediant	Leading note	Tonic

Figure 2.2   The scale of E Major notated on the stave

Cadences

The most fixed cadence in terms of any sense of meaning is what is known as the 'perfect cadence', so-called because it is the most satisfying completion of a standard phrase, resolving from the dominant to the tonic (V-I). This firm resolution to the grounded root of the musical key creates a feeling of completion, and therefore this particular musical pattern signifies that the end (of the phrase, or even the piece) has been reached. By contrast, the 'interrupted cadence' begins on the dominant but moves to an unresolving chord, typically II or VI, both of which are minor triads. The result of this is that the cadence seems to be left suspended, with (often) an unsettling change of modality from major to minor. Musical 'meaning' becomes more prominent when patterns are associated with a particular setting or context: the 'plagal cadence' (IV-I) conventionally accompanies the intoned 'Amen' at the end of a psalm or hymn, and has thus come to take on a religious connotation. The final type of cadence is the 'imperfect cadence', or 'half cadence' (I-V), which leaves the music sounding unfinished. It is usually answered by a resolving phrase (and a perfect cadence).

Yet while music is a comparable structuring system to language, there are differences. In language the use of words fixes an allocated, arbitrary meaning (that which is signified) to each pattern of letters or sounds (the signifier). This is not always the case with music, which generally resists such explicit signification. On the other hand, certain recurring patterns have over time accrued an associative sense. For example, a musical phrase will typically conclude with one of a number of 'cadences' that have become standardized.

Elsewhere, associations are founded thanks to rhythm or instrumentation. Waltzes evoke dancing and are a typical style of music from turn-of-the-century Vienna, when social dancing was hugely fashionable. Military music typically features a strong, regular beat that connotes the regular rhythm of a march; percussive instruments are often used to emphasize the beat, and a melody is often played out over the top on a piccolo. To be sure, these associations have a historical provenance as well, since these instruments (fife and drums) have been used throughout history to control the pace of soldiers marching and to allow spirited tunes to be heard over the noise of the regiment going to war. In terms of signification, these associations become increasingly potent as cultural habits become ingrained, and as popular culture uses stereotypical signifiers to short-cut meaning. The sound of the piccolo and drums has become sedimented as a military sound by its use in countless war films (think *The Great Escape*). Nowadays, it would be very difficult for this combination of instruments *not* to have a military connotation.

In this respect, signs in music (just like in any other context) *mean* not only through a literal 'reading' of what they *denote*, but also through associations that they *connote*. Roland Barthes (1977, pp. 32–51), whom we encountered in the previous chapter, has written about this in 'The Rhetoric of the Image', analysing a photograph of a shopping bag full of food. Although the literal signs in the image (food in a shopping bag, some Italian writing) *denote* certain basic things, the image becomes richer to interpretation thanks to what is *connoted*. Barthes argues that this image connotes qualities like freshness, vitality and, most of all, *Italianness*. Likewise, we could say music's meaning-potential works connotatively: 'The Song of the King' in *Joseph* is just one of a number of song-style pastiches, which also include a calypso ('Benjamin Calypso'), a Parisian ballad ('Those Canaan Days') and a Western cowboy song ('One More Angel'); their Caribbean, Parisian and Western qualities are *connoted* by features of the music. Lloyd Webber's delight at playing with such stylistic pastiche is a feature of his work; *Starlight Express* (1984) includes a number of raps, a gospel number ('Light at the End of the Tunnel'), a Tammy Wynette parody

('U.N.C.O.U.P.L.E.D', based on 'D.I.V.O.R.C.E', 1968) and a blues number ('Poppa's Blues') that self-consciously deconstructs itself ('The first line of the Blues is always sung a second time. / I said the first line of the Blues is always sung a second time. / So by the time you get to the third line you've had time to think of a rhyme'). In each of these examples, meaning is generated through layers of signification, creating, in Jacques Lacan's (1977, p. 153) words, a 'chain of signifiers'. A sign's meaning is constantly 'deferred', reminding us by association of something else, which reminds us of something else, and something else, and so on.

So although music *itself* may not exactly 'mean' anything, it picks up resonances, and as the cultural archive of associations builds, writers and composers make use of these associations to create short-cuts. The use of music to accompany visual gestures (in film or on stage, for example) works on these principles: the plaintive weeping of the sad wife to a mournful solo violin is familiar from silent films and therefore becomes a cultural code; so too is the appearance of the villain to an urgent bass motif which exploits minor sounds and a chord known as the 'devil's chord' because of its earlier sinister connotations. In cartoons, characters are accompanied by what become signature tunes (think Scooby Doo), enabling the cartoon-makers to work in a semiotic shorthand not only within an episode but also throughout the series and beyond.

The leitmotif

Having invoked the important cultural reference of Scooby Doo, we should perhaps qualify that Hanna Barbera's use of a signature theme in this example was itself borrowing from a classic(al) device most commonly attributed to Richard Wagner. Wagner (1813–1883) was a German com-poser who single-handedly sought to establish German opera as great art and his operas in particular as the greatest. He did this by accompanying his life's creative work – a dozen or so significant operas – with a dense theoretical treatise on how musical theatre (or rather, music drama) worked (see Wagner, 1995; Kerman, 1956). He established the theory of the Gesamtkunstwerk, the unified work of art, in which all of the elements combined to create something more powerful than they would alone. Central to Wagner's theory was the idea that characters, events, objects and themes within the drama should be signified in the music through their own leitmotif. Using these motifs as musical building blocks, and varying them according to appropriate nuances in, for example, a character's devel-opment, Wagner constructed complex scores in which the musical motifs wove around one another, interacting, clashing and engaging with each other just like the characters.

The Ring Cycle: Das Rheingold (1869), Die Walküre (1870), Siegfried (1876), Götterdämmerung (1876)

Music and libretti by Richard Wagner

Based on Norse myths and the mediaeval German epic poem 'The Ring of the Nibelungs'

Synopsis: The Nibelung dwarf Alberich forges a magic ring from gold stolen from the Rhine maidens (Das Rheingold). King of the Gods Wotan steals the ring, but trades it to the giants in payment for building the Gods' home 'Valhalla'. The ring is cursed, and attempts by Wotan and his offspring to get it back are bloody and dangerous, eventually leading to the destruction of Valhalla itself. In Die Walküre he arranges for his children Sieglinde and Siegmund to fall in love and bear a child, Siegfried. Once an adult (in Siegfried), Siegfried kills the dragon Fafner to regain the ring, which he takes to Brünnhilde. In Götterdämmerung, Siegfried betrays Brünnhilde and is killed. She throws the ring into his funeral pyre to purge it of the curse and invites the Rhine maidens to reclaim it to restore the order of things. With the ring retrieved, the curse is broken. Valhalla bursts into flame, and the rule of the Gods is ended.

The most extensive development of the leitmotif appears throughout Wagner's four-opera epic, The Ring Cycle, and one of the most interesting themes is the Sword motif, introduced at the end of the first opera Das Rheingold (1869) when the character Wotan forges a sword. From that moment, the distinctive pattern of the leitmotif is associated with the sword, and although the detail of the motif varies with each appearance to reflect different emotions or nuances, its basic structure remains. It consists fundamentally of an octave drop followed by a dotted arpeggio feature. Thus these elements – the octave, the arpeggio and the dotted rhythm – become signifiers of the sword, its power or its effects throughout The Ring.

In the second opera, Die Walküre (1870), for instance, the sword represents a potent tool of connection – and division – between the opera's hero and heroine, Siegmund and Sieglinde. Siegmund has sought refuge in the unhappy marital home of Sieglinde and Hunding. While Hunding is away, Sieglinde realizes that she is curiously drawn to the stranger Siegmund. Once her husband returns, he reveals himself as an enemy of Siegmund, and though he agrees to extend his hospitality overnight, he challenges him to a fight the following morning. Sieglinde realizes that the stranger needs a weapon and remembers that on her wedding day a sword was plunged into the trunk of a tree by a mysterious old man (Wotan). No one has been able to remove the sword from the tree, and desperate to flee from her forced marriage, the sword has become a symbol of Sieglinde's entrapment. Long ago, she pledged her love to the hero who could release it, and now Siegmund does, to gain her devotion and adoration. But as this happens, she realizes that the bond she feels for him is because they are twins; their incestuous union is therefore doomed – the tragic flaw – and the rest of the opera plays out the inevitable tragedy.

Perhaps the most celebrated incarnation of the sword motif comes at the beginning of Act III, in the variation known as the 'Ride of the Valkyries'. Wotan has intervened in the fight between Siegmund and Hunding, smashing the sword to bits and therefore allowing Siegmund to be slain. The Valkyrie Brünnhilde gathers up the pieces, and with Sieglinde in tow, rides across the skies to meet with her sisters, the other Valkyries, on top of a mountain. In this variation, the arpeggio feature is extended to become the basis of a sequence lasting some eight minutes. The theme itself has become – in a different sense – *iconic* because of its intertextual use both in *Birth of a Nation* (1915) and *Apocalypse Now* (1979), a passing on of signification that carries connotations of mythology and power.

As these constructed and associative meanings become established in the cultural psyche, a glossary of sorts does in fact emerge, as we see from the use of underscoring in cartoons. This typically follows indications of pace and direction in the visual action, with fast action accompanied by fast music, and action that moves up or down accompanied by corresponding higher and lower music, a technique known as 'mickey-mousing'. When a character runs up a flight of stairs, the music emulates that sonically by running up the scale. Together with various exclamations, musicalizing the bangs and crashes of the action, or the moods and tantrums of the characters, this use of cartoon music has habituated our understandings of musical patterns and their 'meaning'. Just as language is arbitrarily encoded, the establishing of, for example, spatial characteristics in music (higher or lower notes) is a construct rather than a 'natural' musical feature. Even so, it is surprising how many people associate high-pitched, rapid musical sounds with something small (a mouse) and low pitched, heavy sounds with something large (an elephant).

Les Misérables (1985)

Even if it is difficult to pinpoint exactly *what* makes a certain quality of music evoke mood, emotion or meaning, composers have developed a remarkable ability to make music contribute significantly to the meaning of a scene, which shows in practice how the wealth of associations can coalesce to signify. Take, for example, the score of *Les Misérables* (1985), whose musical numbers evoke by turn patriotism ('Red and Black'), dignity ('Stars'), tenderness ('Bring Him Home') and comedy ('Master of the House'). Granted, each of these songs is positioned in the context of a narrative and sung by specific characters voicing their emotions; the context, characterization and especially the lyrics clearly provides detail to our understanding of what these musical moments *mean*. However, they would not be as effective if the music did not corroborate the signification from those elements – imagine how confusing it would be if Javert sang 'Stars' to the tune of 'Master of the House'! Let's consider this song to explore some of its musical signification.

'Stars' is sung by Javert, the chief of police who has been chasing Jean Valjean for decades having dedicated his life to capturing the fugitive. Javert's understanding of right and wrong is based deeply in his religious values, though having had his sense of belief tested in his previous encounter with Valjean – an 'evil' man who has proven himself more worthy than Javert – he wrestles with his pride, faith and resolve, eventually throwing himself to his death. As a figure of authority, Javert fulfils the classic role in this narrative of the villain (see Figure 2.3).

Figure 2.3   Javert (Philip Quast) singing 'Stars' in the 10th Anniversary Production of *Les Misérables* at the Royal Albert Hall. Sony / BBC Video

---

Les Misérables (1985)

Music by Claude-Michel Schönberg

Lyrics by Alain Boublil and Jean-Marc Natel; English lyrics by Herbert Kretzmer

Based on the novel by Victor Hugo (1862)

Synopsis: When the fugitive Jean Valjean is recognized by arresting officer Javert, a chase begins. Although Valjean evades capture, he is destined to a life looking over his shoulder. Years pass, and the action moves to Paris, where tensions are high as the government cracks down on the poor. Valjean has become guardian to the orphan Cosette, whose mother Fantine died while she was still a child. When he arrives in Paris with Cosette, she falls for the leader of the student rebels, Marius, and Valjean joins their forces. The rebels build barricades and prepare to fight for their rights. Javert – a government officer – infiltrates the rebel hideout in disguise, though he is discovered and the students threaten to execute him. Before he is shot, Valjean frees Javert, showing the clemency of an honest man and shaming Javert, who throws himself to his death. The battle breaks out, and when the first victim Eponine is slain, the students pledge to fight in her name. The fighting is bloody and nearly all the students die, but Valjean saves Marius and reunites him with Cosette. Still a fugitive, Valjean must once again flee, taking refuge in a convent where his health deteriorates. Finally, Cosette and Marius find him and, with their blessing, and with the spirits of Fantine and Eponine beckoning him to heaven, he dies.

The accompaniment to 'Stars' is built on a descending ground bass, a classic musical device found also in Pachelbel's 'Canon', Bach's 'Air on a G String' and Purcell's 'When I am Laid in Earth' from *Dido and Aeneas*. This repeating pattern establishes a firm foundation of strength and emphasizes the obduracy of Javert in his quest. Some of this suggestion undoubtedly comes from the fact that the ground bass has become a conventionalized motif, though it does possess qualities that seem to evoke surety and resolve: equal notes resolutely descend the major scale, and the pattern reliably 'returns and returns and is always the same', at least every time the main theme recapitulates in the opening eight bars of each verse. By contrast, Schönberg has scored a markedly different accompaniment in the strings, which begin the introduction with high-pitched sustained notes and a rippling harp motif. Together, these connote the ethereal quality of the night sky and the twinkling of the stars about which Javert is singing, themselves representing the grace, majesty and wonder of God.

Once Javert has stated his position in two iterations of the A material ('I never shall yield'), his expression changes twice, and musically the significance of this change of thought is clearly marked. First, he considers the reality of capturing Valjean, an overwhelmingly difficult quest. As he acknowledges this ('He knows his way in the dark...') the music shifts into the relative minor key, evoking a sombre feeling. But Javert quickly counters his uncertainty by repeating the same musical motif up a tone to make it major and more optimistic ('Mine is the way of the Lord'). He phrases the rest of this section confidently in a spirited melody suiting the 'path of the righteous'. However, the second musical change marks the complex turmoil in Javert's character and his chilling justification to punish himself for his human weakness. The music here moves into a completely different key, departing from the E major harmonies (remember those seven degrees of the scale?) to introduce A minor, D major and G major before modulating back to the root chord by way of B major. This sequence is unsettling to the harmonic palette of the song, and just as its tonality reflects Javert's turmoil, its metre is disturbed with a half-bar effect interrupting the regularity of the song.

The signification of vocal range and timbre

If this analysis decodes some of the signification of the music, further levels of signification are implied associatively in performance, particularly through the encoding of meaning in the voice. While it might appear that singing style and technique are 'natural', they, like all culturally based articulations, are neither 'natural' nor unchanging; they alter over time in response to new technologies, new compositions and changing tastes. The layers of signification through which the listener interprets the voice include not only the content of the song, but also the timbre and pitch, the singing technique and the musical genre. Singing styles and techniques are also cultural patterns that exist within a geographical, linguistic and historical context. All these facets have an effect on sound production and singing style and therefore feed back into strategies for composition, performance and interpretation.

Les Misérables contextualizes its vocal practices within a specific frame of reference relating to its period (the 1980s), its origins (France and England) and the milieu of its production history (West End). A fashion for a particular type of pseudo-operatic pop, a drive to enhance the cultural status of musical theatre as a form and the availability of particular technological capabilities led to a slew of shows during the 1980s, broadly termed the

'Megamusicals' (see Sternfeld, 2006), that established this vocal aesthetic (*Sweeney Todd*, 1979; *Les Misérables*, 1985; *The Phantom of the Opera*, 1986; *Jekyll and Hyde*, 1990, etc.). The voice of Javert in *Les Misérables* is idiomatic of this aesthetic, and following certain traditions of the classical musical stage, Javert's identity as the formal adversary is indicated in part by his deeper register.

The megamusical

The megamusical is a recent form best represented by the shows produced since the 1980s by Cameron Mackintosh, the Really Useful Group (Andrew Lloyd Webber) and Disney. The production budgets of these shows are often eight figure sums, and there is an expectation that they will sustain runs of several years to recoup such a big investment. The longest running musicals, *Cats* (1981), *Les Misérables* (1985) and *The Phantom of the Opera* (1986), have stayed in the West End and/or on Broadway for upwards of 20 years, becoming must-see tourist events. They are characterized by high-profile marketing campaigns, associated merchandise and, more recently, promotional televised casting competitions. Megamusicals have also been characterized in their sound aesthetic by an electro-orchestral instrumentation and a pseudo-operatic vocal 'belt', elements that give the sound a largesse to match that of the moving machinery and spectacle. Notable production gimmicks have included an ornate chandelier crashing to the stage in *Phantom*, a full-size helicopter landing on the stage in *Miss Saigon*, and a flying car taking off in *Chitty Chitty Bang Bang* (2002).

The patterns of Western European vocal technique and musical genre that have been imagined and re-imagined since the sixteenth century are complex, with layers of sedimentation accrued through this long history. However, the early history of opera was largely influenced by Italian singing style. In the seventeenth and early eighteenth centuries castrati sang many roles including heroic male characters. Female performers were employed in cross-dressed roles too; the sex of the performer didn't appear to be as important as vocal quality or agility. By the end of the eighteenth century, opera had become more commercial, with larger halls, larger orchestras and consequently the requirement for larger, more resonant voices. It was at this point, too, that the modern idea of 'classical' singing was established. At the same time a mythology about the singing of a previous era, referred to as 'bel canto', developed (Potter, 2006, p. 47). From Handel to Rossini, composers required increasing vocal agility from their singers and wrote passages intended to be improvised and ornamented in performance.

By the nineteenth century, most noticeably in the work of Giuseppe Verdi, some patterns had become so established that correlations could be drawn between operatic vocal timbres and character types, although such patterns have many exceptions. Catherine Clément describes the soprano heroine as the 'Persecuted Victim', the tenor as heroic and courageous, the baritone as providing 'organised opposition' and the mezzo-soprano as being resistant or involved in witchcraft or treason (in Smart, 2000, pp. 22–23). The deepest male voices 'act in a sacred field, shamanistic or religious', but the spiritual range in the lower female voice is more difficult to catalogue (p. 24). There is also a synaesthesic association between good (high and light) and bad (low and heavy). We can see that Javert's deep register therefore imbues our understanding of the character with a sense of both the sacred and the dark *and* allies itself to historical/classical ideas in order to elevate the cultural cachet of the musical.

Carmen (1875)

Carmen (1875)

Music by Georges Bizet
Libretto by Henri Meilhac and Ludovic Halévy
Based on the novella by Prosper Mérimée (1845).

Significant productions: Royal Opera House, London (2008), conducted by Antonio Pappano and directed by Francesca Zambello (filmed for Decca in 2008); Broadway adaptation *Carmen Jones* (1943), by Oscar Hammerstein II.

Synopsis: Set in Seville, Spain, the opera tells the story of the gypsy Carmen who seduces the soldier Don José into releasing her from prison, abandoning his childhood sweetheart, Micaëla, and deserting from the army to leave with her and join a band of smugglers. However, she soon tires of him in favour of the exciting toreador, Escamillo. When Micaëla comes looking for Don José he leaves with her to tend his sick mother, but soon returns to find Carmen at a bullfight where Escamillo is performing; Carmen and Escamillo declare their love for each other. When she refuses to leave with Don Jose, he stabs Carmen just as cheers signify that Escamillo has killed the bull. Carmen dies. This onstage murder called into question the term *opéra comique* – how could a tragic ending be part of a comic opera? After Bizet's death the spoken dialogue was reworked as recitative by Ernest Guiraud to form a *grand opéra* version performed at the Paris Opéra.

Carmen (1875) conforms to the expectations Clément outlined. Micaëla, the young, pretty, girl next door who looks after Don José's mother and loves him, is the soprano whose love is unreciprocated. Don José, the heroic tenor, is seduced by the working-class Carmen, rebels against the constraints of the Spanish army and is ultimately destroyed by his passion. Escamillo is a bass-baritone, a successful toreador bearing a voice that has 'reached the ideal of maturity of European men: not too young, not too old' (in Smart, 2000, p. 23). Such characters, Clément suggests, are often in the centre of a conflict, articulate and violent. Finally, Carmen herself, a mezzo-soprano, is not a fresh young voice – and for this one might read her to be sexually active, articulate, capable of violent contestation and in some ways masculinized in her way of life. Clément associates this quality of her voice with the idea of freedom: 'Carmen poses resistance to each and every order: "Libre elle est née, libre elle mourra" [Free she is born, free she will die]. Indeed the best definition of the mezzo is through that freedom – freedom to murder, and freedom to meet death if necessary' (ibid.). Elsewhere, Wayne Koestenbaum (1993, p. 231) identifies the contrast between the two female characters too, describing Carmen as a 'lewd-voiced mezzo almost outside opera's pale' and Micaëla as the 'hometown soprano' who 'sings a seraphic melody while repeating the ailing mother's words'. Perhaps equally important is the fact that in the first version of the opera Don José speaks through much of the first act (in the manner of opera comique rather than opera seria); it isn't until the moment when Micaëla brings him the letter and sings of home that he is also moved to song. Abbate and Parker (2012, p. 187) suggest this reveals a gap between his public and private personae and that he has been holding his emotions in check. He doesn't become the passionate heroic tenor until he is reminded of the pure love of his mother and Micaëla, and ultimately until he betrays them both in chasing the unattainable fantasy of Carmen.

While these vocal ranges contributed to a nineteenth-century construction of character that continued in some twentieth-century works, the introduction of a popular aesthetic as musical theatre mutated through the twentieth century invited a different range of practices. In recent shows with a bias towards operetta, such as *Les Misérables*, the young heroine and hero (Cosette and Marius) sing in soprano and tenor ranges conforming to the ideological patterns of the nineteenth century. However, jazz, blues and rock music (along with the introduction of microphones) upset these associations, and female characters (including heroines) began to be written in much lower vocal ranges and popular styles. This is apparent in *Chicago* (1975) where all the female characters are in the mezzo-soprano or alto ranges. This represents their characters, not least since neither Roxie nor

Velma has the moral character of the 'traditional' soprano heroine, but also because the musical genres they sing and the use of radio mikes makes it inappropriate and unnecessary to use the carrying power of the soprano voice. Even when the tenor range is maintained in rock, pop or soul musicals, it is sung with a different timbre and aesthetic to reflect a popular idiom. Billy Flynn is in the baritone range, while the poor deluded husband, Amos (who sings 'Mr Cellophane'), is in the tenor range. Jazz/blues inflections colour the tone of all these voices but also affect whether the singer sings before, on or after the beat, and whether the singer approaches the note from below or above. The types of ornamentation used are also signified by genre. The end result of this diversity is that vocal range in itself does not signify, but does through the performance of genre. By the start of the twenty-first century the range of voices in musical theatre has become diverse with popular music genres and timbres contributing to the ways voices and characters are represented.

The performance of 'When You're Good to Mama' by Queen Latifah in the film version of *Chicago* is interesting in this regard. Her reinterpretation of the song, evoking 1920s blues singers such as Bessie Smith, brings that musical genre to life, but the idea of a black woman working as a prison warden in 1920s Chicago introduces an anachronism. Todd Decker describes how Latifah's presence in the film invokes a memory of her past 'as a truth-telling female rapper' (in Knapp, Morris and Wolf, 2011, p. 207) that fits in with the unrealistic portrayal of the rest of the film, and it introduces the black gospel voice into a twenty-first-century revival in a way that contemporary audiences recognize, appreciate and enjoy. In musical theatre and opera there is generally the expectation that the timbre and musical aesthetic will work within the musical genre and together the music and voice will signify character, but there are exceptions that demonstrate the changing cultural context. There was general agreement that although José Carreras was a brilliant operatic tenor, his 1990 portrayal of Tony in *West Side Story* (1957) didn't fit the musical genre; his voice was too operatic. Even more oddly than that, Carreras the Spaniard had been cast in the role of an East European American immigrant; in this story of ethnic tension between Latino and European American gangs, the signification of Carreras's accent placed him squarely in the wrong camp.

Reading the performance

We have explored how music can be used to signify in musical theatre, and you should now be able to construct your own semiotic analysis of a musical theatre text. Of course, the signs projected in performance extend well beyond the music, lyrics and script of a musical; everything from costumes to body language to the positioning of characters on stage carries meaning (not always intentional!). In our next chapter we explore in more detail the way in which we experience musical theatre most commonly: in performance.

Further reading – theoretical

Barthes, Roland (1977) *Image – Music – Text*, trans. Stephen Heath (London: Fontana Press).

Elan, Keir (1980) *The Semiotics of Theatre and Drama* (London: Methuen).

Counsell, Colin and Laurie Wolf (2001) *Performance Analysis: An Introductory Coursebook* (London and New York: Routledge).

Further reading – relating to the examples

Kerman, Joseph (1956) *Opera as Drama* (New York: Vintage Books).

Smart, Mary Ann (ed.) (2000) *Siren Songs: Representations of Gender and Sexuality in Opera* (Princeton and Oxford: Princeton University Press).

Snelson, John (2004) *Andrew Lloyd Webber* (New Haven and London: Yale University Press).

Sternfeld, Jessica (2006) *The Megamusical* (Profiles in Popular Music) (Bloomington: Indiana University Press).

Swain, Joseph P. (2002). *The Broadway Musical: A Critical and Musical Survey* (second edition) (Lanham, MD, and Oxford: Scarecrow Press).

3 'Razzle Dazzle 'em': Performance Studies, Reception Theory and the Epic Musical

In one of its most popular songs, the Kander and Ebb musical *Chicago* (1975) shows slippery lawyer Billy Flynn attempting to woo the press. He represents two of America's most notorious killers, Velma Kelly and Roxie Hart, who each murdered their partners. The evidence against them is compelling, and the women face long sentences for their crimes of passion. But Billy is convinced he can get the press on-side. His strategy: performance. 'Give 'em the old razzle dazzle', he sings nonchalantly; 'Give 'em an act with lots of flash in it and the reaction will be passionate.' Performance, the show tells us, is beguiling, and the sheer thrill of its energy and excitement impresses us emotionally and viscerally.

There is a special quality about performance, whose magic seems to transcend the moment of experience. During that moment we have the sense of being 'captivated', or even 'lost', as if time stands still and the immediacy of presence is heightened. Afterwards, 'the memory lingers on', the moment is 'unforgettable' and – according to the powerful promotional slogan used for *Cats* (1981) – it will stay with you 'Now and forever'. But is this *all*? Are we really the suckers that Billy Flynn suggests, mindless morons who experience song and dance and get swept away into a thoughtless fug? If this is really our role when we watch a show, what are we to make of the audience's relationship with performance?

The audience is certainly a crucial aspect of performance, at least according to the director Jerzy Grotowski (1968, p. 32): 'Can theatre exist without an audience?', he asks; 'At least one spectator is needed to make it a performance'. Around the same time another theatre director, Peter Brook (1968, p. 11), wrote: 'I can take any empty space and call it a bare stage. A man walks across this empty space whilst someone else is watching him, and this is all that is needed for an act of theatre to be engaged'. Two such similar statements from such influential figures as Brook and Grotowski demonstrate the importance of the audience's relationship with a show – its reception. This chapter explores 'Reception Theory', a set of ideas originally from literary criticism which relates to the reader of a text; here it has been modified for the particular type of 'reader' that encounters the act of performance.

Before we pursue this we should reflect on the terminology we have used to evoke the idea of 'reading' performances. Of course, we use this term metaphorically: there are similarities in the way we engage with books and performances, though the dominant element of books – language – is only one element of performance. As performance moves away from or beyond language (embracing, for example, the beguiling power of music or the physical grace of dance), those similarities diminish. The idea of 'reading' the performance is one that privileges the script, the playwright and a certain form of literary theatre. It's worth considering other metaphors, and how those might affect the way in which we conceptualize performance. One of Patrice Pavis's books, for example, is called *Languages of the Stage*, implying that we interpret or translate the elements of performance; alternatively, we could see our study as a science which seeks hard facts or truths, some sort of empirical understanding of a performance. But is our relationship with musical theatre really one that demands 'understanding', 'meaning' or 'knowledge'? Perhaps its value is something we sense, experience or absorb; but if so, which sense(s) do we use? Do we *watch* a performance, *listen* or engage other senses – even a sixth sense? Does it differ depending on the performance form (music, theatre, dance), the performance medium (theatre, TV, radio) or the performance mode (aurality, physicality, mediality)? And what is at stake in our relationship with the performance we are watching? Do we have obligations as members of an audience, or are we at liberty to interpret freely, letting anything and everything wash over us?

These are all concerns that scholar Richard Schechner has addressed in developing the academic discipline of Performance Studies. He suggests that performance has seven functions, each positioning its public in a different relationship: to entertain; to make something that is beautiful; to mark or change identity; to make or foster community; to heal; to teach, persuade, or convince; and to deal with the sacred and/or the demonic (p. 46). In each of these scenarios our reception of the performance – our role as its witness – is differently nuanced.

Susan Bennett's book *Theatre Audiences* (1997) turned the focus away from the show (play) as a text and onto the audience, documenting the development of theoretical arguments about how audiences understand performance. Her book offers a good introduction to the role of theatre audiences, exploring first Reception Theory and then the influential writings of Bertolt Brecht. In this chapter, then, we explore some of these ideas.

Reader Reception Theory

Although the prominence of Reader Reception Theory within literary criticism has diminished since the 1960s and 1970s, it has influenced our contemporary understanding about texts, whether literary or performative. Reader Reception Theory is not a single theory, but the combined ideas of theoreticians who turned away from the text to consider the response to that text by readers. Whereas semiotics – the study of signs *within* a text or performance – assumes that there is a stable meaning to a text, the ideas of Reader Reception Theory invite us to consider how meaning can change. Thus the idea of a text being universal and timeless becomes challenged, and – as this might imply – some of our core assumptions are therefore put into question.

Consider the way in which literary history (or for our purposes, musical theatre history) is taught: certain 'truths' become established, fixing a particular version of that history as fact. Over time, thanks to repeated tellings (narratives) of the same story, the general historiography of musical theatre and the prominent examples that illustrate it (the 'classic' or 'great' shows) become fixed. Histories, for example, often evoke a *twentieth-century* form developing in *America* through a desire to better *integrate* words and music in dramatic storytelling. Thus, musical theatre became viewed – unchallenged – as a twentieth-century, American, integrated phenomenon, and classic examples of *the integrated Broadway musical* are repeatedly cited to corroborate that account: *The Black Crook* (1866) is a primitive example; the first integrated musical is *Oklahoma!* (1943); the Rodgers and Hammerstein shows are considered a benchmark; and Stephen Sondheim took the form to its extreme. Thus a 'canon' of musical classics is born, which becomes stabilized and entrenched.

Horizon of expectations

This general trend, stabilizing the identity of a form like the musical, inevitably affects the way audiences perceive it; and the way the musical theatre world operates reinforces this coherent – if restricted – perspective by establishing a 'horizon of expectations'. This is a term suggested by Hans Robert Jauss, one scholar who writes (though not specifically about musical theatre) about our 'preceding experience of the literary work' (quoted in Bennett, 1997, p. 48). He suggests that our thinking about a form is based on a set of assumptions, which guides our preferences, and then moulds our theatre-going practices. Our assumptions about musical theatre, for example, are

---

The canon

People talk of a 'canon', 'canonic works' and 'canonic writers' in all artistic fields. These are the 'great' works (by great writers) that represent the best examples of that field. Although there is no actual *thing* as 'the canon' (no one has formalized these lists), repeated histories of a particular area establish prominent (and dominant) texts and writers, which are seen as examples of excellence and which influence the expectations about an artform. In musical theatre, the idea that 'great' musicals have to be integrated is a mythology that has arisen through repeated assertions of a canon associated with a 'golden age'. However, there are problems in the construction of canons. Although they might represent prominent examples of work, they often privilege certain voices; English language works by educated white males receive particular attention, thereby excluding or marginalizing anyone from outside that demographic (works in other languages, works by women, works by writers of different ethnicities). Likewise, canonic influence tends to obscure experimental or emergent practices, since public expectation seeks repetition of canonic qualities (the tried and tested; the formulaic), even in new texts. Consequently, the canon is nowadays considered troublesome, and although we have to recognize canonic works in order to tell consistent stories about an area, it is important to view the canon as something which restricts and delimits as much as it defines and exemplifies.

---

formulated around what is accessible and high profile. Shows we encounter (by studying, performing or seeing them) are drawn from a small cross-section of the repertoire and generally reflect the canon. Influences like the education system and the media guide us towards those shows using vocabulary that reinforces their value – they are from 'the Golden Age'; they are 'classic' musicals; they are 'West End smash hits' or 'direct from Broadway'. You can see how this tendency might prejudice the chances of new shows emerging, particularly if they are experimental, transgressive or if they represent the voices of marginalized communities.

Instead, we are guided to thinking that musicals *must* be structured in a particular way (a big opening number; a linear trajectory) and must include certain elements (a celebrity/star; a spectacular set) and a certain type of music (Western, diatonic, pop-based). Moreover, our judgements about their value will be based on whether they have achieved certain signifiers of 'success': have they played in the West End or on Broadway?; have they had a long run?; have they made lots of money?

With entrenched assumptions such as these, and with limited choice available, it's not surprising that our own tastes privilege the repertoire of the canon, and that musical theatre practices sustain its values. Consider how we typically experience a musical on Broadway or in the West End, for example. Here is an occasion that is – literally – *significant* to us (i.e., it *means* something). Seeing a show is likely to be an unusual or special event, costing money and time, and often accompanied by other special activities – a day in the city; a meal before the show; a stay in a hotel. The theatre trip is likely to be a featured activity of our day. We look forward to the theatregoing experience, perhaps with weeks of anticipation, and tell friends about our impending trip, sharing our excitement, showing off a little and dressing up to emphasize its significance. Going to the theatre, after all, is an activity that boosts our prestige: it has cultural value, suggests Pierre Bourdieu, and sends a signal that we are classy, literate and have good taste. At the theatre, we encounter signs that add value to this experience, supporting our belief in its worth – glittering lights and spangled marquees; rococo decorations and gold leaf in the foyer; plush seats and lavish interiors in the auditorium. Once the lights dim, having purchased an expensive glossy brochure, hoody or cast recording, we sit in reverent silence and marvel at the technology, spectacle and voices on the stage; we delight in seeing our favourite performer; we text home, tweet, and post Facebook pictures to gain cultural cachet and reinforce our passion for the show. We wear the t-shirt flamboyantly, sing the songs loudly and name-drop shamelessly. All of this is what is called the 'signifying practice' of our engagement with musical theatre.

However, this is just one set of practices, even if it is common in the Western world; we are making the assumption that it is likely to be *your* set of practices and familiar to other people in your social circle. But understanding Reception Theory means recognizing that there are different social circles: different readers, different expectations and different demands; different readings that different audiences bring to a show.

Different audiences

In Jerzy Grotowski's comment quoted earlier, he uses two different words to refer to the witness of the performance. He speaks of both the 'audience' (which stems from the same root as 'audio' and 'audition') and the 'spectator' (from the same root as 'spectacles' and 'spectacular'). It is interesting how these two words emphasize different aspects of reception. For an 'audience' the encounter relates to the ear, to listening and hearing; for a 'spectator' it relates to the eye and to seeing. Though we tend to use these words indiscriminately, their subtle differences alert us to different dynamics. There is another difference: the word 'audience' speaks of a single massed body of people and implies a shared response to the event; 'spectator' speaks of an individual who gathers in a group of many individuals with different responses. Although subtle, these conceptual differences are significant for performance. If we consider ourselves as part of an audience, for example, we probably think of a particular *type* of performance taking place indoors, where we sit in rows, hushed and attentive as the performers take the stage. We are permitted to express ourselves (we laugh, we applaud, perhaps we sing along), but only en masse – any *individual* expression from the audience is unwelcome. And our expression is carefully controlled: we applaud only at certain points (the end of a song; the end of the show); we laugh, clap along or sing along at selectively engineered moments. The ritual of this type of theatre has a rigid framework of rules, and although we adopt its etiquette, its very formality can turn people off. Both Broadway and the West End subscribe to this model, on the whole (as does opera), and most 'musicals' anticipate the audience being in these passive, silent conditions. The 'horizon of expectations' includes us understanding how to engage appropriately with a show.

By contrast, think of situations in which we are spectators – sporting events, carnivals, parades, festivals. These are events in which our relationship with the performance is more active and less formal: we come and go; we wander around or change viewing positions; we chat and even divert our attention away from the spectacle; we may express ourselves more volubly by chanting or singing; perhaps we find a space of our own to express ourselves in dance. Such events follow a very different model of performance – a different horizon of expectations – though just because they are not sited in a Victorian theatre does not mean that they are not acts of theatre. Indeed, many are very pronounced *musical* and *theatrical* acts that can be understood using these theories. When we go to a music festival we watch performers playing out the narrative in song, dance and dialogue; when we watch friends singing karaoke we build our own horizon of expectations; when we witness an event like the Olympics we see at its beginning and end a pageant of music, dance and performance.

These two different types of audience/spectator experience make us *feel* in very different ways. In the first scenario, the more formal, we probably feel a need to behave appropriately, to conform to the expectations of the ritual; we probably associate a certain amount of value with the event, and a particular status because we are attending it. We may feel distanced from our fellow audience members, though we probably appreciate that anonymity and feel at home within the mass. In the second scenario, we may feel more sense of community, a shared passion for the occasion; we may communicate in familiar terms with people whom we have never met; we may feel a sense of *communitas*, a shared identity; and we may pick up on each other's overt expressions of involvement. These are fundamentally different scenarios, and they highlight some of the dynamics at the heart of Reception Theory.

It was the restrictive conditions of the first type of scenario that troubled the German dramatist Bertolt Brecht. In one essay that accompanied his production *The Rise and Fall of the City of Mahagonny* (1932), he expressed his thoughts: 'We see entire rows of human beings transported into a peculiar doped state, wholly passive, sunk without trace, seemingly in the grip of a severe poisoning attack. Their tense, congealed gaze shows that these people are the helpless and involuntary victims of the unchecked lurchings of their emotions' (Willett, 1993, p. 89). The essay targets what he calls the 'apparatus' of opera – the framework of the opera industry with its trappings of glamour, assumptions of high art and promises of social prestige. He criticizes opera for offering audiences productions that leave them passive and hypnotized, and through his own work he determined to re-model this apparatus so that theatre could work as an active agent to galvanize the people.

Although Brecht's comments ostensibly target opera, the set-up he describes applies to musical theatre; we *do* sit watching *Wicked* or *Phantom* as if we are hypnotized, swept away by the music and indulging in our emotions. Although we might not articulate this experience quite so critically as Brecht, to whom we are 'victims' under 'attack' (indeed, we are more likely to value it than criticize it), we certainly lose ourselves to the romance and wonder of musical theatre. This may be because the main intention of most theatregoers – particularly musical theatre audiences – is to be entertained: 'no theatre form is as single-mindedly devoted to producing pleasure', writes David Savran (2004, p. 212). This – at least throughout the twentieth century – has always been a dominant dynamic within musical theatre, and few shows reflect that better than Cole Porter's classic *Anything Goes* (1934) with its 'pure, unadulterated fun [...] pure escapist entertainment' (Whalen, 2013).

Pure escapist entertainment

Anything Goes could be a blueprint for any number of shows from the 1920s and 1930s, a period which really consolidated the idea of the musical comedy as a light-hearted form. Its plot hinges on subterfuge, mistaken identity, minor shenanigans and head-over-heels infatuation. The whole breezy affair is an excuse to throw together a top-notch score with some great song hits for the stars, including 'Anything Goes', 'I Get a Kick Out of You' and 'You're the Top' (the interpolation of other songs over the years

Anything Goes (1934)

Music and lyrics by Cole Porter

Book by Guy Bolton, P. G. Wodehouse, Russell Crouse, Howard Lindsay

Rewritten and revised extensively, different libretti exist from 1934, 1962, 1987 and 2011, each interpolating additional Cole Porter hits from other shows. The original libretto, featuring a shipwreck, was hastily rewritten after a fire killed dozens of passengers on the ship *Morro Castle* just weeks before the show opened.

Synopsis: When Wall Street broker Billy Crocker falls in love with classy Brit Hope Harcourt in a taxi, he can't help following his heart. He stows away on the *S.S. American*, on which she is travelling to England with her fiancé, Lord Evelyn Oakleigh, and is aided by two gangsters who happen to be aboard. Moonface Martin and his sidekick Bonnie procure travel documents for him, though these belong to Public Enemy Number One, Snake Eyes Johnson. When the captain hears that Public Enemy Number One is on board, Billy disguises himself to evade detection. Eventually he is uncovered, and he and Moonface are locked in the brig. Meanwhile, Billy's friend, nightclub singer Reno Sweeney, has been trying to discredit Lord Evelyn Oakleigh so that the engagement can be broken off and Billy and Hope can get together. They spread the tale that Lord Evelyn has been dallying with a young oriental girl, Plum Blossom. When the ship docks and Moonface and Billy escape, they rush to Lord Evelyn's estate disguised as Plum Blossom's parents, and blackmail him into cancelling the marriage. Billy and Hope end up together, Lord Evelyn and Reno fall for each other, and Moonface pockets the payoff, so all ends happily ever after.

like 'De-Lovely' and 'Friendship' shows both how adaptable the musical comedies of this period were, and how important producers considered the showstopping numbers) (see Figure 3.1). The musical for Cole Porter was undoubtedly intended to offer wit, entertainment and a great slice of escapist fantasy. He was after all a millionaire member of the party crowd who spent as much time holidaying on the French Riviera as he did on songwriting, and he evokes this fun-filled high-life in his songs, whether 'driving fast cars' ('Anything Goes') or 'flying too high with some gal in the sky' ('I Get a Kick Out of You'). Meanwhile, he is renowned for his 'list songs' (such as 'You're the Top' and 'Friendship'), and it is in part his structuring of these that washes his shows and their characters with a spirit of carefree delight. These are not emotionally deep storylines, and the characters are perfectly happy to play witty 'list song' games with one another, even when their dramatic circumstances are troublesome. Trading off the increasingly cooky witticisms of their partners, characters revel in dodgy rhymes and topical references as they try to outdo each other: 'You're a Botticelli', remarks Billy about Reno Sweeney, comparing her to classic Italian artwork; she replies, 'You're Keats' (the romantic poet), and his retort is 'You're Shelley' (another romantic poet). Finally, the laugh line comes: 'You're Ovaltine', concludes Reno, comparing Billy not to a celebrated artistic figure, but to a popular bedtime drink.

Unusually, Porter wrote both music and lyrics for his shows (not many writers do this, though Stephen Sondheim and Jonathan Larson are other prominent examples); musically too, he creates patterns which, like the lyrics, seem to resist emotional depth in order to bounce like stones skimmed across the water. Take the B section of the chorus from 'Anything Goes' ('The world has gone mad today', etc.). Here, an infectious syncopated rhythm is repeated for several phrases over a monotonic melody whose only movement is to rise chromatically on the first beat of every bar, coinciding with a significant rhyme. It is fun: simple, but not simplistic.

Anything Goes is actually rather a late example of this sort of breezy, carefree musical comedy, typical of the inter-war period on Broadway, and a real cure for both Prohibition (1919–1933) and the Great Depression (1929–c. 1940). According to Gerald Mast (1987, pp. 194–195), it is 'the best 1920s musical of the 1930s', which is a fair assessment. During this period

Figure 3.1   Only entertainment? *Anything Goes* **at the Theatre Royal Drury Lane (2004). Photo: Alastair Muir. REX Theatre Productions**

the classic musical comedy found its feet, evolving into a formulaic shape that satisfied audiences and producers. The producers found a format that worked, and – generally speaking – American audiences flocked to shows offering light-hearted entertainment with topical references, appealing characters and happy endings.

Musical comedy was carving itself a niche in the popular imagination: firstly, it was an out-and-out American form; secondly, it was modern and very twentieth century; thirdly, it was popular – and by that we don't just mean appealing – it was a cultural form that targeted and delivered to the populace as a whole: theatre for the people. In *Anything Goes* and other musicals of the same ilk, producers had a type of show that could be regenerated countless times with slightly different packaging and a different leading lady. The songs were in a style that all kinds of people loved; the storyline was amusing but not too complex; the show could be enjoyed on a number of different levels; and, most importantly, it didn't require a degree in philosophy or classics to understand.

But a show like *Anything Goes* did not appeal to everybody. By contrast to this *lowbrow* entertainment, a different type of *highbrow* culture found favour with some. Not wanting to associate themselves with the common tastes of popular audiences, highbrow audiences promoted art that was *elevating*, *worthy*, *moralistic* and *complex*. Above all, as Savran (2009) reports, highbrow culture was *not musical theatre*:

> The hierarchy of theatrical entertainments was clearly defined during the first quarter of the twentieth century [...based...] on a binary opposition between the serious legitimate stage and everything else. This guaranteed that literary or text-based theatre (regardless of its provenance) was granted a degree of prestige denied musical or variety entertainments. (p. 105)

Thus we find musical theatre's position within (American) culture to become interestingly compromised by an apparently arbitrary judgement that elevates *drama* whilst denigrating *the musical*.

Of course, there is one obvious area of the musical stage that also dissociated itself from the lowbrow: opera had long since separated itself from musical theatre, as histories of Italian and French opera from the seventeenth century show. These are riddled with stories of bitter cultural rivalries over the prestige of their respective operatic forms. By the early twentieth century, as various popular innovations emerged (musical comedy, jazz, film, radio), opera suffered something of a crisis. In America, though greatly admired by aficionados and highbrow critics, opera (specifically at the Metropolitan Opera House) was attacked by writers like Gilbert Seldes (1957). 'There is a vast snobbery of the intellect which repays the deadly hours of boredom we spend in the pursuit of art,' he wrote; 'We are the inheritors of a tradition that what is worth while must be dull; and as often as not we invert the maxim and pretend that what is dull is higher in quality, more serious, "greater art" in short than whatever is light and easy and gay' (pp. 265–266). Notice how Seldes picks up on the 'horizon of expectations' and cultural assumptions that had developed around opera. His influential championing of popular culture was as much a condemnation of this as anything else. He accused cultural elitists of constructing a false value system whereby tastes for certain types of culture determined social status. To him, the pretension of opera (amongst other things) represented what he called the 'bogus arts': worthless, shoddy and cynical. Across the Atlantic at around the same time, the young Bertolt Brecht was also condemning opera and championing the popular, though his reasons were more political.

Bertolt Brecht

Brecht's involvement with theatre began in the Berlin cabaret clubs of the 1920s. At that time, following World War I and the subsequent collapse of the economy, Germany's problems were enormous. The Weimar government did not seem to have a grip, and unemployment and inflation both spiralled out of control. Brecht viewed the problem not so much as a result of the war, but as a consequence of capitalism. As technologies had developed, factory owners became more powerful, meaning that everyone else – the country's workers – was exploited. More than this, government departments were under the influence of big business, scared to take a stand against the bosses, and therefore susceptible to corruption. So it was the common people's duty to fight, Brecht argued.

A distraction like opera, though, prevented this: it made you forget your problems, numbing your mind so any thought about the inequalities of your social condition would be squashed. Instead, Brecht suggested, theatre should wake up its audiences, galvanize their collective might and call them to action against the corruption. His thoughts echoed the words of Karl Marx in *The Communist Manifesto* (1848): 'The proletarians have nothing to lose but their chains. They have a world to win. Working men of all countries, unite!' (2008, p. 84).

Marx and capitalism

Marx was an economist whose principal theory suggested that society is controlled by the material conditions under which we live. Our current form of society – capitalism – is shaped by a small number of capitalists (the bourgeoisie) exploiting everyone else (the workers, or proletariat). Marx understands the fundamental driving force of society to be its economic set-up, or the 'Base'. Everything else, responding to and informed by the functioning of the Base, he labels the 'Superstructure'. The Base consists of two main elements: the 'Means of Production' and the 'Relations of Production'. The 'Means of Production' refers to an individual's ability to produce goods and hire labour power thanks to their ownership of factories and raw materials. The 'Relations of Production' refers to the economic arrangement between these people (the capitalists) and their labour forces (the workers). This is an unequal and exploitative arrangement. Since capitalists have the ability to produce (the 'Means of Production'), they also have the ability to make profit, by selling the goods created. With profit, they can buy more factories and become increasingly powerful. Workers, on the other hand, have no means, so they resort to selling the only assets they have: their time and their working capacity (their labour). With an excess of workers, the value of this labour can be determined by the capitalists, so the lowest rate possible is offered – enough to survive but not enough to make them independent or affluent. The worker is left constantly having to sell their time and labour to keep afloat, a situation Marx compared to (and referred to) as 'prostitution'.

In the economic climate of Weimar Berlin, cabaret clubs were popular places for disgruntled workers to stand up and protest against the government. Brecht's acerbic poetry, recited to the accompaniment of his guitar, became noticed, and he soon joined a group of avant-garde musicians to create musical theatre that he believed could rouse the people. These *Lehrstücke* or 'teaching pieces' are quite different from conventional musical theatre, both in form and effect: they were blunt and forthright; they did not resort to imaginative romanticism or fantasy; and they presented characters making hard decisions that had clear consequences. Brecht's aim was to show that any decision we made had a *social* effect, but that *indecision* or turning a blind eye had the worst effect of all.

This was a theme he would emphasize throughout his career, and in his classic plays from the 1930s and 1940s (*The Life of Galileo, Mother Courage and Her Children* and *The Caucasian Chalk Circle*), the consequences of indecision and complacency were shown to be socially and personally disastrous. It was also a theme that would resonate for the German people as the Nazi party rose to power. As Holocaust commentators Simon Wiesenthal and Alan Rosenbaum have suggested (quoting philosopher Edmund Burke), 'The only thing necessary for evil to triumph is for good men to do nothing'.

As Brecht formulated his ideas about theatre and its political possibilities, he established a form called 'Epic Theatre' which tried to keep its audience alert and critically engaged; which presented stories about people affected by their situations; and which emphasized how lives could be changed through cause and effect. In order to make his Epic Theatre practically effective, Brecht developed a range of devices to disrupt the conventional experience of watching theatre: performers were seen to be play-acting characters rather than 'becoming' them; costumes, sets and machinery were kept visible to remind audiences that they were in a theatre; messages were hammered home with slogans written on placards or projected onto the set; music was used to jar audiences into keeping alert rather than lulling them into a hypnotized state. Brecht referred to the effect his theatre had on audiences as the *Verfremdungseffekt* (the Alienation Effect), suggesting that through epic devices the audiences could see their own lives from a different (alien) point of view, thereby recognizing their problems and faults. What he put on stage he referred to as *Gestus*, individual actions whose significance was heightened thanks to the historical and social context of the scenario.

The Threepenny Opera (1928)

Despite Brecht's use of song and frequent collaborations with composers such as Kurt Weill and Hanns Eisler, his only work typically seen as a 'musical' is *The Threepenny Opera* (1928).

Brecht took on the commission of writing this when he was asked to translate John Gay's *The Beggar's Opera* (1728), a revival of which had run successfully in London's West End during 1927. Rather than simply translating it for German audiences, the young playwright decided to update and politicize it, adding new songs with music by Kurt Weill. The result was the first high-profile 'hit' of Brecht's career, much-revived and known for its notorious main character Macheath. The signature song '(The Ballad of) Mack the Knife' has become one of the most recorded songs in history, though ironically (following Bobby Darin's 1958 recording) this song entertains audiences rather than waking them up thanks to a performance style that masks its hard-hitting subject matter. In versions by Darin, Sinatra

---

The Threepenny Opera (1928)

Music by Kurt Weill
Book by Bertolt Brecht
Based on John Gay's *The Beggar's* Opera (1728)

Synopsis: London is being terrorized by Mack the Knife (Macheath), a serial killer and rapist who has left a trail of slaughtered young girls and bred fear into people's hearts. Meanwhile, the crooked proprietor of a beggar's agency plans to make as much money as possible out of the forthcoming royal coronation. But when Peachum finds out that his daughter Polly has become betrothed to Macheath, he does everything he can to have him arrested. Unfortunately, Macheath is best friends with the chief of police, Tiger Brown, so the gangster evades detection as events come to a head. Eventually, Macheath is arrested and sent to the gallows, but at the last minute Tiger Brown appears and our 'hero' gets pardoned by royal decree.

---

and numerous other crooners, a big band accompanies the singer, and we really are swept away by their 'razzle dazzle' as they sing about rape, knife-wounds and bodies found in the river.

The Threepenny Opera is an exciting adventure with an anti-hero at its centre, the stuff of crime novels and gangster films. Brecht's stylistic spin on both the play and its performance style, however, made it a classic example of Epic Theatre. Despite Macheath's very obvious criminality, it is the corruption of other characters and state institutions that stands out – the police, the courts and the church are shown not to uphold justice and faith, but to peddle hypocrisy and serve their own ends; the conniving Mr Peachum exploits the poor for profit with his protection racket; and the police chief Tiger Brown is in the pockets of organized crime. In drama-tizing such corruption Brecht is clearly making veiled remarks about insti-tutions in his own country.

Brecht, however, is not simply pointing the finger of blame so that the audience can sit back and accuse others. *The Threepenny Opera* is jarring and uncomfortable because he positions us within the hypocrisy of society, forcing us to notice our own roles in this corruption. And it is largely through the songs – with their discordant music and political lyrics – that he does this. 'What keeps a man alive?', asks one, revealing the answer to be 'selfishness': 'You have to kill your neighbour to survive. / It's selfishness that keeps a man alive.'

Finally, in a dramatic about turn, Macheath is reprieved from the gallows by the intervention of Tiger Brown. This is a completely unbelievable ending, but Brecht and Weill are making a point here too, as the music changes in style and becomes a pastiche of opera. This *deus ex machina* comments on how art – however politically inclined – conventionally offers that satisfying denouement and habitually perpetuates the status quo.

The musical idiom introduced by Weill in *The Threepenny Opera* and subsequently appropriated by practitioners such as John Kander and Fred Ebb in *Chicago* harks back to working-class origins (the folk song), popular musical forms (the music hall, vaudeville or cabaret) and deliberately didactic compositional styles (*Gebrauchsmusik*). The sound is recognizably distinct from the rag- and jazz-infused sounds that Irving Berlin, Cole Porter and George Gershwin were producing in America, the melodious romanticism of Jerome Kern and Richard Rodgers that came to typify the integrated musical or the later heavily produced quasi-operatic style of the megamusical. Instead, these political pieces – expressly *because* they intend their songs to have a conscious effect on their audience's thinking – often have an assumed simplicity and an apparent naivety in their jarring chordal harmonies and oompah accompaniments. In fact, the music is carefully constructed to give off impressions of austerity and functionality and used (both austerely and functionally) to comment on the dramatic or lyric content of the song. Even if the music doesn't itself express a political agenda – perhaps that is something it cannot do, after all – it accompanies, heightens and punctuates the significance of the lyrics.

Although Brechtian theatrical style has become common in more recent musical theatre, we rarely see Broadway or West End shows inciting people to revolution. Though *Les Misérables depicts* such battles, our sympathies are with the emotional loss of the characters, not with the political actions of the students. It is far more an *integrated* than an *epic* musical, and so dominant is the horizon of expectations about our reception behaviour here that we barely think about the social conditions borne by 'the miserables'. Nevertheless, to some extent – even in this show, but more obviously in others like *Chicago* (1975) – the Brechtian performance style initiated in *The Threepenny Opera* has become a key aesthetic of musical theatre. *Chicago* was structured as a vaudeville and originally featured a corrupt vaudeville agent (Henry Glassman – 'the Worm'), who introduced the numbers and explained the show's concept (the character was dropped after tryouts in Philadelphia). While this *structure* allowed its themes and issues (corruption, bribery, scandal) to stand out, the vaudeville *aesthetic* was enjoyed to the full. In a way the show is all 'razzle dazzle', with its provocative attack on celebrity and the media simply a hook for the entertainment of its song and dance, as critics such as Walter Kerr (1975, p. 109) noted: 'The storyline with its built-in satire has really been lost altogether, sacrificed to stunts and soft-shoe'. His remark reveals some of the expectations of audiences in 1975: the emphasis in a musical should be on its *storyline* (implicitly: should be *integrated*), and this show's 'alternative' presentational form somewhat challenged that.

Thus epic musical theatre has never been able to compete with the romanticized sentiment of commercial musical theatre or the art for art's sake of more serious composers. Nevertheless, since the politicizing events of the 1930s (the Depression, the rise of Hitler) which established very forcefully the fact that economics, politics and culture are linked, musical theatre has had its political (and often epic) exponents. Several Gershwin shows comment on Depression politics and the quagmire of American economics, including *Strike Up the Band* (1927), *Of Thee I Sing* (1932) and *Let 'Em Eat Cake* (1933), though these are more in the vein of Gilbert and Sullivan than Bertolt Brecht. Meanwhile, Marc Blitzstein's *The Cradle Will Rock* (1937) deals directly with the corruption of the American steel industry and emulates Brechtian style in both music and form. Later, racial politics informed a number of other allegorical if not epic musicals with social or political messages, including *Finian's Rainbow* (1947), *Cabaret* (1966), *Ragtime* (1998), *Parade* (1998) and *Caroline, or Change* (2003). The work of Kander and Ebb has shown a consistent Brechtian style, most famously in *Cabaret* (1966) and *Chicago* (1975), and more recently in *The Kiss of the Spider Woman* (1993) and *The Scottsboro Boys* (2010) – though their political impact is somewhat light. Other epic shows include John Dempsey and Dana P. Rowe's *The Fix* (1997) and Greg Kotis and Mark Hollmann's *Urinetown* (2001). Together, these form a significant canon of political musical theatre, though their (lack of) political influence proves that, on stage, the plights of others are kept at a distance – they are stories for amusement, entertainment and perhaps even the odd satirical swipe; but, fundamentally, musical theatre succumbs to the 'razzle dazzle' every time. As theatre has become increasingly commercialized, audiences have come to associate the musical not with politics or change, but with sheer entertainment; the complexities of the form have become hidden under a veneer of simplicity, and the cultural value of this extremely value-laden type of theatre has become one that – partly through its reception – perpetuates rather than challenges the might of capitalism.

Of course, much of the impact of any art form depends on the context in which it is created. The conditions in London in the 1980s, for example, were very different from the conditions of mid-nineteenth-century France, so one can hardly view *Les Misérables* without recognizing the difference between one world and the next. In the next chapter we consider how the cultural and historical context of a show's production can inform our understanding of the show as a performance text.

Further reading – theoretical

Bennett, Susan (1997) *Theatre Audiences* (London: Routledge).
Freshwater, Helen (2009) *Theatre & Audience* (Basingstoke: Palgrave Macmillan).
Schechner, Richard (2006) *Performance Studies: An Introduction* (second edition) (London: Routledge).

Further reading – relating to the examples

Block, Geoffrey (2009) *Enchanted Evenings: The Broadway Musical from Show Boat to Sondheim and Lloyd Webber* (second edition) (New York: Oxford University Press).
Swain, Joseph P. (2002) *The Broadway Musical: A Critical and Musical Survey* (Oxford: Scarecrow Press).
Willett, John (1978) *Brecht on Theatre: The Development of an Aesthetic* (new edition) (London: Methuen).

4   'Life Is a Cabaret': Cultural Materialism

It is 20 November 1966. A snare drum roll and a short cymbal splash bring to a close the opening night of John Kander and Fred Ebb's *Cabaret* at the Broadhurst Theatre on West 44th Street. The show has been striking and uncomfortable, positioning its audience in the shoes of the passive German public as the increasingly violent thuggery of the Third Reich played out on the streets of Berlin. In the show, American writer Clifford Bradshaw watches events escalate until he can no longer bear to stay in Germany. His response to the horror is to run away; many people were not so lucky.

How many members of the first night audience saw in this story of Berlin an allegory of America's treatment of racism goes unrecorded, though making this connection was an intention of the original production team. 'To us, at least, it was a play about civil rights, the problem of blacks in America, about how it can happen here', wrote director Hal Prince; 'What attracted the authors and me was the parallel between the spiritual bankruptcy of Germany in the 1920s and our country in the 1960s' (Jones, 2003, pp. 241–242). In *Cabaret*, the prism of international events from one generation magnified the social commentary on the next. The audience was faced (literally) with a huge mirror in which they found themselves reflected: a not-so-subtle indication that, in this show, art was intended to reflect life.

Understanding musical theatre within a cultural context reminds us that artworks – musicals, operas, songs – do not exist as stand-alone objects, but spring from and reflect the culture in which they were created. To discuss this we need to explore an area of theory known as 'cultural materialism'.

This was an idea introduced by British scholar Raymond Williams around 1960. It is effectively a way of historicizing a cultural text, considering it in the context of its own period but bringing to that study a contemporary perspective about society and its social dynamics. Although this approach works particularly well with historical texts that can therefore be 're-read' through contemporary eyes, cultural materialism can also reveal hidden dynamics in modern texts. In particular, these often relate to the treatment of individual or group identities, especially concerning gender, race, sexuality or class. This chapter therefore serves as a stepping stone towards the discussions in the second part of this book, which considers in more detail each of those identity areas.

'Im Kabarett, au cabaret, to cabaret...'

Cabaret (1966)

Music by John Kander, lyrics by Fred Ebb
Book by Joe Masteroff

Based on the play *I Am a Camera* (1951) by John van Druten, which was based on Christopher Isherwood's book *Goodbye to Berlin* (1939)

Synopsis: American writer Clifford Bradshaw arrives in Berlin and takes lodgings at Fräulein Schneider's boarding house, recommended by a stranger he met on the train, Ernst Ludwig. Cliff discovers the Kit Kat Klub, a seedy revue bar where English girl Sally Bowles is the headline act. He spends his days teaching English, and when Ernst offers him money to conduct business for him, he agrees to take documents to and from Paris. Soon, Sally has fallen for Cliff, become pregnant with his baby and moved in with him to live 'in delicious sin' at Schneider's boarding house. Meanwhile, Jewish greengrocer Herr Schultz has been wooing Fräulein Schneider, and towards the end of the first act, she agrees to marry him. At the engagement party, Cliff finds Ernst wearing Nazi insignia and realizes that he has inadvertently been working for the Third Reich. Act Two begins with Schneider breaking off her relationship with Schultz: tensions have mounted and it has become too dangerous to be associated with a Jew in Berlin. Cliff urges Sally to leave Berlin and arranges to take her back to America to raise the baby. But she prefers to stay, and when she has an illegal abortion without asking him, he realizes that their whirlwind romance has really only been a superficial fling. As events escalate, Cliff takes a train and leaves the edgy city behind. Throughout the show narrative scenes are interspersed with scenes in the Kit Kat Klub, whose engaging song-and-dance numbers, led by the charismatic Emcee and a kickline of dancers, comment on the events in the play.

Cabaret is clearly a show that observes and comments on society, and even if the allegorical reflection of America's prominent civil rights issues may not be explicit, the message 'It could happen here too' is forceful. And the show – depicting the milieu of Brecht's early years and using music that *sounds* like it came from the instruments of Brecht's collaborators – set a precedent for the American musical. By now immersed in the conventions of the integrated musical, whose seamless transition between scene and song aimed to elevate emotional connection, this dollop of epic theatre was jarring and uncomfortable. Between 'naturalistic' scenes outside the Kit Kat Klub, in which songs (particularly those of Fräulein Schneider) are conventionally integrated into the narrative, the show inserts stand-alone cabaret numbers commenting on the action. In particular, the effect of 'If You Could See Her through My Eyes' is strong. In the previous scene, Fräulein Schneider has broken off her engagement with Herr Schultz. The situation in Berlin is escalating, and although she feels tenderly for the Jewish grocer, she fears being associated with him amid rising anti-Jewish hostility. At the end of the poignant scene (which includes an excerpt of the integrated number 'Married'), a brick is thrown through the window of her boarding house, showing that the prejudice against Jews has already reached a point of violence. Immediately, the action cuts to the mischievous Emcee in the club, who introduces us to his 'girlfriend', a gorilla (see Figure 4.1). As he tells us of her attractions and the two dance, we are reminded that love can happen between people of difference, and that our prejudices (about people who look different or people who are not like us) are simply born out of ignorance. This is a clever epic device that, through satire, makes a compelling point; and it correlates just as pertinently to the racial tensions of 1960s America as it does to the ethnic tensions of 1920s/1930s Berlin.

By 1993, when the same show was directed by Sam Mendes at the Donmar Warehouse in London, the text took on a very different meaning. Where Joel Grey's Emcee character had been a ghoulish showman, the Emcee played by Alan Cumming was a highly sexualized character flirting with both male and female clubgoers and presenting Weimar Berlin as a

Figure 4.1 The Emcee (Joel Grey) and his gorilla girlfriend in *Cabaret* (1972). Allied Artists

hotbed of eroticism; the show betrayed not a hint of its *intended* civil rights agenda. At the end of the show, Cumming removed his Emcee costume to reveal a concentration camp uniform with a yellow badge and a pink triangle, respectively the signifiers of 'Jew' and 'Homosexual'. This reading of the show took on an entirely different agenda from the original production, although it still reflected the social context. London in the early 1990s (like New York) was steeped in a tension not associated with race but with sexuality. The impact of HIV and AIDS, which had no cure and which was killing even prominent white Westerners (Rock Hudson, Freddie Mercury, Michael Bennett) had really hit home a decade previously, and the result of this disease was a social backlash against the people most closely linked to it, the gay community. Media warnings against the perils of HIV were trumpeted loudly, but alongside this came the negative implication that it was caused by the debauchery of the gay lifestyle, which commonly featured casual and promiscuous sexual relationships. Whether or not this was true, middle-class Westerners became suspicious of these 'others' in their midst, and the taboo about being gay, which had been easing for decades since the relaxation of civil laws against homosexuality, became once more entrenched. To a 1993 audience, *Cabaret* offered a different narrative, in which the allegory of racism in the 1960s was substituted by an allegory of homophobia in the 1990s.

By 2006 such furore had eased significantly, and in a London now embracing gay culture, Rufus Norris's London production, with James Dreyfus as the Emcee, reduced this commentary on the threat of sexuality. Now, a prominent image at the end of the show presented the horror of the concentration camps, as the cast stripped off entirely to reveal emaciated bodies vulnerably awaiting extermination in the gas chambers. Yet the Holocaust is a part of the show's explicit narrative context; in this version the idea of *Cabaret* alluding to anything else vanished; it stayed within its own dramatic parameters. Was this version of the show weakened? Was this *Cabaret*-lite? Or was Norris still situating the production socially, within a context of the United Kingdom (and America) entering an unpopular war with ethnic 'others' in Afghanistan, and a civil scenario in which anti-Muslim sentiment was building on the streets? In this reading, perhaps the actual storyline (of real Germans being sucked into the hate-crimes of the Nazis) mirrored even more closely the contemporary situation. Was this also telling us 'It could happen here too'? If the race riots and burning of mosques in British towns in recent years are anything to go by (events that have escalated since 9/11, but particulary since the London bus bombings of 7 July 2005, and the killing of Lee Rigby in a London street in 2013), it suggests that this may be true.

Cultural materialism

Cultural materialism

Raymond Williams's interest in developing cultural materialism was to understand culture as something other than 'a pursuit of total perfection by means of getting to know [...] the best which has been thought and said in the world' (Arnold, 1869, p. viii). This view had been proposed by nineteenth-century theorist Matthew Arnold, who celebrated certain texts as 'great' art but dismissed others. Culture to Williams was far more than just the works of Shakespeare and the music of Mozart – indeed, far more than just a set of texts, a *canon* of esteemed work. He viewed culture as everything a society collectively thought and said and did. This included art and literature, but since he saw these as expressions *of the people*, he allowed *popular* forms and practices (not just highbrow) to become significant. Beyond this, a society's culture also included the way it behaved, the social interactions it encouraged and the attitudes and opinions that prevailed.

In one of his most important books, *The Long Revolution*, Williams (1961, p. 57) established 'three general categories in the definition of culture' (p. 57): 'ideal' culture, 'documentary' culture and 'social' culture.

'Ideal' culture expresses the values aspired to by a society – 'certain absolute or universal values' (ibid.), which it showcases as exemplary art. This is the culture found in museums and galleries or which we encounter as part of our education. This is culture that *enlightens* us or *improves* us, a value that is clearly signposted since it is preserved in majestic buildings and encased in gilded frames. But for many people lacking the privilege of money, education or class, 'ideal' culture can be out of reach and can become a divisive tool that marks the 'haves' from the 'have-nots'.

'Documentary' culture represents a society or reflects its behaviours to the world; it is 'the body of intellectual and imaginative work, in which, in a detailed way, human thought and experience are variously recorded' (ibid.). This culture has the potential to be far more inclusive, because it can operate locally and include the expressions of real people. Societies document themselves in popular activities such as fetes and festivals, telling their stories in histories or accounts and celebrating traditional practices and folk art. But for Williams, although this is a more inclusive category of culture, it is still incomplete: this may be the expression of a society, but it is the selective expression of what they choose to represent and how they wish to be seen.

'Social' culture moves beyond an encounter with objects or practices to 'clarif[y] the meanings and values implicit and explicit in a particular way of life, a particular culture' (p. 57). When we use language, fashion our hair, decorate our bodies or interact with technologies in certain ways, we are making cultural statements that reveal something about us. Such statements are very localized, both in time and place: the behaviour of one generation may be unfamiliar to the next, and the attitudes of one community may be different from the next. From outside a cultural community it can be difficult to understand what Williams calls the *structure of feeling*, the 'felt sense of the quality of life at a particular place and time'; he likens his own position in observing cultural groups to that of a visitor or a 'guest from a different generation' (p. 63).

Thus for Williams a true understanding of culture can come only from a holistic consideration of all of these aspects: 'The more actively all cultural work can be related, either to the whole organization within which it was expressed, or to the contemporary organization within which it is used, the more clearly shall we see its true values' (p. 70).

So what does this mean for musical theatre? Let's take a look at the 1935 opera *Porgy and Bess*.

Porgy and Bess (1935)

Porgy and Bess (1935)

Music by George Gershwin.
Lyrics by Ira Gershwin and DuBose Heyward

Based on DuBose Heyward's novel *Porgy* (1925) and its adaptation as a play by DuBose and Dorothy Heyward (1927)

Significant productions: Original Broadway production (1935), directed by Rouben Mamoulian; Glyndebourne Festival (1986), directed by Trevor Nunn (re-staged at the Royal Opera House in 1992, subsequently adapted for film by Nunn and Yves Baigneres); Cape Town Opera (2012), directed by Christine Crouse.

Synopsis: Set in the fictional 'Catfish Row', South Carolina, the story centres on Porgy's love for Bess. Bess begins the story as Crown's woman, but after Crown murders a gambler during a crap game, Porgy takes her in and protects her. The entire community is made up of poor black people, within which Porgy is a disabled beggar, regarded as the lowest of the low. The story focuses on the humanity of this community, and particularly that of Porgy. But there isn't a happy ending: first Crown and then Sportin' Life (the local drug dealer) tempt Bess away. The show ends as Porgy (only able to perambulate on a wheeled cart) sets off for New York to win her back.

A basic reading of *Porgy and Bess* using the narrative and semiotic codes we have encountered in Chapters 1 and 2 enables a reasonable understanding of the text. The story follows a conventional narrative: boy meets girl, boy loses girl, boy resolves to get her back. The stylistic codes reveal a hybrid form, part operatic and part Broadway jazz. The characters are a community of black folk in the American deep South. Visual clues signify poverty through clustered buildings in disrepair; the uneducated slang of the language reveals a lack of opportunities for the characters; musical signs signify blackness through referencing spiritual and jazz tropes. Beyond this, many symbolic allusions in the material embellish this basic semiotic reading: Porgy's disability is a magnified emblem of the bad lot he has in life; the temptation of Bess by shady characters adds a religious connotation; the elevation of the (black) 'Gullah' slang into a (white) operatic idiom gives universal value to their tale. All of this heightens the text, turning a personal story into a heroic challenge, and an individual plight into the struggle of a whole race. *Porgy and Bess* stands as a canonic example of American culture; it is a *great work of art*, 'ideal' culture.

But it is also 'documentary' culture. Like its source novel and play, *Porgy and Bess* attempts a realistic re-creation of tenement life in a black community from America's deep South: the depiction of life is violent, evoking poverty and a quiet, powerless desperation amongst the people. DuBose Heyward, a white Southerner, was in part writing from his own experience. Although not a member of the community he was depicting, his familiarity with Charleston and its black communities meant he could offer a reasonably authentic snapshot of tenement life. George Gershwin was a middle-class Jewish New Yorker whose background, education and erudition were far from the world depicted in the opera. Yet he had a fixation with black culture and visited Folly Island near Charleston several times in preparation for writing the show. He made great efforts to try and understand the music and setting for the work and to incorporate stylistic musical effects to represent the black characters. He used the structure and framework of nineteenth-century opera infused with 'the humor, the superstition, the religious fervour, the dancing, and the irrepressible high spirits of the race' (Woll, 1989, p. 171) to reflect the poor rural black setting. This resulted in an eclectic mix of operatic ensembles and spirituals ('Leavin' for the Promise' Land', 'It Take a Long Pull to Get There', 'Oh De Lawd Shake De Heavens' and 'Oh Dere's Somebody Knockin' At De Do'')[1] alongside songs with jazz rhythms and blues intervals that became well known outside the opera ('Summertime', 'Oh, I Got Plenty o' Nothin'', 'There's a Boat Dat's Leavin' Soon for New York' and 'It Ain't Necessarily So'). His almost anthropological observation of the community added to the show's folk authenticity. In *Porgy and Bess*, art reflects life, albeit heightened and expressed stylistically in the idiom of 'folk opera'. Calling it this recognizes both its authenticity and class: this is a document not only of Southern life but also of the writing team's aspirations to highbrow art.

Beyond the internal reading of the text and the consideration of its authorial production, though, a cultural materialist reading reveals how *Porgy and Bess* resonates as an expression of 'social' culture. Viewed from this perspective, further contextual considerations spring into significance.

The Metropolitan Opera was keen to produce the work, but Gershwin chose to have it staged by the far smaller, socially conscious Theatre Guild. Newspapers weren't sure whether to send their drama or music reviewers to the original production, as the show fell between the two. What this reveals about the social encoding of 'opera' at the time is interesting. Music critics disliked the show's musical comedy elements, while drama critics disliked the operatic recitatives (Woll, 1989, p. 171), views which reveal the gulf between cultural responses to theatrical forms. On the other hand, John Mason Brown's *New York Evening Post* review of the premiere, though mixed, reported: 'It is a good thing, a memorable production…and one of the far-famed wonders of the "Melting Pot".' He identifies the Russian director and designer, the two Southerners who wrote the book and the 'two Jewish boys who composed its lyrics and music, and a stage full of Negroes who sing and act it to perfection' before concluding that 'the result is the most American opera that has yet been seen or heard' (quoted in ibid., p. 173). Here we see dynamics of race writ large in the psyche of Americans at the time. And the reference to 'American opera' points to how important it was in this period for America to define an identity for its own culture that was distinct from Europe's. *Porgy and Bess* becomes an exemplar of the melting pot of America's ethnic identity, emblematic of a fresh start for American race relations, a blurring of boundaries between popular and highbrow cultures and – especially following President Roosevelt's attempts to revive America following the Great Depression – idiomatic of an America that was looking for a 'New Deal'.

However, despite the attempts of the writers, the employment of an entire cast of African American singers (only the white characters don't sing) and the operatic range of the work, there has often been a perception of racism in *Porgy and Bess* and concern about its appropriation of black music. This stemmed from criticism that white middle-class writers (of the creative team, only the chorus mistress, Eva Jessye, was black) were attempting to represent poor black characters, and to do so, were systematizing and reinterpreting what had been black music. Some critics of the opera – as they had with the play – asserted that Heyward dealt only with stereotypes who drink, take drugs and fight. This negative critique continued until after the Civil Rights Movement became established in the 1960s and 1970s (Graziano in Everett and Laird, 2008, p. 101). Yet it not only offered opportunities for black performers, but also gave those black performers a voice within a musical genre regarded as high class, elitist and, above all, white.

Like *Show Boat* (which has many of the same issues), it continues to be performed on musical theatre and operatic stages as new interpretations articulate its relevance to twenty-first-century audience. The opera is a powerful work that has become part of the operatic repertoire, while the songs and the story are part of mainstream cultural experience. It returned to Broadway in 2012 with most of the recitatives replaced by speech, while a recent complete production by Cape Town Opera Company toured the world. The South African production reflects a new life for the work in which a different black community with different though associated issues is allowed to 'speak' through the operatic text. The work in this production appeared to speak not only about a historical moment in the United States, but about the plight of South Africans during apartheid. Thus its cultural significance lives on in different contexts, relating to each in different but no less complex social ways.

Reading the text from a cultural materialist perspective emphasizes not so much the activities of the *plot*, but the significance of its *production*: the long saga of race relations in America; the dynamics of Broadway as a centre of production; the effects of the Depression and Roosevelt's New Deal policies; Gershwin's interest in a culture so distant from his roots; the fixation of a Jew of immigrant descent with ethnic 'others'; the cultural merging of popular jazz and highbrow opera; the fact that the characters depicted in his tale would have little access to the art form. These are all signifying factors (note the terminology of semiotics here) that bring meaning to this cultural text.

Very often there will be a relationship between the plot and the production, as there is in this example which deals coherently with race issues within and without the show. Indeed, the impact of a show can often be most pronounced when there is an obvious *ironic* serendipity between the internal and external dynamics of a piece (as there was with *The Cradle Will Rock*). But, of course, cultural materialism can expose precisely the opposite, perhaps revealing the absence of something significant from the narrative of a show, or flagging up an inherent anomaly between what is produced and its context of production. In the next example, we consider how the staging of a very recent show reveals a great deal (not always deliberately) about the society in which it is produced.

Here Lies Love (2013)

The David Byrne/Fatboy Slim musical *Here Lies Love* (2013) portrays the life of Imelda Marcos, former first lady of the Philippines (1965–1986) and, from 2010, political representative of Ilocos Norte (see Figure 4.2). Following tryouts of material throughout 2006 and 2007, it was released as a concept album in 2010, before being staged at the Public Theater in New York in a space transformed into the ambience of a contemporary club. Most audience members viewed the show in what is known as an 'immersive' way, standing on the dance floor of the club while the action took place around them on raised platforms and at either end of the room. The show used a contemporary technological aesthetic, with club-like lighting, powerful dance music and multiple video screens around the playing space. Live video projection emulated TV newscasts, moving rostra changed the shape of the stage areas and the audience was encouraged to dance throughout the performance.

To frame the biographical story of a political matriarch within the milieu of a contemporary club scene may seem rather anachronistic, though the justification for this is Imelda's passion for clubbing during her 'handbag democracy' days. The project is clearly attempting to define a new type of musical theatre that capitalizes on the immersive experience of clubbing and moves away from a traditional Broadway sound – the jazz of the 1920s/1930s; the melodious string sounds of Rodgers and Hammerstein; the

Figure 4.2   Imelda Marcos (Ruthie Ann Miles) in *Here Lies Love* at the Public Theater, New York (2013). Photo: Sara Krulwich. *The New York Times* courtesy of Eyevine

---

Here Lies Love (2013)

Concept and lyrics by David Byrne

Music by David Byrne and Fatboy Slim

Based on the life of Imelda Marcos, and influenced by Ryszard Kapuscinski's book about the Ethiopian dictator Haile Selassie, *The Emperor: Downfall of an Autocrat* (1978). First released as a concept album (2010)

Synopsis: Imelda Romualdez is a poor Philippine girl looked after by her nursemaid Estrella Cumpos. When Imelda wins a beauty contest to become 'Rose of Tacloban', she moves to Manila and starts dating political journalist Benigno Aquino. She is feted by society for her beauty, and when she and Aquino split up, she meets Senator Ferdinand Marcos, who courts her flamboyantly for 11 days before proposing. Marcos grooms her to be the perfect senatorial wife, and when he wins the presidential election in 1966, Imelda effectively shares the presidency. But their behaviour is criticized by detractors, including her former boyfriend Aquino. While terrible poverty blights the Philippines, Imelda lives a jet-setting lifestyle and authorizes lavish building projects. Travelling the world, she lobbies for Philippine interests with an entourage of glamorous ladies and a mantra of 'handbag diplomacy'. The press discovers her humble origins in an interview with her former friend Estrella; furious, Imelda summons Estrella to the palace, and when she refuses to be bribed into silence, Imelda puts her under house arrest. Near the end of his second term of office, Marcos engineers civil unrest and is implicated in a terrorist bombing that kills most of the political opposition. He instigates martial law and censorship to keep control, jailing the remaining opposition, including Aquino, but maintaining power. In jail, Aquino conducts a hunger strike, and when he has a heart attack, Imelda arranges for him to seek asylum in America. But seeing from afar the Philippines descend into further chaos, he takes the dangerous decision to return in 1983. He is assassinated on his arrival. The public outcry at his funeral begins the long revolution of the Philippine people against the Marcos regime. When votes are rigged in a 1986 election, the people campaign, and after four days of peaceful protest, they oust the leader and his wife, who are air-lifted to safety by American forces.

---

pseudo-operatic rock of the megamusical. Its production team is a collaboration of well-established experimenters: David Byrne has long been known and respected as an innovative musician, whose fronting of the 1980s band Talking Heads was just one interesting facet of an illustrious career; the club DJ Fatboy Slim (real name Norman Cook) has built a strong reputation in the United Kingdom and internationally as the role of the celebrity DJ has grown; and the Public Theater has long been an off-Broadway venue not

afraid to push the boundaries of conventional theatre. This show's significance then – what allows it to get away with the bold incongruities of this
theatrical conceit – is in the makeup of its concept; it passes as 'ideal' – or
at least interestingly worthwhile – culture.

Of course, the show is also very clearly a documentary of Imelda
Marcos's life, though in referring to 'documentary' culture Raymond
Williams does not explicitly mean biographical, fact-based or verbatim
examples of work; in Williams's terms, the 'documentary' nature of *Here
Lies Love* is also in its use of a particular contemporary idiom *and* the
incongruity of the style and subject matter. This cultural expression comes
from a world in which the glamour and hedonism of the music industry
gets juxtaposed or even confused (through countless media images) with
the politics of international poverty, war-mongering or decay: think of the
celebrity adoptions of orphans from developing countries by celebrities
like Madonna; the way performers like Bob Geldof and Bono have used
rock as a soapbox for international aid; or the way teenage pop sensation
One Direction were flown out to Africa as part of the UK-based Children
in Need charity telethon. Make what you will of these odd scenarios and
the curious juxtapositions of wealth and poverty, exposure and awareness
and pity and guilt.

In the end, *Here Lies Love* is less innovative as a production than it promises. Although overcoded with a stylistic club sound, the songs are actually
fairly standard musical theatre constructions, more or less integrated into
a rise and fall narrative. The narrative offers plenty of opportunity for the
sort of emotional expression that is common currency in musical theatre,
from the dreams of a young girl ('Here Lies Love') to the heady feelings
of love ('Eleven Days'). And tracking the story of a famous political figure
has been a common pursuit of the musical stage, from *I'd Rather Be Right*
(1937) through *Fiorello!* (1959) to *Evita* (1978), which this show seems to
emulate.

At various points the audience becomes significant to the narrative, as
it implicitly plays the part of the crowd at political rallies, entertainment
events and public festivals. But this becomes one of the more troubling
aspects of the show, since the call to engage in the immersive *experience*
overwhelms the politics of the diegesis. Towards the end of the narrative,
Philippine leader Ferdinand Marcos and his political adversary fight for
the presidency, both delivering powerful political speeches. The audience
becomes the supportive crowd at first one and then the other rally,
invited by powerful dance music to create an atmosphere of euphoria and
implicitly gesturing support for the politics of (both) leaders indiscriminately. When Marcos subsequently massacres the opposition and when

his policies lead to devastating poverty around the country, the impact does not hit home; audience members are blind to the fact that moments before they have willingly and enthusiastically – but mindlessly – danced to his tune.

What does this expose about 2013's structure of feeling? A contemporary cultural zeitgeist in which atrocious acts of horror are meaningless? A pervasive obsession with immediate self-indulgence? A worrying commitment to style over substance? Or an artistic form (the musical) that is destined to always be *Only Entertainment* (as Richard Dyer ironically titles one of his books)? Just as the different productions of *Cabaret* and *Porgy and Bess* reflect the culture of their context, *Here Lies Love* inadvertently says a great deal about contemporary ambivalence and social unawareness.

Cultural materialism and Marxist thought

At the heart of cultural materialism is the return to Marx (1904, pp. 11–12) and his statement, 'It is not the consciousness of men that determines their existence, but [...] their social existence that determines their consciousness'. In other words, it's not what we *think* that shapes the world, it's the way we are forced to live.

The way we live, according to Marx, is intrinsically unequal, imbalanced in favour of the powerful capitalists and confirmed by an ideological belief system that encourages us to accept the status quo. One aim of cultural materialism is to try to make visible the ideological forces that perpetuate inequality and to recognize in cultural products how those ideologies are sustained and confirmed. Though we might imagine musicals to be rather innocuous (*Only Entertainment*), it is often surprising how ideologically loaded they can be. The reality that we don't notice in these ideologies means that we can easily be influenced by them; and the fact that musical theatre often appeals to impressionable people (children and teenagers, for example), means we absorb ideological agendas without thinking about them or noticing how forceful their power can be.

In the second section of this book we consider several ways in which ideologies have been constructed to validate the unequal status quo and cultural texts (like musicals) endorse these ideologies. As such, and in common with other arts, musical theatre can be considered a tool of the state, through which problematic ideas are perpetuated, and class struggle is suppressed. In particular, we look at how ideologies of identity marginalize certain groups of people – women, non-Western societies, ethnic groups and minorities – so that the powerful can prevail.

Ideology, ISAs and consent

It is surprising no one does anything to change things: clearly the monetary reward for selling our time and labour is inadequate – we go into debt, we scrape an existence and we can see gross inequalities, even in developed countries, between the haves and the have-nots. Why do governments do nothing to improve things? Why don't we demand higher rates of pay? Why not stage a revolution? Well, of course, sometimes these things do happen, but generally the people, the governments and the capitalists seem resolved to keep things as they are. This reveals complexities in the capitalist arrangement that have been explored by post-Marxist writers like Antonio Gramsci (1891–1937) and Louis Althusser (1918–1990). Gramsci suggested that the reason the status quo was maintained was because of 'hegemony' and 'consent', the domination of one group over others and their willing acceptance of it. He suggested that the bourgeoisie maintains power because it constructs ideologies that people accept; the people *consent* to be treated as they are because they get the impression that it is in their interest. Althusser took this further, suggesting the situation was entrenched through 'Ideological State Apparatuses', mechanisms that support capitalist ideologies and instil these into the people as commonsense values. The government is an 'ISA' which visibly makes the rules, but to Althusser, other ISAs like the education system and even the family reinforce ideological ways of thinking. 'Family values' are normalized in society, yet these promote certain ideologies – marriage, monogamy, fidelity and heterosexuality – that not only perpetuate the status quo but also disenfranchise anyone who does not conform, thereby abnormalizing and implicitly punishing non-conformity. Although capitalists are the main beneficiaries of this system, they can maintain power only because we agree (consent) to this inequality. Thus we are as much to blame for the inequality and injustice; the power of ideology is such that we rarely think about these complexities, remaining unaware that we could make a change.

Further reading – theoretical

Knowles, Ric (2004) *Reading the Material Theatre* (Cambridge: Cambridge University Press).
Storey, John (2006) *Cultural Theory and Popular Culture: A Reader* (third edition) (Harlow: Pearson Education).
Williams, Raymond (2001) *The Long Revolution* (Letchworth: Broadview Press).

Further reading – relating to the examples

Bush Jones, John (2003) *Our Musicals, Ourselves: A Social History of the American Musical Theater* (Hanover and London: University of New England Press).

Kroenert, Tim (2010) 'Imelda Marcos the Musical', *Eureka Street* 20(7): 29–30.
Leve, James (2009) *Kander and Ebb* (New Haven: Yale University Press).
Noonan, Ellen (2011) *The Strange Career of Porgy and Bess: Race, Culture, and America's Most Famous Opera* (Chapel Hill: University of North Carolina Press).

PART II
Interpreting Contexts

5 'You've Got to Be Carefully Taught': Orientalism and Musical Theatre

In the first part of this book we explored ways in which musical theatre *means* – through its narratives, its sign-systems, its interaction with audiences and its cultural context. We discussed four theories – Narrative Theory, Semiotics, Reception Theory and Cultural Materialism – and we encountered the important influence of thinkers like Roland Barthes and Karl Marx. We finished Part I by introducing you to the concept of *ideology*, a set of ideas that guides behaviour and practices. Through looking at Louis Althusser and Antonio Gramsci's ideas we saw how ideology controls us and how we also consent to this control. We noted in particular that ideology privileges certain groups of people over others, and that this leads to situations in which certain behaviours, lifestyles or identities are seen as 'normal' while others aren't.

In Part II we are going to explore some of the identity politics that arise from this situation, noting how the voices of the dominant have historically been heard, whilst the voices of others have been marginalized. However, we also discuss how, through cultural texts like those of musical theatre, dispossessed voices have been able to reassert themselves.

Our first discussion, in this chapter, considers how the West developed a powerful voice while the rest of the world was sidelined. We explore this through the critical lenses of Orientalism and Post-Colonialism. We see how Western attitudes to other cultures have constructed not only relationships of power, but also attitudes of authority affecting the way we see the 'other'. Ultimately, this has led to a global spread of Western hegemony that is beginning to be challenged only now. Next, in Chapter 6, we consider how capitalists and producers have made money not only from these relationships, but also from the artistic practice of musical theatre, maximizing profits along the way. We consider various strategies that producers have taken from other industries, leading to a global musical theatre industry which mimics their exploitation and which really does reflect big business. In the final chapter in this part of the book, we explore how some of the powerful foundations of Western thinking that allowed such cultural domination by the West have been challenged in the late-twentieth century's turn to postmodernism. We consider whether developments in artistic form can generate developments in artistic production: the way that the form is produced, consumed, traded and experienced.

South Pacific (1949)

One of the most thankless roles in musical theatre for a young actress is the part of Liat in *South Pacific* (1949). You have to be beautiful, of course – Liat is the mesmerizing object of hunky Lieutenant Cable's desire; but you don't get a chance to do much else. Liat is the daughter of the comedy character Bloody Mary, and doesn't speak English; in fact, she doesn't speak. Nevertheless, she communicates very gracefully through dainty hand and head gestures, and through a language of love which doesn't use many words. Cable does all the talking (well, singing) in this relationship, serenading her with 'Younger Than Springtime' before setting off on a mission only to be killed in action. Liat, the pretty Polynesian, is the *silent* exotic, the fantasy encapsulation of 'otherness'. 'What a lovely cross-cultural match', writes Rick Ayers (2008) in *The Huffington Post*: 'Liat speaks not a word in the whole musical, only smiles and takes the Yankee to bed. She's underage; he's a pedophile. What a fantasy of the white western male, the submissive, exoticized and eroticized Asian "girl" to, to what? Well, to screw of course'.

South Pacific (1949)

Music by Richard Rodgers

Book and lyrics by Oscar Hammerstein

Based on James Michener's collection of short stories, *Tales of the South Pacific* (1947)

Synopsis: This World War II story is set on an island in the South Pacific where a team of US marines has been stationed. Military nurse Nellie Forbush falls for French plantation owner Emile de Becque, who lives on the island. When she discovers that the charming Polynesian kids on Emile's plantation are his children from a previous marriage, she is horrified that a white Westerner could have had a relationship with a native. Nevertheless, her feelings soften, and eventually she moves in with Emile and becomes stepmother to his kids. Meanwhile, one of the marines falls in love with the beautiful islander Liat; despite Lieutenant Cable's attraction to her exotic beauty, he rejects her because of her skin colour. Cable goes on to be killed in action, causing us to regret the waste of young lives in war and missed opportunities brought about by prejudice.

South Pacific is far from the worst offender when it comes to depicting oriental characters as *different* – though Rodgers and Hammerstein shows have a surprising number of racially contentious characters, like the ridiculous Bloody Mary here and Ali Hakim in *Oklahoma!*, or the king in *The King and I* (1951), who is just not schooled in Western ways. This is significant: schooling is key, and to their credit, Rodgers and Hammerstein acknowledge this in one of their songs from *South Pacific*. Here, in the context of a storyline that shows both Nellie Forbush and Lieutenant Cable falling for foreigners but balking at the idea, Hammerstein offers his thoughts on racism through the voice of Cable. Racism is not something you are born with, he contends, but something that 'you have to be carefully taught'. So challenging was this sentiment in 1949 that Rodgers and Hammerstein risked the show's success to keep it in (see Most, 2000). This mattered to them, although *South Pacific* treads a fine line between objectifying its ethnic characters and humanizing them; within the (cultural materialist) context of its time, the attempt to challenge racism was at least progressive.

Orientalism

The history of relations between the West and the East is long and complex, and it has affected the way peoples from different countries think about and value their own cultures, histories and identities. Rooted in different religious mythologies, mindsets and cultural practices, an inevitable sense of difference has prevailed. To Western eyes, the Orient has been alluring, exciting and exotic; as soon as explorers from the West started travelling to the East, they noted the differences in lifestyle, looks and beliefs and found mystique in this alien 'other'. As a result of the global expansion of trade, and especially links with the Middle and Far East, interest developed in exports from this exotic other world. Traders brought back spices, materials and foodstuffs; poets fetishized the people as beautiful and exotic, and across the arts, orientalized features and borrowings became widespread. Such borrowings from other cultures raise issues of power and representation; yet the exchange of culture and knowledge can provide a catalyst for new and exciting work. As such the dynamics of orientalism have the potential for both socially problematic and artistically progressive results.

Since these other cultures had been discovered through exploration, Europeans saw them as curiosities, interesting specimens from a different world; a sense of superiority over their discoveries could easily be turned into *authority*. Where Western skin was the noble white of the affluent merchant or aristocrat, the 'other' was differently coloured, and therefore differently cast as lesser to the European norm; where Western language was elegant and developed from centres of learning and prestige, the 'other' spoke gutturally and barbarically, suggesting to Western ears inferior linguistic and therefore mental faculties. Where Westerners were hard working, civilized, educated, free thinking and moral, the 'other' was lazy, sensual, immoral and decadent, acting on instinct and emotion rather than through thought and education. The 'other' is everything that the Westerner is not, and when standards of Western success mark status, anything alien becomes lesser. Within this framework we can see how relationships get out of hand. Slavery, for example, could be justified because native black subjects were assumed to be inferior to whites and incapable of being educated; colonizing powers imposed legislative methods and cultural practices in order to improve them.

In 1978 Edward Said wrote a seminal work that critiqued the relationship between Western culture (the Occident) and the East (the Orient). He described the relationship, in which Europeans assumed their cultures and practices were universal and natural, as one which articulated 'a relationship of power, of domination, of varying degrees of a complex hegemony' (Said in Williams and Chrisman, 1994, p. 133), and he suggested that this power imbalance was brought about by a perception of the East which at the same time exoticized and debased the 'other'. He called this perspective *Orientalism*, but argued that it was only an *idea* of what the East is, not a reality: an ideology that established its hold during the colonial period (from the late 1840s until the 1990s), sustained by socio-economic and political institutions of power. Said argued that it was more than a fantasy, calling it 'a created body of theory and practice, in which, for many generations, there has been a considerable material investment' (p. 133).

The way people from oriental cultures were portrayed derives from a sense that all 'others' are homogenous and anonymous, so that they remain an ideal and unchanging abstraction, a group that embodies instincts and emotions very different from those of westerners. But Said's argument is more complex. He demonstrates how writers, educators, academics and institutions assimilated ideas of the Orient into their work so that the literal control of native people (the colonial conquest of the East) was matched by the implicit denigration of the 'other' in cultural language, imagery and rhetoric. By the end of the nineteenth century the designation of the area east of Europe as 'Oriental' 'implied no necessary connection between actual experience of the Orient and knowledge of what is Oriental', he wrote; 'the cumulative effect of decades of so sovereign a Western handling turned the Orient from alien into colonial space' (p. 148).

There are many works that can be considered offensive to – or at least ignorant of – oriental cultures. In his exploration of musical orientalism,

Figure 5.1 Being Japanese: Geraldine Ulmar as Yum-Yum in the original production of *The Mikado* (1885). Billy Rose Theatre Division, The New York Public Library for the Performing Arts, Astor, Lenox and Tilden Foundation

Derek B. Scott identifies several, from Purcell's *The Indian Queen* (1695) to Delibes's *Lakmé* (1883) and Iggy Pop's 'China Girl' (1977). Over time, rather than presenting genuine expressions of the art of any particular place, a range of signifiers began to appear that sedimented the alien, exotic and oriental into stereotypical banalities. The height of this orientalism occurred around the turn of the twentieth century. Gilbert and Sullivan had a huge success with *The Mikado* (1885), an operetta ostensibly set in Japan and using comic Japanese names and references to satirize Victorian English manners. The assumed formalities of Japanese culture are ridiculed in the flippant treatment of things like execution, and characters – especially the women – are crassly orientalized (see Figure 5.1). The Three Little Maids from one of the show's most popular songs, for example, come across as chirping, indistinguishable little girls, both modelled as Japanese stereotypes and refined by an English education system. Sidney Jones followed this with *The Geisha* (1896; set in Japan) and *San Toy* (1899; set in China). They showed very little difference in the way their 'exotic' music and characters were represented. The characters Ping, Pong and Pang in Puccini's *Turandot* (1926), as Scott (1997) discusses, are Chinese stereotypes. The exoticism of China is represented by an instrumental palette of harp, celeste, glockenspiel and gongs, and by a harmonic texture of pentatonicism and augmented triads. These, along with parallel fourths, came to represent the Orient in music and, as Scott points out, can be heard in Frederic Norton's *Chu Chin Chow* (1916), Albert Ketèlbey's *In a Chinese Temple Garden* (1923) and contemporary versions of *Aladdin*.

Madame Butterfly (1904)

The musical and thematic stereotypes of orientalism are also present in the story of *Madame Butterfly*. The events take place entirely in Nagasaki at the turn of the century (at the time of composition), giving the opportunity for exoticism in a set design showing a Japanese house, terrace and garden with the beautiful Nagasaki bay in the background. Exotic costumes (kimonos), hair styles and makeup are worn by the heroine and her relatives, and the image of the small submissive, compliant and loyal oriental woman conforms to the pattern already established and to which many future representations will adhere. Japanese sensibility is partially represented through the misunderstanding that occurs between Butterfly and Pinkerton, but the expectation that Butterfly will accept an arranged marriage and then remarry when her 'husband' goes back to his country invokes a partial and partisan understanding of Japanese custom. The code

Madame Butterfly (1904)

Music by Giacomo Puccini

Libretto by Luigi Illica and Giuseppe Giacosa

Derived from several sources, including the short stories *Madame Chrysanthème* (1887) by Pierre Loti and *Madame Butterfly* by John Luther Long (1898), the dramatization by David Belasco (1900) and events in Nagasaki in the early 1890s

Significant productions: First performed at La Scala, Milan, in 1904, Puccini kept revising the work – there are five different versions – and since its successful performances in the fifth or 'standard' version, other works have derived from it. Most notable is the musical theatre transposition to Vietnam by Claude-Michel Schönberg and Alain Boublil, *Miss Saigon* (1989).

Synopsis: The story is set in Nagasaki and concerns a visiting naval officer, Colonel Pinkerton, and a 15-year-old Japanese girl Cio-Cio San (known as Madame Butterfly). Pinkerton has arranged a marriage of convenience, while Butterfly believes this to be a love match and has converted to Christianity to celebrate the wedding. Her uncle finds out about the wedding and curses them both, causing the wedding guests to leave. The colonel completes his tenure in Nagasaki and leaves, but Butterfly waits for him. In the meantime the marriage broker arranges another marriage for her, which she refuses, and the American Consul visits her to tell her that Pinkerton is due to return with his new wife. When he discovers that she has had a son by Pinkerton, he can't bring himself to tell her this news. Pinkerton arrives (with his wife), but hasn't the courage to face her because he realizes his mistake. Instead, his wife Kate meets Butterfly and offers to take and raise the child. Butterfly, in shock and shame at his desertion, and in desperation for her child, agrees on condition that Pinkerton shows himself. She blindfolds the child and makes him wait for his father before killing herself. The different customs and moral practices of the two cultures are revealed as the main protagonists misunderstand each other's intentions and feelings.

of honour that depicts Western morality as well as Japanese sensibility is apparent in Butterfly's steadfast refusal to accept a new husband, and her eventual suicide. The focus on Butterfly's perspective ultimately reveals Pinkerton and the Consul to be at best misguided and at worst cruel, heartless and fraudulent. The exploration the opera undertakes, therefore, demonstrates an early awareness that colonial power leads to personal conflicts arising from cultural difference and that the victims of such situations are disproportionately women and children subjected to male sexual power. Even while audiences enjoy the exotic experience of empathizing with Butterfly, the focus on her emotional journey provides a critique of the colonial trade practices at home.

This is a more sophisticated approach to the East than that shown in many of the other musical comedies mentioned, and contains a more nuanced approach to the representation of the 'other', though its appeal still relied on the fashion at the time for Japanese imagery, and the sexual availability of the exoticized female. As Chadwick Jenkins (2002) reports of David Belasco's play, 'The lack of familiarity with Japanese culture served not only as a point of interest but also as a form of insulation from the play's tragic conclusion'. He cites *The London Times* review from the time, which commented, 'In any other than an exotic setting, the dramatic episode would be intolerably painful'.

There are two layers, then, in the audience's interaction with the piece. Firstly, the audience is attracted to the character due to an interest in the erotic and exotic 'other'; secondly, the audience is insulated from Butterfly's tragedy because of being culturally distanced. In the music, though – especially during Butterfly's long vigil in Act 2 – Puccini provided a possibility of identifying with her through textures and timbres that sound oriental yet familiar. Her tragedy and Pinkerton's villainy are thus magnified and felt more profoundly. This may account for the work's continuing popularity and its adaptations into other formats such as the West End musical *Miss Saigon* (1989).

Butterfly's score contains references to Japanese melodies gathered during Puccini's research. He studied recordings and publications and discussed Japanese music and culture with the wife of the Japanese ambassador to Rome. Kimiyo Powils-Okano has identified at least ten authentic melodies in the score, including the national anthem *Kimi ga yo* during the wedding ceremony between Pinkerton and Butterfly (see Gerbino, 2002). However, the structure of the work and the sonic images of Japan rely on the stereotypical pentatonic and whole-tone scales associated with 'a rather broadly defined and exotic east' (ibid.). More importantly, the representation of Butterfly herself often uses quite naïve music which, '(whether or not based on authentic Japanese music) seems to project the image of an infantilized world, epitomized in the delicate and fragile musical idiom of the infantilized heroine of Puccini's opera, Cio-Cio-San, the girl-bride, "bimba dagli occhi pieni di malia" ("a child with eyes full of seduction")' (ibid.).

This feminization of the Orient is addressed by Nasser Al-Taee, who argues that female characters in Turkish and Arabic operas were often portrayed as available, seductive and 'a locus of often dangerous desire which Europeans apparently could not resist' (in Baur, Knapp and Warwick, 2008, p. 19).

He continues: 'Within the colonial enterprise, she is doubly threatening as an oriental and as a woman, and she must be dealt with accordingly.' In other words, in the narratives of opera, she must die. In a period when middle-class European wives were imagined as unsexed domestic servants, the oriental woman was depicted as a male fantasy figure. One might go even further in observing Butterfly's small size, young age and feminized exoticism, and the naivety of the music, to note again the almost paedophilic gaze of the orientalizing tendency (which we saw with *South Pacific's* Liat) that positions the West as dominant 'master' and the East as submissive 'child'.

Post-Colonialism

We have seen how a fascination for the Orient led to the incorporation of Eastern stylistic features, themes and characters in Western shows. Yet the way in which the East influences Western culture is often only partial, filtered by Western sensibilities through the perception of these cultures as different, foreign and strange. A process of transposition occurs here which could be best illustrated through the parlour game 'Chinese Whispers'. Here, players sit around the room and one player whispers a phrase to the next, with each player passing it on to their neighbour until the final iteration of the phrase is announced out loud, usually grossly distorted from the initial whisper. How interesting that this game, which for our amusement mimics the processes of orientalism, should be given a title that situates its comic potential as an articulation of the Orient (a 'Chinese Whisper'). Think how this is also problematic: alongside the casual fun come assumptions about language, culture and difference – ultimately, we end up laughing *at* difference, and in its name alone, this game entrenches the idea that the language (culture) of the East is something to be mocked.

Said felt that representations of the Orient that compounded this imbalance had to be reconsidered, a project known as Post-Colonialism. Since the 1970s works from the colonial period have been revisited to understand how portrayals of the East promoted or subverted a reading of the 'other' as inferior, emotional and immoral, and whether that representation revealed or critiqued the imbalance of power. Through this project, the voices of 'others' have found more articulation, subverting established dynamics of power and voicing alternative perspectives.

Three phases have been identified in the development of post-colonial identities. Firstly, during colonization, the culture of the invading power was adopted. Secondly, indigenous peoples used European genres and styles, but adapted them to their own concerns, revisiting pre-colonial history and reviving folk cultures and native voices. Thirdly, creators began to take ownership of new hybrid forms that expressed post-colonial identities. Works in this category often reveal identities as fluid and narratives as contradictory to reflect the ideological instabilities resulting from colonial oppression and the need to revise identity construction in the present.

Pacific Overtures (1976)

Pacific Overtures (1976)

Music and lyrics by Stephen Sondheim

Book by John Weidman

Synopsis: *Pacific Overtures* explores the relationship between the West and Japan. It is set in Japan in 1853 and documents the events leading up to the opening up of Japan for trade after it had been closed to the outside world since about 1600, and its subsequent development into a world power. American warships led by Commodore Perry entered the bay at Okinawa to the consternation of the Japanese, who had banned all interaction with foreigners and forbidden them access. The problem Japanese leaders faced was how to convey this to the Americans, and how to enforce it with only swords for weapons. The leading Samurai send a minor noble, Kayama, to negotiate, who enlists the help of a fisherman brought up in America, Manjiro – who knows how to 'manage' Americans. The pair arrange the meeting in a specially constructed Treaty House with mats laid so that the Americans' feet never touch Japanese soil. After the meeting the Japanese think they have been successful but the Americans have simply determined to return with a larger force. In Act 2 representatives not only of the United States but also of Britain, France, Holland and Russia arrive to begin trade negotiations. Gradually Kayama becomes more and more Westernized while Manjiro joins an underground resistance force, ultimately assassinating his old friend Kayama. Meanwhile, other unpleasant consequences such as prostitution and rape have been brought in by the Westerners. The new young emperor finally seizes control and decides that Japan should modernize. He opens up trade and in the final scene the modern Japan of Suzuki, Toyota and Mitsubishi, and the colonization of the West by Japanese goods is revealed.

Pacific Overtures, set mainly in 1853, deals with a period immediately preceding that of *Madame Butterfly*. The story is again written from a Japanese perspective and uses Japanese theatrical forms in its construction. Thus there is a sensitivity to the plight of Japan, in an approach that to some extent reverses the tendencies of orientalism. Yet even while the morality of the work clearly deplores the cultural encounter that ripped Japan from its isolation, it still trades on a sense of the exotic – the oriental 'other'. As in *Madame Butterfly*, there is an attempt at authentic musical representation and performance practice, and an equal criticism of both Japanese and American cultures: the Americans are represented as monsters with guns, while the Japanese are ridiculed for the arcane structures of their culture.

The use of a Japanese theatrical style (a combination of Kabuki with Nō and Bunraku puppet theatre) and a largely Asian American cast shows a production team attempting to avoid orientalism while dealing with a culture they could not entirely represent. Aware of musical clichés and the exoticism deplored by Edward Said, Sondheim attempted to find 'a syntax that could be made to sound Japanese to Broadway audiences, but would avoid the clichés of Broadway's ready-made orientalist idioms' (Knapp in Baur, Knapp and Warwick, 2008, p. 164). Although the parallel fourths and fifths and the pentatonic and whole-tone scales that represented oriental cultures from *The Mikado* (1885) to *South Pacific* (1949) still appear – after all, Sondheim needed to be intelligible to a Broadway audience – Sondheim's aim was to construct the show from the smallest, simplest elements in a reflection of a Japanese approach to creation (Banfield, 1994, p. 261). Thus he developed a musical language reflecting the timbres, patterns and simplicity of the Japanese poetry form, the Haiku (see ibid., pp. 262–267). He used these and other aphorisms in the words of the Madam in 'Welcome to Kanagawa' and in some of the narrator's lines; meanwhile, 'Poems' uses the structures of a poetic exchange, a tradition associated with the Haiku in which an opening three-line poem is answered by a completion in two lines of seven syllables (see Knapp, 2005, p. 274). Instrumentally, the *shakuhachi* and *shamisen* create the atmosphere of Japanese theatre even though they are not authentic to any one Japanese theatrical form. Further references to Japanese cultural idioms include the use of circularity and repetition to reflect the Japanese idea of timeless cycles of life. The repeated references to the 'ships in the bay' during 'Chrysanthemum Tea' show circular musical structures, as Banfield (1994, p. 279) observes. Though these derive from a Western popular song tradition, the focus on repetition alongside the cycles of the narrative demonstrates a conceptual strategy for the work. Raymond Knapp suggests that the whole structure of *Pacific Overtures* is like a series of nested Matryoshka dolls (with the Haiku as the smallest doll), around which individual episodes 'are as much parable as narrative, and present themselves within their particular musical construct as but variations of neighbour episodes' (Knapp in Baur, Knapp and Warwick, 2008, p. 165). In this way we can read each number as a condensed expression of the whole show.

Indeed, so Japanese in its perspective is *Pacific Overtures* that it is the American, British, Dutch, Russian and French admirals who are caricatured in 'Please Hello' through stereotypical music and accents, and a form of 'pidgin English'. The two most apparent musical styles pastiched are an American patriotic march and a Gilbert and Sullivan patter song for the British admiral. The Dutch admiral offers chocolate, 'vindmills', tulips and a 'vooden shoe', the Russian bear is represented as a boor who constantly reminds the others 'Don't touch the coat', while the French admiral proposes 'détente' and kisses everyone even as explosions continue around the talks. This reverse type of orientalism may represent how these Western cultures are seen in the eyes of the Japanese – or simply how a Western audience imagines they would be perceived. As such it demonstrates ironically the superficiality of our understanding of alien cultures.

Yet as this show's narrative explores, identity and its articulation are extremely complex, and complex identity signification can be a challenge. Music that is unfamiliar in the work, however authentic, can restrict an audience from identifying with the piece, thereby promoting an unthinking orientalist perspective of the 'other' as strange (Baur, Knapp and Warwick, 2008, pp. 165–166). In this show, as Sondheim has pointed out, 'the language becomes more Western – as does the music – after the invasion' (quoted in Zadan, 1994, p. 212), reflecting American influence on Japan. Music now seems more familiar (and therefore appealing) to a Western audience, though it presents unpleasant aspects of Western culture such as the poisoning of the emperor by his mother, the introduction of prostitution in 'Welcome to Kanagawa', the misunderstanding that leads to rape in the beautiful 'Pretty Lady' and the burlesque stereotypes of 'Please Hello'. Even though the increasingly Americanized music voices the processes of acculturation to the dominating forces and disidentification with authentic indigeneity, the (Western) audience inadvertently associates with the familiarity of Western tropes and entrenches the 'otherness' of the East. Other aspects of the show present similar challenges, as Banfield discusses: the depiction of communities meeting forces the representation and articulation of language as a barrier. But to represent someone struggling with a language or struggling to communicate can imply all sorts of negative connotations about intelligence, cultural status and treatments of power.

By this point in the twentieth century, and in a work as sophisticated as this, the understanding of cultural difference has progressed to represent the 'other' in far more nuanced ways, though as we see, the representation of difference is fraught with challenges. In a sense the importance of the representation of the oriental is in what it can help us to understand about ourselves, though that doesn't absolve us from the charge of denigrating other cultures through our unknowing caricatures. One significant aspect of *Pacific Overtures* that reflects upon 'ourselves' (i.e., America in 1976 when the show was written) is that it was staged in the bicentenary year of America's founding as an independent nation. The patriotic celebration of national identity would thus have been thrown into relief by this story of the Western treatment of overseas indigenous communities. Just as the Berlin of the 1930s in *Cabaret* tacitly evokes the race relations of American Civil Rights in the 1960s, this negotiation between Japan and America in 1853 tacitly evokes the relations between indigenous Americans and the Euro-American claimants to the land mass in 1776. *Pacific Overtures*, then, is a contemporary political critique of America during a time of overt celebration.[1]

Our use here of a text by the white male Westerner Stephen Sondheim deserves some consideration, since once again we have effectively marginalized or silenced the voices of the 'other': why haven't we used a musical written by Eastern practitioners, or an opera voiced in indigenous terms? This alerts us to the fact that musical theatre (as it is perceived) still overwhelmingly privileges Western forms: when we think of musical theatre we probably associate it with Broadway or the West End, both English-speaking centres stemming from European cultural roots; likewise, opera houses of the world invariably produce operas in Western formats by composers of European heritage. Even in oriental centres of culture, the dominance of Western practices is striking: the world-renowned Takarazuka showbar just outside Osaka in Japan models its performances on Western practices (see Karantonis, 2007); in Korea a burgeoning fascination for Western musical theatre has even led to new Broadway shows being developed and tried out in Seoul (see Savran, 2012). Of course, there are many indigenous musical and theatrical practices which exist 'in the shadows' (to borrow again from Rodgers and Hammerstein). Some, like the opera *Pecan Summer* (2010) by indigenous Australian composer Deborah Cheetham, find in mainstream (Western) cultural forms the opportunity for the 'other' to speak; others, because of the anathema of Western commercializing practices to their traditional cultural expression, continue to be less visible. Some practices, especially in the 1970s and 1980s, have offered raw material for well-meaning Westerners to bring indigenous culture to Western attention, though some of these practices have themselves been critiqued because of the unequal power balance between the annexation of oriental cultures and their performance by and for audiences who might not understand their full relevance. Consider, for example, the debates surrounding Peter Brook's *The Conference of the Birds* (1972) and *The Mahabharata* (1985), both of which explored the theatrical languages of non-Western cultures, but from within a framework of what might be seen as 'worthy European art'. Such interplay between different international performance paradigms is therefore a rich area of interest, though one steeped in contention (for more on the issues of Intercultural Exchange, see Pavis, 1996). And even when themes of cultural and ethnic identity have filtrated into musical theatre in respectful, integrated ways, as might be argued with a show such as *West Side Story*, such projects have been criticized as no more than contemporary expressions of orientalism (see Sandoval Sanchez, 1994).

Multiculturalism, interculturalism and hybridity

As we will see in the following chapters, these ideas of the power imbalance between colonizer and colonized have been applied to other parts of society; since the Western colonizing power was always the white European male, the same understanding of 'otherness' has been discovered in representations of women, children and people of other sexualities to reveal marginalization within all societies. In the latter part of the twentieth century a number of 'multicultural' and 'intercultural' theatre and music exchanges began to occur – a situation encouraged by the movement of peoples around the world which resulted from war, famine, asylum seeking, post-colonial emigration, economic or cultural exchange, personal relationships and marriage. Diasporas have spread cultural practices as groups of people with similar heritages became established in new countries in the post-colonial period bringing their cultural practices with them. In addition, technology has allowed performances to be shared across a much wider area and cultural practices to be disseminated in festivals all over the globe.

Thus the idea of a binary distinction between West and East has become far more blurred, and these intercultural expressions enable the articulation of individuals and communities who consider themselves as belonging to more than one culture simultaneously. It is no longer possible to think about orientalism as a binary of opposition or emancipation, and this is evidenced in world music, whose practices can no longer be viewed as merely the result of cultural imperialism or economic domination (Guilbault, 2001, p. 176). The critique of this binary suggests that we can no longer think of geographical spaces as having defined and stable boundaries. Firstly, cultures spread around the world as global corporations and work forces meet economic demands; secondly, since cultures are no longer isolated or populations rooted in a specific location, the idea of culture as homogenous and fixed is no longer viable. In the same way, race cannot be regarded as having fixed cultural characteristics. In a sense, perhaps, by reviewing the opening up of the last great isolated culture, *Pacific Overtures* documents the end of an era in which race and nation might have been conceived through defined and separate cultural practices.

Although the colonial and the post-colonial are still important as they reveal the ways in which such diasporas have developed, the cultural exchange has moved on. Cross-cultural and intercultural exchanges have been replaced (to some extent) by hybrid practices that reflect the experience of individuals whose own identities derive from pluralistic cultural practices. A continuation of the melting pot that began in the United States in the early twentieth century and in the United Kingdom in the 1950s has led to works that reflect the experience of, or speak to, diasporic communities through hybrid practice. Such works in the United States incorporate Spanish language and South American music, as well as African, Japanese, Chinese and Eastern European cultural influences. In the United Kingdom the sources are different – Indian, Pakistani, Caribbean, African, Oriental and South American – but the incorporation and reflection of diversity produces a similar variety of hybrid theatre practices.

In the Heights (2008)

So far we have focused, in this chapter, on the idea of the oriental 'other' as Japanese, though at the start we recognized that orientalist theory can relate to other nationalities and even minority groups within a mainstream culture. Examining *In the Heights* (2008) allows us to consider orientalist theory in relation to a Latino/a culture within the United States, where according to the 2000 census this group is the second largest ethnic racial group, numbering 35.3 million (Sebesta, 2007).[2]

In the Heights (2008)

Music and lyrics by Lin-Manuel Miranda

Book by Quiara Alegría Hudes

Synopsis: Set under the Washington Bridge in the Upper East Side of New York City, this show contains overt references to *West Side Story*. It portrays a contemporary immigrant community, of largely Spanish-speaking people who arrived from various Caribbean islands including Cuba, the Dominican Republic and Puerto Rico. The families on the block, all of whom for various reasons are short of money and at points of transition in their lives, operate a cab company, a corner store selling lottery tickets and a beauty salon. Over the course of a very hot Fourth of July weekend the power fails, police are called to a battle, and Abuela Claudia wins the lottery and dies. Usnavi (the hero), who inherits the winnings from Abuela Claudia, decides not to use them to move back to the Dominican Republic, but to stay running the barrio cornershop surrounded by his friends and family.

The musical was a huge success on Broadway in 2008, nominated for 13 Tony awards and winning 4 including Best Musical. The narrative, rather than incorporating Latin American or Latino/a stereotypes into a white (or indeed black) American story, is set in a contemporary community whose characters have mixed heritage. The characters share a sense of displacement between their minority status in New York and their 'other' culture which many have never visited. As Sam Thielman (2007, p. B7) remarked in *Newsday*, 'This show revolves around heirloom memories of Cuba, DR [The Dominican Republic], Puerto Rico and other places that are deeply missed by people one or two generations removed from them'. The reviews point to the innocence of the characters, the thin plot and the lack of urban credibility but identify the 'terrific title number that opens the show' (Isherwood, 2007) and a blend of 'hip-hop with salsa and merengue, pop and traditional Broadway' that doesn't shrink from 'corny exuberance' (Rooney, 2007, pp. 52, 54).

Lin-Manuel Miranda, who also played Usnavi in the original production, and Quiara Alegria Hudes drew on their own experiences and hybrid identities and worked with the company to conceive the show. But the work borrows from a Broadway heritage too; it is a contemporary *West Side Story* not simply because of the Puerto Rican characters, but also because Miranda and Hudes, with director Thomas Kail and choreographer Andy Blankenbuehler, reflexively remind audiences of this heritage. The hip-hop movement through which everyday tasks are accomplished is a reminder of the incorporation of everyday movement in the dance style of *West Side Story*, and the setting of the love scene on the balcony of a New York tenement is an iconic image knowingly recreated. The 'Dance at the Gym' is reflected at the Salsa club, where jealousy leads to a stylized fight that explodes onto the streets.

Elizabeth Titrington Craft (2011, p. 57) documents the marketing phenomenon that led to the success of *In the Heights* using YouTube and other online platforms to stimulate 'viral' marketing, 'reaching out to pan-Latino communities of MiGente or Latina.com' or to fans through Facebook and twitter. But its most important legacy is that it articulated diverse hybrid ethnic histories to audiences who could 'express pride in seeing their Latino heritage onstage' (p. 64). Rather than a Western production creating a stereotype of the 'other', this production, and others in community theatres in the United States and United Kingdom, are exploring a response to the issues of orientalism through recognizing the diversity and hybridity of identity within individuals and post-colonial communities. These people are no longer the 'wretched', as they were labelled by sociologist Frantz Fanon (1961) some 50 years ago, though they are still minorities. What *In the Heights* demonstrates is the potential for new hybrid and multicultural voices to emerge, to reflect our contemporary multicultural societies.

One of the most important features of the orientalist exchange is the way that representing an alien culture helps the home culture to perceive its own idiosyncrasies, promoting the potential for self-criticism. Though this is no justification to stereotype, exoticize and feminize the Orient, it does provide opportunities to analyse what we still consider problematic; how race and gender are linked in representations of the exotic; and the paradoxical catalyst for change that arises from what might be considered outdated or problematic practices.

When looking back at works that are problematic because of their representation of other cultures, and especially the orientalist patterns of perceiving, it is important to remember how cultures are continually changing. What was acceptable in one era is not acceptable in another. This can make some works difficult to perform. The song 'You've got to be carefully taught' and Nellie's distress when she discovers that Emile's children are of mixed race deals with the issue of race openly, but its naivety has to be seen in the context of a different American society. Equally, hybrid patterns of representing multi-racial cultures in contemporary shows will doubtless be problematic to future societies for other, as yet unimagined reasons. The important idea to explore from this is that within our societies there are patterns of responding that appear 'natural'; it is not until they are problematized by the reflection from another culture that our own prejudices are revealed. The feminization of the orient was not considered problematic until it was pointed out, and so we must continually challenge how our own representations of others might be perceived and what that might say about us.

Further reading – theoretical

Pavis, Patrice (ed.) (1996) *The Intercultural Performance Reader* (London and New York: Routledge).
Said, Edward (1978) *Orientalism* (London: Routledge and Kegan Paul).
Williams, Patrick and Laura Chrisman (1994) *Colonial Discourse and Post-Colonial Theory: A Reader* (New York: Columbia University Press).

Further reading – relating to the examples

Banfield, Stephen (1994) *Sondheim's Broadway Musicals* (Ann Arbor: University of Michigan Press).
Lovensheimer, Jim (2010) *South Pacific: Paradise Rewritten* (New York: Oxford University Press).
New York City Opera Project: Madama Butterfly, http://www.columbia.edu/itc/music/ NYCO/butterfly/index.html, accessed 6 May 2013.
Sebesta, Judith (2007) 'Just "Another Puerto Rican with a Knife"? Racism and Reception on the "Great White Way"', *Studies in Musical Theatre* 1(2): 183–197.

6   'I Wanna Be a Producer': Globalization, Capitalism and Consumerism

While the main action of Rodgers and Hammerstein's *Carousel* (1945) recounts the tragic tale of Billy Bigelow and Julie Jordan, the secondary couple, Carrie Pipperidge and the sardine entrepreneur Enoch Snow, provides an element of light relief. Given Enoch's trade, there are plenty of gags about him smelling of fish, but his modest livelihood – suited to provincial New England in 1873 – harbours a great ambition: to establish a sardine empire. 'Goin' to build a little sardine cannery', he tells his fiancée; 'then a big one – then the biggest one in the whole country. Carrie, I'm goin' to get rich on sardines' (Rodgers and Hammerstein, n.d., p. 125). Enoch explains his strategy for success, envisaging his cottage industry becoming a nationwide corporation through textbook capitalist expansion: 'When I make enough money outa one little boat', he says, 'I'll put all of my money in another little boat'. His enterprise expands, his profit increases, and before long he is the capitalist owner of 'a great big fleet of great big boats!'

Around the same time, another young man was growing up in Greenfield Township, Michigan. Like Enoch, he harboured ambitions that would lead both to enormous success and to new efficiencies of economic production. It's interesting to speculate whether Enoch would have had the business acumen to pull his expansion off, and whether he was destined, post-*Carousel*, to become a major player; Henry Ford certainly succeeded, and his global empire survives today.

This chapter explores ideas surrounding global economics, or globalization. We discuss how developments in production (the way we produce or manufacture things) and commoditization (the way we turn things into sellable commodities) have become two main motors powering globalization. Then we consider how technological development (innovation) led to new ways of thinking about the world (ideology) and behaving (material practice). In discussing globalization, we consider a number of strategies that have been developed by producers to maximize efficiency and profit in the system. We consider the production-line economy of Ford's car manufacturing, the franchising economy of McDonalds' global empire, the vertical integration of the Disney Corporation and the commodifying practices of the jukebox musical. In the words of one cheeky commentator, 'Money makes the world go around'. If this all sounds very Marxist, it is because globalization, according to Dan Rebellato (2009, p. 12), is 'the rise of global capitalism operating under neoliberal policy conditions'.

Globalization: innovation, ideology, material practice

The journey towards globalization began with the industrial revolution and rapid innovation in technology. Improvements in transportation developed trade domestically and overseas such that industry could take advantage of 'the interconnectedness of different parts of the world' (Magee and Thompson, 2010, p. 2). Railways and canals connected factories and docks; international shipping developed vessels capable of carrying great loads; undersea telegraph cables enabled efficient communication; and trade routes with short cuts like the Suez Canal 'compress[ed] time and space, and accelerate[d] the "interdependence" of societies and states' (ibid.).

This trade growth was underpinned by strong ideological and political ideas; and although the literal economic development of globalization advocated *interdependence, interconnectedness* and *mutual trade* – apparently benign concepts – the ideology of globalization relied on structures of power in which the West became dominant over the rest.

We saw in Chapter 5 how Westerners perceived and represented the newly accessible space of the Orient. The construction of this space as an exoticized world of 'otherness' – part fascinating, part threatening, but above all uncivilized and unenlightened – would not have been possible without a contrasting view of the West, and particularly Britain, as Great (it's in the name, after all). This reflected the political commitment to building an empire that was an 'expansion of England' (Seeley, 2010). As Catherine Hall (2000, p. 2) explains, Britain established colonies and ways of living modelled directly on society at home; the Brits 'took their name to "empty" parts of the globe which they settled and made English throughout'. Of course, those parts of the world weren't really 'empty'; but the suppression of that particular bit of information was significant.

Although we now frown on the arrogance and brutality with which the empire was built (indigenous populations were often forced off their land, coerced into slavery or simply killed), Britain's dominance was seen as a God-given right and championed by an incessant cultural message. 'Britannia, rule the waves!', cried Thomas Arne's 'Rule, Britannia', in which Britain arises from the sea 'at heaven's command', to be given a 'charter [... to] rule the waves' by 'Guardian Angels'. Edward Elgar and A.C. Benson's message was even clearer: 'Wider still, and wider shall thy bounds be set; God, who made thee mighty, make thee mightier yet!'

If innovation enabled expansion, and ideology supported it, it was behaviour – material practice – that consolidated globalization. Magee and Thompson discuss how the British world of the imagination was brought into being by a mass migration of Brits settling in far-flung countries. It is this migration, they claim, that was the real force of power behind the great colonial enterprise of the Victorian era. Even when relocated to the other side of the world, British migrants clung to their cultural understanding of Britishness, meaning that even today, majority populations in the former colonies (Australia, Canada, South Africa) speak English, adhere to a British sensibility, subscribe to Christianity and acknowledge the British monarch as Head of State. In fact expat communities are often perceived to espouse more conservative British values than the liberal ones at home. It's a situation wryly observed in the Gilbert and Sullivan operetta *HMS Pinafore* (1878):

> In spite of all temptations
>
> To belong to other nations,
>
> He remains an Englishman! (p. 112)

So the colonial project was far from *just* a money-driven enterprise, though it was certainly about the power and authority of the British brand. It was also about conceptualizing Britain as global (and the globe as British) and creating conditions for this to be enacted. These were as much cultural and social manoeuvres as economic ones.

HMS Pinafore (1878)

Gilbert and Sullivan's long run of successes appeared between 1871 and 1896, at the height of the British Empire's dominance. Their comic operas referenced not only classical themes (like opera), but also the contexts and mores of contemporary society. The beginning of their collaboration is marked by two shows that explicitly reference the sea-faring might of the Empire; *HMS Pinafore* (1878) and *The Pirates of Penzance* (1879).

In these satires, Gilbert and Sullivan are observant commentators on the ironies and contradictions of society, even if they show a cultural blindness caused by their own position within that society. The

---

HMS Pinafore (1878)

Music by Arthur Sullivan

Book and lyrics by William Schwenk Gilbert

Synopsis: The good ship *Pinafore* is harboured in Portsmouth and expecting a visit from First Lord of the Admiralty, the Right Honourable Sir Joseph Porter, K.B.E. Amongst the good-natured crew, we meet Ralph Rackstraw, who is in love with his captain's daughter, Josephine. Though she reciprocates his love, their difference in social status prevents a relationship. The same is true for 'Bumboat Woman' Mrs Cripps ('Little Buttercup') and Captain Corcoran; though he thinks fondly of her, his rank far exceeds hers, and according to class expectations of the time, any romance would be out of the question. However, Buttercup is hiding the secret that, as a nursemaid many years ago, she inadvertently confused two babies, meaning that a child of lowly rank became Captain, and an heir to the nobility became a modest sailor. Corcoran and Ralph turn out to be the swapped children, and each must now replace the other. Thanks to this, Ralph can now marry Josephine and Corcoran can marry Buttercup.

---

complex nuances of the world they depict, self-consciously referred to as 'Topsyturvydom' by Gilbert, demonstrate the paradoxes of Britain's social make-up, and *Pinafore* and *Pirates* reveal a great deal about the Empire's colonial posturing.

HMS Pinafore is a comedy of manners, steeped in the hierarchy of the British class system, and builds its character relationships into this framework. The aristocrat Sir Joseph Porter is at the top of the pecking order. Beneath him, Captain Corcoran has a certain social standing (he is related to a peer) that his daughter Josephine inherits. At the bottom are the sailors and the bumboat woman Little Buttercup. The lines of deference are clearly drawn.

Nevertheless, it is a mark of the British navy's gallantry that all men are regarded as equal, a theme woven throughout the show. 'A man is but a man, whether he hoists his flag at the main-truck or his slacks on the main-deck', comments Ralph (Gilbert and Sullivan, 1997, p. 90). Accordingly, Sir Joseph Porter writes a song extolling the principle 'that a British sailor is any man's equal, excepting mine' (p. 97). The hypocrisy is evident, and remarked on by the straight talking of social outcast Dick Deadeye: 'When people have to obey other people's orders, equality is out of the question' (p. 98). Nevertheless, the sentiment is significant, and recurs when Sir

Joseph tries to use this argument to ensnare Josephine for himself: 'Love is a platform on which all ranks meet', he asserts; then sings: 'Never mind the why and wherefore, Love can level ranks' (p. 108).

Although this satirical storyline may be an inward-facing commentary on the arbitrary privileging of Britain's hereditary class system, its staging on board a ship draws awareness to the hierarchies of colonialism, and the lyrics of at least one song pick up on this dynamic with reference to a familiar refrain:

> Shall we submit? Are we but slaves?
>
> Love comes alike to high and low –
>
> Britannia's sailors rule the waves,
>
> And shall they stoop to insult? No! (pp. 101–102)

In lyrics like this, *HMS Pinafore*'s commentary on global Britishness is rather ambivalent, suggesting a liberal attitude to equality while elevating the national status. Read in these terms the song quoted earlier, 'For He Is an Englishman', reveals this ambivalence. Ralph Rackstraw is caught absconding with Josephine in the middle of the night; it's a court-martial offence, though to escape conviction Rackstraw plays the trump card: 'I am an Englishman; I can get away with anything.'

If this national arrogance legitimates actions without criticism, the hostile invasion of other countries and the barbaric violence of Empire-building is easily sanctioned as a privilege of birth. However, a further rhetorical dynamic in both *Pinafore* and *Pirates* obscures the violence of colonialism. For both the Royal Navy in *Pinafore* and the gang of mercenaries in *Pirates* are depicted as completely harmless gentlemen with virtue and integrity. The crew of Pinafore are never actually seen doing any crew work (whether invading other lands or ruling the waves); and the pirates of Penzance 'make a point of never attacking a weaker party' (p. 123). Moreover, the soundtrack to this behaviour in the works of Gilbert and Sullivan is an accompaniment of charming, melodic music, emphasizing refinement and grace. Thus the composite impression of Britain's maritime power at the height of the Empire is that it is neutral and benign.

In theatrical terms globalization is not only apparent in the themes of these operettas, but also in the practice of touring the world with cultural products, an enterprise which was becoming increasingly common. Once *HMS Pinafore* became a success, two additional companies were sent out to tour the provinces. At the same time numerous companies mounted the work without permission in the United States. The UK tours were authorized and the income from them fed back to the D'Oyly Carte company to invest in new works. However, the income from the unsanctioned and unlicenced US productions was lost. To counter this D'Oyly Carte opened a production on Broadway in 1879 and began touring America with 'authentic' productions. By the time of *Pirates of Penzance*, Gilbert, Sullivan and D'Oyly Carte were determined to protect their work from unsanctioned productions, so they opened almost simultaneously in London and on Broadway, thus securing copyright in both countries. This meant that they could ensure the quality of productions on both sides of the Atlantic and earn income from all productions of their works.

This example raises some of the key issues of globalization – where does the money go? And what is the effect of the cultural product on the location, the workers, and the producers?

Copyright and intellectual property

Authors and producers make a large investment in writing, developing and mounting performances, from which they hope to make a profit. Copyright legislation (one aspect of intellectual property law) protects their investment by restricting anyone else from reproducing, performing or publishing the work; the result of complicated national and international law is that if you want to mount a performance you need to buy a licence. The licence fee is split between writers and producers according to their contractual arrangements so that their creative efforts are rewarded. This remuneration is likely to encourage creativity as well as recompense the creators for existing work. However, since the costs and the requirements of the licensors may be prohibitive, it can also be a barrier to the work being performed.

In the late nineteenth century international intellectual property laws had not been harmonized, so copyright protection in one country didn't extend to another. To establish copyright in both countries Gilbert and Sullivan premiered their work in the United Kingdom and the United States. This is no longer necessary because of world trade agreements, but in practice such agreements are enforced more strictly in some countries than others, and piracy of intellectual property is rife – which is why you can buy fake designer goods more easily in some countries than in others. The Internet has had an enormous impact on the international trade in creative products; since file sharing and downloading of music and film became possible the structure of intellectual property law struggled to keep pace with technology, and some people argue that it is no longer beneficial.

The global expansion of the nineteenth century would inevitably come to an operational end as the limits of colonialism were reached; in any case, an ideological backlash during the first half of the twentieth century meant that the subjugation of some nations by others became outlawed. Nevertheless, just as new technologies and developing infrastructure in the nineteenth century led to the massive global expansion of the British Empire (innovation, ideology, material practice), other technologies and developments in the twentieth century have facilitated very different types of globalization.

The production-line

Whereas Britannia ruled the waves throughout the nineteenth century, the twentieth century's global project has been an American story. The significant difference between nineteenth- and twentieth-century global-ization is that the global powerholders are no longer nation states, but multinational corporations like Walmart, Ford, Microsoft and McDonalds, all companies whose annual revenues rival the gross domestic products of countries.[1]

The Ford Motor Company was incorporated in June 1903, offering Henry Ford a place to develop his designs. He was keen to tap into a big middle-class market, but he was aware that the price of automobiles was prohibitive for the modern American family. Ford's great success came with the design of an affordable family car, the Model T Ford, and the production method he used in its manufacture. Rather than having two or three workers putting together a car from start to finish, which was a slow process that required specialized skill, Ford created an 'assembly line' to increase efficiency and keep labour costs down. Each worker was assigned a specific component to add to the vehicle as it moved along the line; workers had a set time to complete their task before the car progressed and the next one arrived for the same component. Productivity increased exponentially, and by 1924, Ford was producing 10 million identical vehicles – approximately half the number of cars in the world.

The Fordist model of production quickly spread to other indus-tries, assisted by a parallel method of industrial efficiency championed by Frederick Winslow Taylor: scientific management. Both systems sought to reduce inefficiencies in production through strategic man-agerial control. America became fixated with mass-produced consumer goods that were affordable and standardized. The benefit to everyday Americans was that commodities and experiences were newly available in a culture that was also benefitting from the energies of mass production. On the other hand, these production methods encouraged the exploitation of cheap and unskilled labour, meaning that workers were kept on low wages and had few prospects of elevating their position. Workers became less able to move to other (skilled) employment and less able to negotiate for better pay since they could be easily replaced. There was a downward pressure on wages and an increasing alienation of the workforce, but the production model increased the availability of goods. This is the model that China has followed, and without unionization to counter the downward pressure on wages, Chinese goods have flooded the market, closing factories in countries where wages and living standards were better. This is the major problem of a twentieth-century global economy linked to a production model based on unskilled labour. The flow of goods encourages imports from countries where wages for unskilled and unregulated labour are cheap. It creates unemployment for an alienated and increasingly poorly paid working class while the profits generate enormous wealth for the heads of global corporations.

Despite this, the mass production process brought about enormous shifts in the way people thought about and consumed culture. In particular, as industrial efficiency became marked by production lines of faceless workers, cultural forms – especially those driven by new technologies – reflected the patterns and rhythms of production. One critic notably saw these patterns in the faceless composition of the chorus line, 'The aesthetic reflex of the rationality aspired to by the prevailing economic system' (Kracauer, 1975, p. 70):

> When they formed an undulating snake, they radiantly illustrated the virtues of the conveyor belt; when they tapped their feet in fast tempo, it sounded like business, business; when they kicked their legs with mathematical precision, they joyously affirmed the progress of rationalization; and when they kept repeating the same movements without ever interrupting their routine, one envisioned an uninterrupted chain of autos gliding from the factories into the world. (Kracauer, 1992, p. 52)

Anyone who has seen the films of Busby Berkeley such as *Golddiggers of 1933* (1933), *Footlight Parade* (1933) or *Dames* (1934) will recognize in the patterns of his choreographed dancers this sort of modernist expression: an aesthetic that reflects technology and production.

Franchising

The next production development to change the world economy derives from America's fast-food market, whose innovation was to expand through a system of franchising. This involves an individual (a franchisee) buying into the identity, branding and product of an existing company (the franchisor) to trade off that company's success. Effectively, the franchisee buys a licence (for the intellectual property of the brand) that includes a very tightly regulated series of requirements to replicate the brand. In this arrangement, the original company benefits by being seen to expand, usually into a different geographical area; consumer awareness of the brand increases, and further franchises are established. It's also useful to local economies, since franchises bring employment and income to the local area. But the ability of the franchisee to be creative with the product or employee relations is very limited, and a high percentage of profits is paid as a licence to the original company, limiting the potential for growth or development by the franchisee but allowing the original company to expand.

Although the idea of the franchise was not invented by burger entrepreneurs, it is they who have capitalized most on the system, McDonalds being the clear frontrunner with over 37,000 franchisees worldwide. In order for this system to work effectively with consumers, every single restaurant has to offer the same commodity: the snacks on offer, the packaging, the ambience, the efficiency of the service and, of course, the logo of the golden arches. The McDonalds model has itself become enormously influential, and is theorized in George Ritzer's book *The McDonaldization of Society* (1993). Ritzer attributes the success to 'efficiency, calculability, predictability and control' (p. 14), and discusses how these principles have been appropriated beyond the fast-food industry to create a model for McDonaldizing (amongst other things) contact lenses, flat-pack furniture and even universities.

The idea of licencing intellectual property – which is the basis of franchising – is not a new practice in the theatre; we've mentioned earlier the licensing arrangements for mounting a new production. A company buys a licence which allows it, in return for a royalty payment, to stage a show using the libretto and score. We've also seen that by touring the production the producer maintains control of quality and consistency, ensuring that all audiences can see a similar product. This generates profits for them and increases awareness of their brand. But touring is very expensive for the producer, who takes enormous financial risks in paying performers to travel to different locations around the country or the world to reproduce their performance for new audiences. The franchise model offers a way of securing the aesthetic quality of the production and its brand without taking on unsustainable financial risk.

Friedrich Kurz is the German impresario who brought Andrew Lloyd Webber's *Cats* to Hamburg by negotiating a franchise arrangement with the Really Useful Group. The Really Useful Group maintained control over the production (though it was translated into German) and received licence income. The production was so successful, bringing a reported £20 million to the city by 1988 (Thorncroft, 1988) that the producer transformed a neglected part of the red light district, employed performers, stage crew and musicians and galvanized the revitalization of musical theatre in Germany. As a result, Bochum's council built a new theatre for Kurz to open a pro-duction of *Starlight Express* in 1988 (Ford, 1988), and the council offered him an empty theatre to open a production of *The Phantom of the Opera* in 1989.

This franchising practice (known derisively as McTheatre) is not one that has been followed to a large extent in musical theatre – the vertical inte-gration model that we discuss later on in the chapter has gradually become more common – but both these models require certain aesthetic features of the musical product in order to translate easily to new markets. In general these are large-scale musicals that have a high proportion of music, dance and spectacle since these translate more easily to non-English speakers and a developing tourist trade than an intricate plot or witty interplay. It was works with these characteristics that began to be termed 'megamusicals' in the *New York Times* during the 1980s. The term relates not only to the aesthetic contents of the work, but also to the material conditions of the production and the global brand marketing, whichever production model the producers utilize.

The downside of this process, as we've seen with workers in other indus-tries, is to alienate them from creativity. This feature of the production has been discussed by theorists such as Charles Lee (2008), and Jonathan Burston (1997) refers to

> specific commercial, technical and aesthetic models which ensure the meticulous replication of any given production across a number of international venues. The megamusical's rationalising, industrial logic [...] reproduces technical and artistic production detail with such rigour as to significantly delimit the interpretative agency of local musical performers. (p. 180)

Burston goes on to qualify the fact that the term McTheatre invokes 'as much the new experience of working on what was perceived as a "theatrical assembly-line" as it did the (often only imagined) experience of attending a show that conformed to the expectations of a cultural McDonalds' (p. 188). Elsewhere, other theorists such as Susan Russell (2006), also a performer, have explored the experiences of working in the machine of a megamusical:

> In order to distribute his product, Cameron Mackintosh created a series of assembly lines that mass-produce images. [...] *Phantom* actors everywhere embody the same dramatic interpretations as their counterparts in the original Broadway cast. When a new actor enters the Broadway show, they are taught how the original actor did the role, and the new actor is expected to simulate a frozen image that is retrieved by management from a documented past. (p. 99)

She confirms that a production 'Bible' standardizes not only design features and blocking for the show, but also 'facial expressions, vocal inflections, physical bodies, gestures, and choices of movement' (p. 100).[2] In the main, and especially as the complexity of moving scenery has been computerized, performers in large-scale spectacles have increasingly become cogs in the wheel; if they stand in the wrong place they are in danger of being hit by the moving flats. On the other hand, for audiences seeking a product they recognize and in which they can be secure, this is indeed a standardized product: we buy into what we already know.

The franchise model allows very limited leeway for the franchisee to vary the product, but it does feed investment into the local area, developing new performers and building a new industry, because some of the profit stays in the new territory. It doesn't necessarily encourage development of local culture, but can provide a catalyst and some of the infrastructure for it to develop over time (as happened in Germany).

Vertical integration

The third production model, vertical integration – the model that many of the largest producers of global musicals now follow – doesn't have all of these advantages for the local economy. Think back to the example at the start of this chapter in which *Carousel*'s Mister Snow wanted to invest his profit from fishing into enlarging his fleet. Perhaps having enlarged his fleet he noticed that the canning factory to which he sold his fish was fixing their price – a fact that affected his business, but over which he had no control. His response, if he had earned enough, might be to buy the canning factory so that he could control the price of fish. He would be securing the employment of his fishermen and the use of his boats and improving his market access. He could reduce the price to the consumer because there would be fewer companies taking a cut. Subsequently he might realize it would be convenient to control the distribution of the cans to the shops, so he might buy a few trucks or a distribution company. Now there are fewer overheads to increase the price of his fish, so this model of vertical integration has greater efficiency and the potential for more profit. Of course, that assumes Mr Snow is a true capitalist who doesn't want to pass on savings to his customers.

Rather than three companies – the fishery, the cannery and the trucking company – all having employers and employees, there is now only Mr Snow's empire. Almost as many employees are working, but they are all working for him. In theory the price of the goods could go down for consumers, who recognize Mr Snow's brand and know what the quality will be. But the money is no longer spread between three local economies; it's now all in Mr Snow's bank. Next, perhaps Mr Snow decides he wants to buy another fishery elsewhere in the world and takes a loan against one or more of his companies. There is now interest to pay on the debt, so either the prices start to rise or the workers have to be paid less. When he realizes that the fishery in one country can generate the fish he needs at a cheaper price than his American boats, he considers whether to lay all his workers off and shift his business out to the cheaper country. And so the spiral of globalized markets and big corporations begins.

When Disney decided to enter the musical theatre market first with *Beauty and the Beast* (1994) and then *The Lion King* (1997), it recognized the need for vertical integration (owning its own productions rather than franchising them to other producers). It invested heavily in setting up its own theatre wing, taking a financial risk – it was big enough to do so – but controlling the quality and the money flow. It owned everything, from the creative product to the production to the Broadway venue, and even down to the store selling Disney merchandize. As it rolled out productions to theatre capitals worldwide, its profits rose exponentially and the power of its brand increased. Yet unlike in the franchising model, where a degree of the profit can be felt in the local economy, with vertical integration all the profits were channelled back to US Disney headquarters. Even though local performers and staff were employed in countries all around the world (which is an economic and cultural benefit), and full theatres generated their own momentum and economic benefit in those locations, more of the profits flowed back to the corporation in this model than in the franchise model.

The Lion King (1997)[3]

Music by Elton John and Hans Zimmer, with choral arrangements by Lebo M

Lyrics by Tim Rice

Originally produced as a cartoon film by the Disney studios in 1994

Significant productions: Original Broadway production (1997); productions in Tokyo, London, Toronto, Hamburg, Los Angeles, Sydney, The Hague, Shanghai, Seoul, Paris, Johannesburg, Taipei, Las Vegas, Singapore, Madrid, São Paulo.

The film *The Lion King* was one of a series of film musicals (including *The Little Mermaid*, 1989; *Beauty and the Beast*, 1991; and *Aladdin*, 1992) that reinvigorated Disney's flagging success in the family market. *The Lion King* marked Disney's second venture onto Broadway, following their success with the very literal stage adaptation of *Beauty and the Beast* (1994). Disney's investment was officially $10 million, a record at the time,[4] and its popularity has been immense. Over 65 million people have seen the show in 28 countries worldwide, and the Broadway production alone has generated $1 billion at the box office.

Synopsis: Based loosely on the story of *Hamlet* it tells the story of the young cub Simba who is destined to become the king of the pack following the death of his father, but who must first prevent his wicked uncle Scar from taking over the Pridelands.

The jukebox musical: 'Thankyou for the music'

We have mentioned the merchandise that has become such a large part of Disney's branding, and such a feature of the Broadway tourist trade. Nowadays it is no longer sufficient to go and see a show; one is also encouraged to spend heavily on branded goods from t-shirts to mugs to cuddly toys. The acknowledgement that spin-off souvenirs could assist in accumulating profit for producers came early, with the popularity of the cast album in the 1940s. By the time the big commercial producers of the megamusicals were beginning their global manoeuvres, merchandise of all kinds was being peddled. Cleverly this development began to exploit commodities for dual usage, turning, for example, the effective promotional material of West End and Broadway shows (the posters and logos) into must-have souvenirs: the marketing artefacts become not only adverts for the shows, but also profit-making commodities that consumers want and will display. T-shirts, baseball caps and tote bags become not only expensive mementoes of the West End experience but also generate further advertising for the productions thanks to consumers carrying and wearing them willingly on their travels. This phenomenon is known as commoditization, and it is a tactic of all the biggest commercial producers, from Disney to Cameron Mackintosh to Judy Craymer, producer of *Viva Forever!* (2012) and *Mamma Mia* (1999), the focus of our next discussion.

The jukebox musical

The 'jukebox', 'catalogue' or 'compilation' musical dates as far back as John Gay's *The Beggar's Opera* (1728). They appear in three guises. First, 'dead rock star' shows like *Elvis* (1977), *Buddy* (1989) and *Jersey Boys* (2005) tell the story of a singer or band as a frame to include their song repertoire in scenes showing auditions, rehearsals, recording sessions or performances. They often weave a dramatic dynamic into the show, either through emphasizing the rags-to-riches storyline or by capitalizing on some tragedy in the celebrity's life. A plane crash (*Buddy*) creates pathos and allows for a poignant song to conclude the drama before the finale showcases a feel-good concert of greatest hits. Second, there are shows which construct a fictional narrative strung together with well-known songs from a variety of sources. This is the classic structure of a burlesque, popular since the nineteenth century and most obviously seen in the British pantomime, which celebrates current and popular song hits through a simple fairytale story of romance with a comedy twist. More recently, innovations on this theme have burlesqued other source material or concocted light, generic narratives around which to hang the songs: *Return to the Forbidden Planet* (1989) is based on Shakespeare's *The Tempest* and features a soundtrack from the 1960s and 1970s; *Boogie Nights* (1997) and *Priscilla Queen of the Desert* (2006) offer compilations of disco music with storylines based around performers, and *Rock of Ages* (2006) raids the glam rock repertoire to tell a tale set in an LA club. Again, it's significant that these stories often revolve around performers, giving ample excuse for song and dance. The third type of jukebox musical, which has become common more recently, creates a fictional story weaving together the repertoire of just one artist or band: *Mamma Mia!* (1999) uses the songs of ABBA, *Our House* (2002) trades on the music of Madness and *We Will Rock You* (2002) celebrates the music of Queen.

Even at the time ABBA released their first singles, commoditization had begun. Here were some songsters with musical talent whose value was that they could entertain; historically they might have toured villages as wandering minstrels, offering entertainment for food and lodging, or perhaps a little bit of money to keep them going. However, in capturing their music on disc the act of performing became part of a production process, creating a commodity (a record) which could be sold. Since this recording means that the experience of the performance can be replayed even in the performers' absence, an element of its authenticity – its *aura* (Benjamin, 1992) – is lost. The record, though, can be mass-produced a million times and sold at a price that seems reasonable to consumers – democratizing the product – but generating profit (a million times) for the capitalists.

Commoditization

The principle of commoditization works on the basis that capitalism can turn anything into profit-generating merchandise (a commodity). In basic Marxist terms, this is a process whereby the *use value* of products in a market economy (carrots for eating, clothes for wearing, etc.) becomes trumped by the *exchange value* in a capitalist economy (the exchange of something not inherently useful for money). Capitalism is largely engineered on this mechanism, since we as workers have no option but to turn our time and bodies into valuable assets that we can exchange for money, though the power balance is such that capitalists determine the arbitrary value of that time and energy. Commoditization works in much the same way, and the products of the pop industry that are commoditized in *Mamma Mia!* are a good example of how effective and profit-generating this mechanism can be.

The really clever part of commoditization is the point at which producers double-sell us products that we already possess. In the case of ABBA, 'Mamma Mia' (the song) was released internationally as a 7" single in 1975, and appeared on the band's third album (*ABBA*), released the same year. Almost immediately it also appeared on ABBA's first *Greatest Hits* album, a compilation of songs that had all previously been released on both single and album. Within the first year, then, consumers could buy three different releases of the same recording, meaning that producers could make three lots of profit out of one act of labour. Not content with this, the song was then further released on subsequent compilations including *ABBA the Singles: The First Ten Years* (1982), *ABBA Gold: Greatest Hits* (1992), *Thankyou for the Music* (1994), *The Definitive Collection* (2001), *ABBA 18 Hits* (2005), *The Complete Studio Recordings* (2005), *Number Ones* (2006) and *The Albums* (2008); this list doesn't include other multi-artist compilations on which the song has appeared, various platforms on which it has been released (7" and 12" vinyl, LP, cassette, CD, mp3, video, DVD, etc.) or many cover

---

Mamma Mia! (1999)

Music and lyrics by Björn Ulvaeus, Benny Andersson and Stig Anderson

Book by Catherine Johnson

Significant productions: Original West End production (1999); productions on Broadway and in Toronto, Chicago, Sydney, Melbourne, Las Vegas, Netherlands, Madrid, Germany, Seoul, Essen, Antwerp, Moscow, Tokyo, Hong Kong, Sweden, Ireland, Mexico, Oslo, Serbia, Switzerland, South Africa, Paris, São Paulo, Shanghai, Buenos Aires, Manila.

Synopsis: *Mamma Mia!* is a jukebox or catalogue musical that weaves the popular hits of Swedish supergroup ABBA into the story of a young girl looking forward to her wedding day. Sophie lives on a Greek island with her single mother Donna. She is engaged to Sky, but desperately wants her real father to walk her down the aisle. As it happens, Donna doesn't know who the father is, and after a bit of snooping, Sophie realizes this is because it could be one of three men Donna had relationships with around the time she became pregnant. Secretly, Sophie invites all three to the wedding, a plan that causes chaos and upset, though eventually Sophie realizes that her real parentage is immaterial. She decides not to marry, Donna marries one of the Dads, and life on the Greek island returns to normal.

---

versions by numerous other artists. In 1999, this song and the ABBA back catalogue in general found a new lease of life in the stage show – and then film – *Mamma Mia!*. If the stage show is successful there are limitless opportunities for selling more merchandize again: more posters, t-shirts, baseball caps and tote bags; and more CDs, DVDs and mp3s, all creating profit for the producers and writers.

The jukebox musical reveals the music industry to be big business – and a business with which theatre producers collaborate to maximize the efficiencies of global capitalism. This type of standardization and commoditization taps into the profligacies of our leisure time. At leisure, consumers spend freely and become carefree about excess, an attitude which the leisure industry promotes. In harnessing some of our most positive human emotions (excitement, enjoyment, awe) through feel-good experiences (nostalgia, spectacle, thrills), producers make us willing participants in spending money excessively. Not surprisingly, the musical theatre industry has grown as new venture capitalists have recognized its potential to generate profit, tapping into the spending power of the most vulnerable markets – children and families. Leaving the theatre, we are routed through a gift shop selling CDs, cuddly toys, t-shirts and baseball caps, which we buy to mark the occasion; then – just at the most charged point of heady excitement – we tweet, or facebook friends and family. You couldn't get more effective advertising than that.

All exploitation?

If globalization has enabled capitalism to reconceive the world for its own benefit, co-opting culture (the culture *industry*) into its machinations, then we are left in a rather demoralizing position. Does the musical have no future other than as an accomplice to the global conquest of capitalism?

We've considered several economic models and the dynamics of profit, branding and exploitation. Each of these models has found its exemplars in musical theatre: the production-line aesthetics recognized by Siegfried Kracauer and evident in Busby Berkeley's work; the franchise models of Kurz's Lloyd Webber productions in Hamburg; the vertical integration models of Disney; and the commoditizing practices that keep perpetuating profit for all these organizations. These models are undoubtedly triumphs of capitalism over art, though there are subtle differences between the economies of goods and those of culture. Cultural goods are slightly different in that they rely on the creativity even of the most alienated workforce, so even while Siegfried Kracauer argued that the Tiller Girls' kick-lines and Busby Berkeley's chorus girls were a reflection of the production-line process, those performers were more skilled than the alienated labour on whom Ford relied. Likewise, though megamusical performers may feel like part of a machine, frustrated and alienated by the limits placed on their creativity, the production model is not entirely Fordist since each performer creates and embodies a part of the goods exchanged.

Dan Rebellato offers a more positive spin, inviting us to view culture not as part of a globalizing force but as part of a balancing and positive alternative energy, 'cosmopolitanism'. Rather than being primed by profit-seeking motivation or exploitative dynamics, reducing the human to a worker and brandishing the profit-power of 'things', cosmopolitanism harnesses an ethical stance that trumps economics even at a global level. For Rebellato (2009, pp. 74–75), 'the theatre has a number of important formal complexities that make it particularly suitable for developing and sustaining the ethical imagination'. In short, theatre at bottom is still populated by people on the stage and people in the auditorium: real bodies communing in a space of shared expression.

However much we might see corporations as exploiting consumers, this is not a process in which we are completely gullible. 'It just isn't the case', asserts Maurya Wickstrom (2005, p. 102), 'that consumers are merely duped with a sleight-of-hand trick. They are, rather, playing, allowing forms to shift into each other, "indulging" a mimetic pleasure'. How else do we explain the attraction of Disney to adults? We know that when we stand next to Mickey Mouse and have our photo taken, *he's not real*; and we know that we are paying inflated prices for fairly mundane nick-nacks when we buy the souvenir mementoes from Disneyland or Times Square. What Wickstrom points out here is that the sort of capitalism into which we have now entered in the globalized age is one in which the consumer is utterly complicit, knowingly playing along, because the benefit we perceive is complicated, related to our identity and to the way we value ourselves. In owning *this*, in saying we have done *that*, in facebooking a picture of ourselves next to Mickey or at *The Lion King* on Broadway, we gain 'cultural capital' (Bourdieu, 1986) amongst friends, peers and observers. We get something from the experience – something we discuss in detail in Chapter 14 – or we wouldn't continue to pay the price.

Further reading – theoretical

Adler, Steven (2004) *On Broadway: Art and Commerce on the Great White Way* (Carbondale: Southern Illinois University Press).

Burston, Jonathan (1997) 'Enter, Stage Right: Neoconservatism, English Canada and the Megamusical', *Soundings* 5: 179–190.

Rebellato, Dan (2009) *Theatre & Globalization* (Basingstoke: Palgrave Macmillan).

Further reading – relating to the examples

Kidd, Kenneth B. (2004) 'Disney of Orlando's Animal Kingdom', in Sidney I. Dobrin and Kenneth B. Kidd (ed.), *Wild Things: Children's Culture and Ecocriticism* (Detroit: Wayne State University Press), 267–288.

Sternfeld, Jessica (2006) *The Megamusical* (Bloomington: Indiana University Press).

Wickstrom, Maurya (2005) '*The Lion King*, Mimesis, and Disney's Magical Capitalism', in Mike Budd and Max H. Kirsch (eds), *Rethinking Disney: Private Control, Public Dimensions* (Middletown, CT: Wesleyan University Press), 99–121.

7   'What's the Buzz?': Meta-narratives and Post-linearity

There's a moment in *Jesus Christ Superstar* (1970) when the Apostles realize the enormity of events. First Mary Magdalene, then Peter, then everyone pleads with Jesus: 'Could we start again, please?' Their whining in this song is fairly consistent with the characterizations they are given throughout the musical. Aside from Judas, these hapless hippies don't really have a clue about anything – they follow their leader, but all we hear are either expressions of blind faith ('Christ, you know I love you!') or vague questions ('What's the buzz? Tell me what's a-happening'). The one time they could be of use to Jesus – at the Last Supper – they are shown drinking themselves into oblivion.

Too late, they realize that events have gone out of hand: Judas is about to betray Jesus, leading to events that have become enshrined in the mythology of the Christian religion. 'Could we start again, please?' Of course, they can't; and Jesus's response is to keep silent and walk away.

There are probably many circumstances in our lives when we wish we could start again, though unlike in a computer game, we can't just press a restart button. However, that's not quite true, because there are many times when we do start again – at least after a fashion. Charity Hope Valentine, the quirky central character of *Sweet Charity* (1964), seems to start over repeatedly, with a different relationship every week. Indeed, her restart is written into the musical, as the opening scene replays again in the final scene: she strolls through the park with her boyfriend, Oscar. He panics, and just as her previous flame Charlie did in the first scene, he pushes her into the lake. For Charity, this may be a never-ending cycle of romantic disappointments, but the idea that we wipe the slate clean and start over again is one that, in fact, explains many of our experiences in life.

This perhaps contradicts (or at least complexifies) the assumptions we started with in Chapter 1, that a narrative, like life, has a beginning, a middle and an end, and that it plays out in one continuous trajectory. Increasingly, the cultural texts of the twentieth century have called this into question, as Hollywood films attest: sometimes, the cycles of our life trap us within never-ending repetitions of the same scenario (*Groundhog Day*, 1993); sometimes, we wonder what might have been had one tiny encounter played out differently (*Sliding Doors*, 1998).

Indeed, the uncertainties of life might well be considered a puzzlement, which is one of the reasons we have historically sought answers to the great philosophical questions like 'Why are we here?' and 'What's life all about?', as Monty Python ask in their musical film *The Meaning of Life* (1983). The presence of a God has been one of the most enduring solutions to these philosophical questions, but as Python query, 'Is God really real, or is there some doubt?'. In the opening number, the irreverent pranksters promise 'to sort it all out', beginning a satirical romp through the seven ages of man and poking fun at every point along the way; as doubts and uncertainties continue to niggle – and as the God hypothesis does not explain *everything* – the very existence of a higher being is increasingly called into question. Monty Python don't really discover whether God is real, though in other musical theatre texts that question at least receives a response: *Carousel*'s Billy Bigelow arrives at the pearly gates to find not 'Mr and Mrs God' (as Hammerstein originally intended), but a 'Starkeeper'; Dorothy Gale from Kansas skips for miles through the dangerous hinterlands of Oz only to discover that her God is a hoax; and Jerry Springer – well, his meeting with God is something we will discuss later. Tim Rice and Andrew Lloyd Webber's *Jesus Christ Superstar* presented their contribution to the provocative debate, at almost exactly the same time, curiously enough, that Stephen Schwartz and John-Michael Tebelak did likewise in *Godspell* (1971), and John Lennon did by claiming that The Beatles were 'more popular than Jesus' (Cleave, 1966); that caused a real hullaballoo.

Such questioning of Western civilization's guiding principles – to understand the world in which we live; to better ourselves; to be humble in the face of God; to conceptualize life following a linear trajectory with a beginning, a middle and an end – illustrates what theorist Jean-François Lyotard calls 'the postmodern condition'. He observed that many of the stable doctrines organizing our understanding of the world were, by the late twentieth century, being challenged and were losing their stability. He wrote about our 'incredulity towards meta-narratives', referring to the *grands récits* or 'big stories' that have traditionally influenced the way we think and behave. Where the prevailing attitudes of the Victorian period, built upon religious, social and moral ideologies, had led to imperialism and cultural domination, the emerging tendency of the late twentieth century was to challenge those ideologies and unpick the divisive, power-based dynamics resulting from colonialism. Gradually, as the moral authority of colonizing countries began to be questioned, power has been relinquished. With this, perhaps inevitably, has come a questioning of the very 'truths' that initiated colonialism in the first place. Was that charter for Britannia to rule the waves *really* given 'at heaven's command'? Or were such deeply rooted beliefs simply ideologies that gave licence to the actions of the Empire, and the moral authority of a 'great white way'?

In the field of drama, this incredulity has become explicit as practitioners and commentators have moved away from conventional givens (character, plot and script), and turned to theatre pieces that do not resemble traditional dramatic plays. Such abandonment of staple dramatic conventions is the subject of Hans-Thies Lehmann's *Postdramatic Theatre* (2006), in which he explains how practitioners have thrown aside ingrained assumptions about drama in the wake of World War II and started anew. In effect, they have started again, and in so doing, people like Bertolt Brecht, Tadeusz Kantor, Heiner Müller and Sarah Kane have created new paradigms for the postmodern world.

This chapter explores how dramatic form has been reshaped, fractured and fragmented in response to the questioning of conventions, to create the sort of postmodern text with which we are familiar today. We consider how the guiding principles of religion have been shaken in *Jesus Christ Superstar*, how traditional structuring principles of opera and musical theatre have been disbanded in *Einstein on the Beach* (1976) and how artists have sought to 'mash-up' a *bricolage* of existing material to create popular cultural texts like *Moulin Rouge* (2000).

Before exploring these texts in more detail, let's consider what we mean by 'postmodernism', taking a look at three of the most prominent theoretical explanations: Jean-François Lyotard's *The Postmodern Condition* (1979), Fredric Jameson's *Postmodernism, or, The Cultural Logic of Late Capitalism* (1991) and Jean Baudrillard's *Simulacra and Simulation* (1981).

Postmodernism

The term 'postmodern' has been widely used for decades; indeed, it has become so common that its precise meaning is hard to gauge thanks to the variety of ways in which it has been used. The main uncertainty is whether 'postmodern' refers to a cultural style whose qualities we can categorize, or to a period following in the wake of modernism.

There are certainly recognizable attributes associated with postmodernism. Postmodern texts and practices are prominent in popular or mass culture, where they are enabled by developments in new technology and new media forms. Characteristic features include a fascination with quoting material from other sources (sampling in pop music), piecing together texts like a patchwork quilt (like a mash-up) and playing around with ideas of truth, the real and the imaginary (virtual reality). In terms of quintessential postmodern texts or phenomena, the aesthetic of MTV on television, films like *Pulp Fiction* (1994) or *The Matrix* (1999), books such as Joseph Heller's *Catch-22* (1961) or *Fear and Loathing in Las Vegas* (1971) by Hunter S. Thompson, art by practitioners such as Gilbert and George or Banksy, celebrity culture in general and pop culture icons like Michael Jackson and Lady GaGa are regularly cited as postmodern. At the same time, postmodernism has a dynamic relationship with commercialism and commodification, so there is no surprise that some of the defining advertising slogans of the 1980s and 1990s seem to express postmodern ideals: Coca Cola's 'It's the Real Thing' is a good example, pastiched by U2 in their song 'Even Better Than the Real Thing', a postmodern comment on a postmodern commodity, a knowing, self-conscious manipulation of the 'chain of signifiers'.

In reaction to modernist principles, postmodernism has embraced the move away from traditional representation, creating increasingly fragmented images of the world and dispensing with many conventions. Indeed, many would say that a feature of postmodernism is its triumph of style over content, surface over substance, meaninglessness over meaning. But creating this rupture between art or culture and the concept of meaningfulness or representation has been possible only because postmodern thinking has also challenged the ideologies that established the conventions in the first place: where modernism valued high art, postmodernism champions popular culture and mass entertainment forms. Unlike the 'genius' of the modernist period, the postmodern artist becomes either the epitome of the common people (The Beatles) or a self-consciously constructed personality whose performativity is part of his/her celebrity (Elvis).

Postmodernism is certainly playful, and some of the most obvious examples of postmodern culture carry their playfulness on their sleeve – many a student room has been adorned with a poster of the Mona Lisa smoking cannabis, for example; while postmodern artists and musicians regularly pastiche one another, as M-J Delaney's 'Newport State of Mind' (2010) did with Jay-Z's 'Empire State of Mind' (2009), which in turn sampled a riff from the soul hit 'Love on a Two-Way Street' (1970). In Delaney's song, the lyrics mimic Jay-Z's (about New York) with reference to Newport, a small town in Wales: 'Concrete jumble, nothing in order, not far from the border, when you're in Newport'. More famously, Alicia Keys' alternative version of 'Empire State of Mind' created another postmodern homage. On the other hand, some of this playful and apparently superficial postmodernism – graffiti artist Banksy's work, for example, however flippant – is extremely committed to politics. The charge that postmodernism is all surface over substance is therefore one that underestimates the potential of

---

Modernism

Modernism refers to a period of cultural development from roughly 1850 to 1950 characterized by Matthew Arnold's definition of culture: the 'pursuit of our total perfection by means of getting to know [...] the best which has been thought and said in the world'. Modernist principles develop the idea of society progressing from the Dark Ages through the Renaissance to the Enlightenment period. Such lofty ambitions might be seen as positive, civilizing values; but for modernists the pursuit of perfection requires them to both exceed previous limitations and to break away from traditional depictions of the world: thus painters such as Picasso flatten the traditional image of a face; writers like James Joyce spew out train-of-thought anti-narratives; composers like Schoenberg, Webern and Berg jettison conventions of musical tonality; and playwrights like Samuel Beckett question character, plot and action. All these people create art that is somehow extreme (excessive) in nature, and in transcending 'normal' confines the art is elevated to a status of high cultural value, its artists defined as geniuses who transcend conventional human ability. In this sense, modernism might also be accused of elitism, and a backlash against modernism's highbrow status might be seen in the increasing acceptance of popular culture and the expressions of the common people as the twentieth century progressed.

---

popular culture. And in some of the following examples of popular culture we can see its power at work.

Lyotard, Jameson and Baudrillard

Lyotard's *The Postmodern Condition* (1984) has been significant in formulating an idea of how postmodernism emerged from modernism. For Lyotard, one of the things that defined modernism was its acknowledgement of and commitment to meta-narratives or *grands récits*. These – the spirit of the enlightenment that has guided our quest for knowledge; the faith in a God who can explain the origin of all things – have been powerful influences as the West has developed and determining principles in the way we lead our lives. Lyotard suggests that the turn to postmodernism has brought about a *distrust* in these narratives, such that we now question them instead of accepting them unreservedly. Along with other theorists such as Jacques Derrida, Lyotard points out that each of these meta-narratives relies on us accepting – illogically – the existence of some transcendental force, such as God. We blithely accept transcendental concepts like 'truth', 'meaning' or 'sense'; without these, the power of the meta-narrative collapses. As Lyotard (1984, p. 20) suggests of all meta-narratives, they 'allow the society in which they are told, on the one hand, to define its criteria of competence, and, on the other, to evaluate according to those criteria, what is performed or can be performed within it'. This Lyotard considers dangerous, since it can sanction problematic and often divisive ways of thinking that privilege some while disenfranchising others. Meta-narratives form the basis of *ideology*, and we have already seen how that can be problematic. But think how, even in our apparently harmless study, we have been conditioned, not least by our quest for meaning throughout Part I. Lyotard's work causes us to reflect on how reliable the idea of meaning might be: is our whole system of representation and our way of understanding it no more than a house of cards?

American theoretician Fredric Jameson, meanwhile, suggested that the postmodern attitude is an inevitable extension of the drive towards capitalism by Western powers. He relates this to capitalism's connection to colonialism, noting how Western countries gained power by conquering other people and colonizing their territory. European countries did this by creating Empires and spreading their might over the world, and perhaps most significantly, the story of America is tied up in the way that settlers steamrollered across the open spaces of a vast continent, pushing the frontier of 'civilization' further west and banishing the indigenous population, the native American Indians. By the twentieth century there was no more land to grab in America, so in order to keep increasing territory and turn it into profit-generating capital, the settlers had to think of clever ways to colonize more space. This they did in 1969 when, symbolically, America claimed ownership of the moon, confirming its success in the 'Space Race' and opening up the possibility of satellites, space stations and eventually perhaps the colonization of other planets. Nowadays (in our postmodern world) many of our cultural experiences rely on the technologies that the colonization of space enabled. Conquering 'the final frontier', as one TV show called it, allowed capitalists to make millions, and before long they found another form of space which could give apparently endless new territory to turn to profit: cyberspace. In the wake of this new territory opening up, the possibilities for making enormous profits have exploded, enabling companies to form (Facebook, Google) that would have been inconceivable before and whose whole mechanics operate in a virtual world created and empowered by the Internet.

Jean Baudrillard's theories pick up on the way that media technologies perform a similar trick of creating dimensions that don't really exist. He notices how a paradigm shift has taken place between the early twentieth century – when to experience the world one had to travel and visit places – and now – when we can see the world whilst sitting in our front rooms, thanks to the marvel of modern television and the Internet. But Baudrillard worries that the images we see might be distorted, *versions*, perhaps, of the 'truth', but edited and photoshopped to create a fantasy world that does not really exist. Is the landscape really as beautiful as that holiday programme suggests? Do those photos of the moon landings really *prove* that Neil Armstrong landed on the moon? Baudrillard has caused controversy by suggesting that the Gulf War didn't happen and that America exists only in our imagination; these are clearly provocative comments, but to understand them, consider what we know of the Gulf War, a city like New York, an event such as 9/11 or the moon landings. If we were not present we can only rely on the edited and selected images of (powerful, capitalist) media companies which *construct* rather than *report* the news. We know New York, for example, from a series of iconic pictures, sounds and characters that have bombarded us through popular culture: it's the 'concrete jungle where dreams are made', it's the 'city that never sleeps', it's the playground of the rich, it's a mecca for dazzling entertainment, corporate success and financial power – but this is in effect an enormous sales pitch for a city that is itself a (profit-generating) commodity.

As Baudrillard's ideas gained currency, culture picked up on the idea that the real world is one hidden underneath a sort of mask – exactly the story of *The Matrix* (1999), whose 'real' world is a disappointing desert beneath the illusion of the virtual. Interestingly, a reference to *Simulacra and Simulation* (as well as to other narratives of other worlds, like *Alice in Wonderland*) features in one of the first scenes of the film, when Neo stashes money in a hidden compartment inside Baudrillard's book. Many other films – *The Truman Show* (1998), *Pleasantville* (1998), *Vanilla Sky* (2001), *Inception* (2010) – create similar narratives in which the 'real' and the 'imaginary' are confused, and in doing so, those certainties of 'truth', 'meaning' and 'sense' are again confronted and called into question.

The three perspectives of Lyotard, Jameson and Baudrillard cause us to reconsider the stories we tell about the world, particularly in the light of narrative theories that we have explored in Chapter 1, and the power of capitalism that we have encountered throughout our critical journey. In this chapter the three shows we consider each challenge 'truth', 'meaning', 'sense' or other meta-narratives through their intriguing postmodern approaches to storytelling: one confronts the existing 'truth' of a well-known tale; one constructs a narrative through a patchwork *bricolage* of intertextual references; and one rejects altogether the need for narrative coherence.

Jesus Christ Superstar (1970)

Jesus Christ Superstar (1970)

Music by Andrew Lloyd Webber

Lyrics by Tim Rice

First released as a concept album in 1970. Based on the story of Christ's last seven days

Superstar was written with a rock score that challenged musical theatre expectations. The show attracted controversy thanks to its portrayal of Judas Iscariot as a tragic figure, and its presentation of Christ as a celebrity figure like John Lennon or David Bowie. It confronted the sensitivities of religious groups and offended many Christians.[1] Yet for Rice and Lloyd Webber it marked the beginning of a long period of dominance in commercial musical theatre, and for musical theatre in general it marked the beginning of the 'British invasion' of Broadway by the megamusical.

The meta-narrative of Christianity has guided Western lifestyles for the past 2,000 years. Representations of Christ and religious iconography have constituted the basis of many works of art, not just in sculpture and painting, but also on the stage in works like Handel's *Messiah* (1741), Britten's *Noye's Fludde* (1957) or the Medieval Mystery Plays. The subject, then, is not new; we have been immersed in the moral and ethical codes of Christianity for generations. Our calendar, behaviour, ruling system and even language reflect the prominence of this meta-narrative, and it is only recently that we have begun to distance ourselves from it, adopting the self-identity in many Western countries of a 'secular' society. Nevertheless, the vocabulary of this meta-narrative is pervasive, pastiched by a popular culture that is both conversant with and irreverent to the ideas of Christianity – think of Madonna's greatest hits album *The Immaculate Collection* (1990). Within this *grand recit*, the story of the last seven days of Christ must be the most famous ever told.

The major innovation of *Jesus Christ Superstar* is to sideline the central character of Jesus, and concentrate on Judas, which humanizes his plight. Tim Rice (1970, n.p.) points to Bob Dylan for this inspiration, in the song 'With God on Our Side' (1964). Towards the end of the musical, Judas comes back from the grave to explain his actions, a narrational device formerly available only to Jesus through his resurrection and the subsequent documentation of his life. This reflection runs throughout *Superstar* as other characters take the spotlight: Pontius Pilate's dream exposes sympathy and understanding for Christ; the Apostles confess their fears when they sing 'Could we start again please?'; meanwhile, in the language of contemporary capitalist culture, characters knowingly sing about 'Jesusmania', 'mass communication' and 'PR'. Jesus is even established as the character of a Hollywood scenario when the crowd reassures him, 'You'll escape in the final reel'. No longer is this narrative structured 'in order to resolve some fundamental antagonism by rearranging its terms into a temporal succession' (Žižek, 1997, pp. 10–11); in what Dick Hebdige (2002, p. 1982) refers to as an 'anti-teleological tendency', this postmodern text distances its audience from the immediacy of plot to draw attention to the conceit with which it is told.

One of the most accessible ways to encounter *Jesus Christ Superstar* is to watch Norman Jewison's 1973 film, whose opening sequence is fascinating. The sequence starts with slow-paced long shots of a barren landscape, showing the dusty wilderness of the Middle East. The accompanying music is unfamiliar in its modality and instrumentation; it *sounds* ancient and 'other'. Together, the images and the sounds give the impression of age and authenticity. This film is going to be truthful, we deduce. As the sequence continues, the camera encounters the ruined walls of ancient buildings, confirming the idea that the film will uncover an ancient story. A glimpse of scaffolding around the ruins reminds us that we are in the present, though we can still believe that this relates to a sort of archaeological dig at this location. Even when the instrumentation becomes contemporary – an electric guitar and a synthesized keyboard – the mood of the music is still plausibly Middle Eastern.

Suddenly, the quiet of this ancient place is shattered: the electric guitar bursts into an unexpected rock riff, and the camera picks up the dust cloud of a vehicle tearing through the desert. The music is jarring and discordant, a rude interruption to the tranquillity that has gone before; the vehicle bounces recklessly across the terrain. It is a Middle Eastern bus – there is Arabic writing on the side – but when it pulls up outside the ruins and a crowd of young people emerge, we notice that they are Westerners. These are not archaeologists with a sense of care, or tourists full of awe and respect; they are hippies, who emerge with the hedonistic irresponsibility of a youthful counter-culture, as if they are colonizers of this almost virgin landscape, sticking two fingers up to the sanctity and propriety of a place that seems holy. More than this though, they are storytellers – actors, complete with props and costumes. This changes our perspective: no longer do we anticipate a truthful or authentic narrative; this is going to be made up, constructed. Now the scaffolding amidst the ruins has a different significance: this story is about to be *re-built*.

This arrival by a travelling group of performers, and their departure at the end of the film, frames the narrative, distancing it from its historical contextual reference. Immediately, though, the clean slate is filled with signs, references which in a Barthesian sense signify far more than their obvious denotations. The hippies emerging from the bus carry connotations of the permissive society, the breaking through of counter-cultures, the rise of youth culture and sex, drugs and rock 'n' roll. The casting of a black actor as Judas and a white actor as Jesus – which might at first seem a crassly simplistic expression of racism – draws attention to race contradictions in the meta-narrative of Christianity: how come Jesus is *always* pictured as neither Jewish nor Middle Eastern, but white? And Judas and Jesus resemble rock icons Jimi Hendrix and John Lennon, a connotation whose force does nothing so much as distance this narrative from any semblance of a religious story: in *Jesus Christ Superstar*, the Gospel is dead.

So, a hotchpotch of signifiers is given free rein in this film, with costumes that both seem appropriate (Jesus's shroud) and incongruous (Herod's posse's wigs and shades). As tanks are seen appearing over the sand-dunes (see Figure 7.1), they are not just indicative of conflict, or the might and violence of the Roman Empire, but of the metaphorical rape of countries by other and more insidious colonizers. To a 1973 audience the tanks would certainly have gestured to American forces, who were at that time deep in the heart of Vietnam. As Fredric Jameson (in Cahoone, 2003, p. 566) has suggested, 'this whole global, yet American, postmodern culture is the internal and superstructural expression of a whole new wave of American military and economic domination throughout the world: in this sense, as

Figure 7.1   Judas (Carl Anderson) faces an incongruous phalanx of tanks in *Jesus Christ Superstar* (1973). Universal Pictures

throughout class history, the underside of culture is blood, torture, death and terror'.

In 2012 *Jesus Christ Superstar* was once again the focus of attention as Andrew Lloyd Webber developed the latest in his series of talent show TV contests, in which unknown performers audition for a coveted role in a new revival. Now with the trappings of a commercial TV channel's design budget and a new set of references from *X Factor* and other mass TV franchises, the text is turned into an even more postmodern commodity as it is re-invented for performance around stadium venues. In this guise, the text becomes even more severed from the sense that it tells the story of Christ: audiences flock to see not theatre but – in a confusing play of signifiers – superstars performing *Superstar*. The winner of the TV contest plays Jesus, singer-songwriter Tim Minchin, fresh from his West End success *Matilda* (2010), plays Judas, Spice Girl Mel B plays Mary Magdalene and radio DJ Chris Moyles plays King Herod. These cultural references clearly pick up on the intentions of the original material to consider Jesus as a celebrity, but as the codes of celebrity status endlessly refer to each other, the text becomes a bubble of cultural self-reflection in which the postmodern 'play of signifiers' is circular and self-perpetuating.

Moulin Rouge (2000)

Baz Luhrmann's film *Moulin Rouge* (2000) is the third of his 'Red Curtain Trilogy' of films, each bearing the authorial stamp of a vivid design aesthetic, and each a postmodern revision of a classic tale. *Moulin Rouge* itself is nominally a retelling of the Orpheus myth, though that is perhaps its least significant reference point. Within the film, in almost all of its signifying modes, references abound.

Like *Superstar*, *Moulin Rouge* pitches the historicity of a former period against the pervasive imagery of contemporary culture. Although set in turn-of-the-century Paris, the film bounces to the rhythm of late-twentieth-century popular music. Here, the horizon that guides our interpretation of signs, both in terms of the world constructed and the characters that inhabit it, is created from a patchwork quilt of already-established cultural references. Paris at the turn-of-the-century is a dark and brooding city; the Moulin Rouge is a decadent and hedonistic whirl of excitement; artists are struggling bohemians fuelled on alcohol and narcotics; and love is a feverish passion more akin to a disease than a feeling. These are all stereotypes born from countless images at the periphery of our perception – the

---

Moulin Rouge (Fox, 2001)

Original Score by Craig Armstrong

Screenplay by Baz Luhrmann and Craig Pearce

Directed by Baz Luhrmann

Starring Nicole Kidman, Ewan Macgregor

Based loosely on *La Traviata* (1853) by Giuseppe Verdi and Francesco Maria Piave, and drawing from the Greek myth of Orpheus

Synopsis: Satine performs at the Parisian nightclub the Moulin Rouge and is promised to the rich aristocrat the Duke in exchange for his pledge to bail out the club from bankruptcy. But when struggling writer Christian meets Satine, they begin an affair that risks the club, their careers and, ultimately, their lives. As the company of the Moulin Rouge stages a fantastical extravaganza funded by the Duke to keep the club afloat, he discovers their affair and attempts to kill Satine on stage. She is saved, only to die from tuberculosis, breaking Christian's heart and sealing the tragedy. The film is constructed to a patchwork sound-track of pop music from the 1960s to the 1990s, remixed in different styles and often pieced together using just snippets of each song. Unlike some of the other shows discussed in this chapter, *Moulin Rouge* has a far more coherent storyline – albeit superficial; but its soundtrack and visual aesthetic owe a lot to the televisual style of MTV.

---

paintings of Van Gogh, Toulouse-Lautrec and Degas, the novels of Émile Zola and Victor Hugo, the early films of Georges Méliès and – from a slightly earlier reference – the well-documented indulgences of the romantic poets Shelley and Byron.

If Ewan Macgregor's Christian is a modern Byron, Nicole Kidman's Satine is a composite of several twentieth-century femmes fatales: at times Marlene Dietrich ('I Want to Be Alone'), Marilyn Monroe ('Diamonds Are a Girl's Best Friend') and Madonna ('Material Girl'), Luhrmann positions her in recognizable poses and costumes from an archive of film and video imagery. Other characters reference different personalities, some from fictional stories (the evil, moustachioed aris-tocrat), some from real life (Toulouse-Lautrec himself), and some played by celebrities (the Green Fairy played by Kylie Minogue). Most of all, though, the intertextual references from which the story is constructed come from music, pieced together in the style of MTV from a host of well-known song snippets.

It's significant that both the construction of the narrative and the aesthetic style of the imagery are reminiscent of MTV, because this has been called 'the quintessential example of postmodern media production':

> From its fast, fragmented production editing to its underlying visions (sexual moral relativism, for example), MTV represents the 'cutting edge' of postmodernism applied to consumer media. MTV's editors 'collage' the shows together into a jumpy, stream-of-consciousness presentation that leaves older viewers baffled by its pace and apparent incoherence. But to the postmodern 'generation-X' crowd who make a steady diet of it, MTV's randomness is normal. MTV's twenty-four-hour parade of images, pseudo-documentaries, hedonistic dating-scenario game shows, music videos, and cutting-edge advertisements relentlessly assault one's visual and auditory senses, leaving viewers feeling fragmented and transient within a decentered plural-reality: the postmodern world. (Hurd, 1998)

This patching together and sampling of material is evident throughout *Moulin Rouge*, from early references to *The Sound of Music* to a club collage of iconic diva songs ('Lady Marmalade', 'Material Girl', 'Rhythm of the Night', 'Diamonds Are a Girl's Best Friend') to witty, even ridiculous cover versions of well-known classics ('Like a Virgin', 'Roxanne', 'The Can Can'). In the most obvious example of song-sampling, 'The Elephant Love Medley', no fewer than 13 songs create Satine and Christian's flirtatious encounter on the rooftop.[2]

Perhaps one of the reasons that *Moulin Rouge* resonated so effectively with young audiences was because it tapped into the zeitgeist and in particular a new paradigm of engaging with culture brought about by the rise of the Internet, the increased use of media platforms and mobile communications and – eventually – the habit of multi-platforming, a behavioural tendency that replicates the aesthetic of MTV-derived models.

Einstein on the Beach (1976)

Hans-Thies Lehmann recognizes the significance of music in finding alternative strategies for structuring experiences within a temporal framework, and accordingly, contemporary music theatre has engaged extensively with the postdramatic. As Copeland (2012) suggests, it is the structures and patterns of the contemporary (postmodern) world that provide a context for this sort of work, and referring to German postdramatic practitioner Heiner Müller, he writes: 'Müller's plays often sample chunks of text from already existing works which constitute a "creative commons", our shared cultural birthright. In this sense, his work anticipates today's Internet influenced aesthetic of the mash-up and the remix'.

Yet perhaps surprisingly a fascination with structures and patterns rather than content and narrative has pervaded twentieth-century music; as an abstract form, music lends itself to such experimentation. In the early twentieth century, modernist composers such as Schoenberg, Berg and Stockhausen constructed formalistic music that turned its back on the romantic indulgences of the late nineteenth century. Their inheritance is evident both in the music theatre of Luciano Berio, Mauricio Kagel and Sylvano Bussotti and in the reaction to modernism of the musical 'minimalists' Terry Riley, LaMonte Young, Steve Reich and Philip Glass, for whom the external presentation of structure was paramount.[3]

Before *Einstein on the Beach* (1976), Glass had been developing two new strategies for his repetitive process music. First, he would write a few very short phrases – sometimes just two notes – to be layered or superimposed by two or more instruments or voices. As instrumentalists play these short

---

Process music

The group of four composers, Riley, Young, Reich and Glass, created music with externally apparent structure as a direct reaction to the inaudible structures of 12-tone music. The process through which their music was created became both form and content as in *Pendulum Music* (1968) by Steve Reich. In this work several microphones are swung between four speakers and emit a squeal of feedback as they approach the speakers. As gravity reduces the swing, the movement reduces and consequently so does the sound – thus the process and structure of the musical sound-making is revealed. This sort of externally apparent process can be found in the works of many performance artists in New York from the same period, such as Laurie Anderson, and in its own way, it brings a performative dimension to what might otherwise be considered simply music. As such, our understanding of what constitutes musical theatre – perhaps in this sense more commonly referred to as 'music theatre' – develops further.

Einstein on the Beach (1976)

Music by Philip Glass

Direction by Robert Wilson

Text fragments by Christopher Knowles, Samuel M. Johnson and Lucinda Childs

Choreography by Lucinda Childs

Synopsis: This opera intentionally dispenses with any notion of plot. It contains a number of images and figures from history, including the physicist Albert Einstein, who for part of the work sits in front of the stage playing the violin. Glass (1988, p. 32) refers to the work as a 'portrait opera' of Einstein that was constructed as a poetic vision rather than as a narrative. It was structured using dramaturgical devices, such as an epilogue and a finale, and also by contrasting dynamic qualities (fast sections against slow sections, for example). The dramaturgy consists of three visual themes or images: 'a landscape seen at a distance', which is represented by several 'Field/Spaceship scenes'; 'still lifes seen at a middle distance', which are a series of 'Trial scenes'; and 'portraits seen in close up', which are interjected physical duets that are known as 'the Knee Plays' (p. 33). These three perspectives rotate throughout the four acts. Some of the choral libretto is sung to the solfège musical notation system (doh, re, mi, etc.); other parts to numbers;[4] the choir also performs complex hand and body movements at a very precise rate. At other times a poetic text with many repeated sequences and recurring cycles is spoken over the music (ibid.). The physical gestures of the work fall into two patterns: everyday gestures, such as walking and pointing, that are repeated in a metronomic fashion, slowed down or accelerated; and sections of dance that use more abstract gestures also contained in repetitive patterns and structures. The music is also constructed through processes of repetition that arose from a minimalist aesthetic, normally referred to as 'repetitive' or 'process' music. The intention was to allow individual meanings to emerge in the imagination of each audience member as a result of the combination of images. *Einstein on the Beach* is one of the three operas by Glass that reference significant personalities: its follow-up *Satyagraha* (1980), with a libretto in Sanskrit, focuses on religious leader Mahatma Gandhi. The third, *Akhnaten* (1983), refers to the Egyptian Pharoah Akhenaten.

phrases, the texture of the intervals between the phrases alters, and new highpoints and melodies can be discerned by the listener that are not written into the musical score, but which emerge anew with each iteration of the performance. For each listener at each performance these might be different. This relates to ideas in Roland Barthes's essay 'The Death of the Author', which we explore in detail in Chapter 12, in which he suggests that the listener rather than the author has agency in creating meaning. The second strategy was to extend the variability of these phrases by using cyclic and additive structures alongside modulation and cadence: a group of five notes might be played several times, then a sixth note added and repeated several times, then a seventh and so on in an additive process; then the phrase might reduce through a similar process. No matter how the notes are grouped, each time the phrase length changes, the rhythmic pattern changes too. As the phrase extends or reduces, the pattern inter-acts differently (both melodically and rhythmically) with other phrases being played by other instruments. Rhythmic cycles are created by super-imposing two patterns that gradually move away from each other through additive or reductive processes. The cycle completes when the music comes full circle and the parts are in the same relationship to each other as they were at the start. A familiar example of the cyclic process can be found in Steve Reich's 'Clapping Games'.

Using a combination of these methods Glass could compose very long durational works very quickly – works that relied on the listener hearing the process and discovering melodic and rhythmic patterns within the texture. For *Einstein on the Beach*, Glass combined these methods with altered and extended cadences (slightly less radical than the music he had been experi-menting with until that time). However, the key elements remained – of music created through an audible process that required the listener to dis-cover melodies and harmonies in the inner workings of the harmonic and rhythmic patterns.

Einstein on the Beach also relies on its visual aesthetic, and Robert Wilson's contribution in this regard was fundamental; it was his understanding of theatre as a visually aesthetic form and his drawings that created the stimulus for the piece in the first place. Likewise, the contribution of choreographer Lucinda Childs should not be overlooked, especially since her choreography has been re-created for every significant production of *Einstein on the Beach* since the premiere (at the Brooklyn Academy of Music in 1992 and internationally in 2012–2013).

Although the piece has no ostensible narrative, Glass does offer a scenario for the audience to make sense of the progression of scenes, though this is a fairly insubstantial trajectory ('the opera begins with a nineteenth-century train and ends with a twentieth-century spaceship'). Instead, the piece is constructed as music, with a theme and variations. The cerebral or intellectual encounter with theatre which has become conventional is rejected in favour of a more immersive experience, as Robert Wilson (2012) suggests:

> We're used to seeing opera and theater that has narrative and tells stories, where action is following the music or action is following a text. It's something that you can easily comprehend, understand. Here, it's a work where you go and you can get lost. That's the idea. [...] You don't have to understand anything.

Indeed, understanding anything is made particularly difficult given the abstract libretto of numbers and solfège sounds. Glass (1978) explains how these are influenced by and form a part of the music: 'When numbers are used, they represent the rhythmic structure of the music. When solfège is used, the syllables represent the pitch structure of the music. In either case, the text is not secondary or supplementary but is a description of the music itself' (p. 67). In some ways, as Glass recognizes, the use of numbers is appropriate for an opera that references the great physicist and mathematician Albert Einstein; in this sense there is a thematic link to the subject matter. However, Einstein is hardly a character in the piece even though various figures resembling him appear throughout the opera, played by various performers, sometimes simultaneously. The most prominent figure of Einstein is a violinist, seated just outside the main frame of the stage, partway between the orchestra and the stage performers, observing the action and events from a distanced position, and symbolically contributing the most significant thematic music, the repeated violin motif.

Without the stabilizing influence of a coherent narrative, characters or language, the work can seem inaccessible, 'impenetrable or plain boring', as Mark C. O'Flaherty laments. However, writing in the online magazine *Civilian Global*, O'Flaherty (2013) asserts that the aesthetic attitude required of *Einstein on the Beach* is simply unusual to a theatre-going experience; in other moments of our lives we do engage with 'a diet of repetitive, sparse techno and postmodern culture generally'. Here, Glass and Wilson's move away from dramatic conventions catches us off-guard and defamiliarizes us, but that in itself merely redefines what theatre can do.

Further reading – theoretical

Brooker, Peter (ed.) *Modernism/Postmodernism* (London and New York: Longman).
Cahoone, Lawrence (ed.) (2003) *From Modernism to Postmodernism: An Anthology* (second, expanded edition) (Oxford: Blackwell).

Lehmann, Hans-Thies (2006) *Postdramatic Theatre* (New York and Abingdon: Routledge).

Further reading – relating to the examples

Glass, Philip (1988) *Opera on the Beach* (London and Boston: Faber & Faber).
Kinder, Marsha (2002) 'Moulin Rouge', *Film Quarterly* 55(3): 52–59.
Rice, Tim and Andrew Lloyd Webber (1970) *Jesus Christ Superstar: The Authorised Version* (London: Pan Books).

PART III
Performing Identities

8 'Marry the Man Today': Feminism and the Performance of Identity

'Marry the man today and change his ways tomorrow' – so sing Sarah and Adelaide towards the end of *Guys and Dolls* (1950) seeing this as a strategy for getting married. And marriage is the goal for many female characters throughout the history of musical theatre. Because of such heteronormative stories that equate 'happy ever after' with marital bliss, and women as the weaker 'other' in a Western society formed for and by white heterosexual men, musical theatre has had a complicated relationship with gender and sexuality. Opera has an equally troubled pattern of storytelling as Catherine Clément identifies in *Opera, or, the Undoing of Women* (1979). She demonstrates, using examples from the characters of nineteenth-century opera, that 'good' girls get married and 'bad' – and for 'bad' read 'sexually active' – girls die.

In this part of the book, we're going to explore how identities are represented onstage, and what those identities say about how society views particular groups of people. In Chapter 5 we saw how racial 'others' were imagined as exotic and different. In this section we consider how that applies to other identity groups within our own societies; in this case, women (this chapter), young people (Chapter 9) and alternative male sexualities (Chapter 10). Significantly, the groups we are looking at are 'others' to white, male and heterosexual normativities, reflecting the fact that society is viewed from the position of a dominant patriarchy. Clearly we could explore other equally disenfranchised communities, applying these ideas to the representation of diasporic communities within Western society, or lesbian women and so on, but that is for you to do when you look at other musical theatre texts.

We begin from the premise that identity is performed and that viewing the performance of identity by others influences how we view our own identities. At the same time theatre positions men and women on stage in front of us, thereby turning their bodies into objects of attention and causing us to regard them in particular ways. This feature of theatre (shared with film, fine art and sculpture) has influenced its stylistic aesthetic, the *language* of the stage: bodies are displayed as figures of aesthetic appeal, ornaments we are invited to gaze at. It is impossible not to be aware of the extraordinarily good looks and honed bodies of actors (of both sexes) in medical dramas, sitcoms and soaps, for example. Equally, it is comparatively rare to see a female singer in pop music who is not a particular size and shape – even though her size and shape can have no bearing on her musical ability. Musical theatre draws attention to this aesthetic even more than non-musical theatre, and since it also explicitly frames the voice in its aesthetic (another gendered entity that we consider in Chapter 13) the fault lines between humanizing and objectifying individuals can be very fragile. Because performance in theatre is viewed as a reflection of life, the dynamics of gender that operate offstage become inscribed with what appears on the stage (and of course on television, in films and music videos too), where the performance of gender is magnified and exaggerated, and therefore powerfully influential.

On the other hand, the performers onstage have agency, they are not simply objects as they would be in a fixed medium like a painting or a sculpture – and this is where the Marxist framework breaks down, as we suggested at the end of Chapter 6. Performers are not simply labourers producing cultural goods for the capitalist market. Their presence and their performance of their own identity on and offstage interact with the performance of character so that on some occasions the heteronormative status quo of musical theatre is subverted or at least questioned.

In this chapter we explore some of these dynamics of power, predominantly in the way they are enacted or confirmed on the stage but with reference to the way such images interact with real life. As case studies, we use the opera *La Traviata* (1853) and the musical *Wicked* (2003).

Three waves of feminism

It may not have escaped attention that the majority of writers mentioned in this book, and even in this chapter on feminism (with the notable exception of *Wicked*'s librettist Winnie Holzman), are male; perhaps it seems odd that we should dwell so heavily on texts created by men in a chapter on feminism. However, this is significant: men have far more of a voice than women, and this is all tied up in issues of power.

For centuries men have been placed in greater positions of power than women, asserting authority, and benefiting from greater opportunities. In Western society, men have the dominant voice, and the power position this gives them therefore shapes the world according to male thinking. This imbalance of power in favour of men, this patriarchy, is a societal setup that is deeply unjust, and at times the violence with which the rights of the patriarchy have been asserted have led to horrendous situations of abuse and oppression for women. Nowadays, in Western countries at least, the pendulum has swung back to create a more just society and more equality between the sexes; however, even if the wounds caused by patriarchal authority are not so evident, the dominance of its power still asserts a firm grip.

The first concerted attempt by women to reclaim a sense of equality was made in the late nineteenth century in both Europe and America as women (suffragettes) campaigned for the right to vote – literally, to have a voice. More widely, the actions of the suffragettes expressed their revolt against a number of social and legal inequalities (education, equal pay, maternity benefits) which, over time, began to be eroded. Gradually, the fight for women's suffrage gained momentum and increasing success worldwide gave women the vote in various countries, signifying a symbolic equality of women with men in the eyes of the law, and paving the way for the gradual erosion of many other oppressive restrictions. The American state of Wyoming was the first high-profile success for women's suffrage, in 1869, and the rest of America followed to allow equal voting rights for (white) men and women by the time of the presidential election in 1920. Britain capitulated in 1918 when voting rights were extended to women over 30 years of age, and by 1928, this age limit was reduced to 21. Other countries acquiesced throughout the twentieth century including France, Italy and Japan after World War II, and many of the African nations following their liberation in the 1950s–1960s. To their shame the European state of Liechtenstein delayed until 1984, and one Swiss province until 1990; following Qatar's decision to allow women voting rights in 1997, many of the Arab states have now adopted equal suffrage. Currently, Saudi Arabia is one of the few democracies yet to grant women the right to vote, though it has pledged to lift its restrictions for the elections of 2015.

The battle for suffrage is recognized as the first 'wave' of the feminist movement. Once voting rights had been gained and other legal and social restrictions began to be eroded, it became clear, however, that Western countries still maintained ways of thinking that undermined women's rights and that a different set of issues needed to be addressed. The momentum for this 'second wave' began with the publication of *The Second Sex* by Simone de Beauvoir in 1949, but really gathered pace during the 1970s. Activists found encouragement in the works of writers who had been influenced by de Beauvoir's (1973, p. 301) assertion that 'one is not born, but rather becomes, woman'. Among the writers leading the second wave were Betty Friedan (*The Feminine Mystique*, 1963) and Germaine Greer (*The Female Eunuch*, 1970) for whom 'there could be no liberation [...] as long as we were required to cram our breasts into bras constructed like mini-Vesuviuses, two stitched white cantilevered cones which bore no resemblance to the female anatomy' (Jardine, 1999, p. 3). Thus 'bra-burning' feminists publicly abandoned high heels, false eyelashes, makeup and other 'instruments of female torture' (Schechner, 2006, p. 160). Miss America and Miss World pageants were disrupted by protestors campaigning against the objectification of women. Meanwhile, following industrial action by women workers in Britain, the government brought its Equal Pay, Sexual Discrimination and Employment Protection Acts into effect in 1975, making it compulsory for companies to provide maternity benefits and making it illegal for them to sack workers who became pregnant. The 1970s in Britain ended with the first female prime minister Margaret Thatcher being elected to office, and with this – a symbolic coup yet something of a feminist own goal – the second wave began to wane. Nevertheless, the legacy of its battles in the 1970s endured throughout the 1980s as feminism's holistic voice dealing with universal women's concerns became fractured into a number of more focused agendas from Liberal, Marxist, Radical, Lesbian and Black feminists, each of which had very nuanced perspectives on their own feminisms and for each of whom 'the personal [was] political' (Hanisch, 1970).

As the 1980s progressed, a third wave of thought began to emerge, which expressed discomfort that feminism tended to position women in the role of victim to the male patriarchy. Where second wave feminists saw bras, high heels and stockings as emblems of exploitation and abuse by men, third wave feminists began to reclaim them as symbols of liberation and self-expression. Greer's oppressive cantilevered Vesuviuses became by 1990 the expression of a new style of feminist, as the pop megastar Madonna donned outfits that embraced sexuality, provoked outrage, challenged gender statements and knowingly referenced the feminist debate. Increasingly, third wave feminists reconceived the identity of women, firstly, by championing strength, independence and self-will, and, secondly, by drawing attention to universal issues affecting women, particularly in developing countries where personal and sexual freedoms continue to be abused.

For this wave of feminists, seeking to discard the identity of victim, it has been important to reclaim the female body and those 'instruments of torture' from patriarchal control, so a feature of feminist expression since the 1990s has been to display open sexuality and to voice sexual desire as a woman's right, thereby negating the ability of the patriarchy to objectify women. This has not come without its complexities, however, and whilst third wavers might embrace Madonna as 'a revolutionary pop star who taught us that we could be sexy and strong', second wave feminists accuse her of 'trading on her sexuality [...] in hot pants and a crop-top'

(Strauss, 2012). Madonna's overt sexualization of her own identity seems to comment intelligently on gender politics but also risks slipping into the very exploitation it challenges. This is particularly the case since she is deeply embroiled in the capitalist (not only *patriarchal* but also *misogynist*) ideology of the music industry, whose images and branding increasingly commoditize women. Music videos often show men in positions of extreme dominance and women in sexualized, near-naked poses as the subjects of violent behaviour. Here – as in other media – women are feminized, sexualized and imaged as victims, all for the profit of the (male, patriarchal) capitalists who condition our mindset. Furthermore, Western culture promotes in young women the attitude that they can be who they want to be, wear what they want and voice their own sexuality unproblematically, leading to a normalization of sexualized behaviour and self-display, even by vulnerable and impressionable young girls. Thus the independence and self-expression that strengthens women in third wave feminism is undermined and appropriated by the patriarchy.

This complex situation is best illustrated by the 'Girl Power' of The Spice Girls, who championed independence and self-confidence. Yet they did this through stereotyping sexualized behaviour and packaging their bodies and identities into objectified commodities. From their first hit, 'Wannabe', their output inhabited this paradox, with assertive statements and an aggressive posturing ('Yo, tell you what I want, what I really really want') combined with a depersonalization of identity promoted in their names (Scary, Sporty, Posh, Baby and Ginger) and other indicators. Later in 'Wannabe' the lyrics commoditize the women as if lining them up for sale: 'We got M in the place who likes it in your face / We got G like MC who likes it on an / Easy V doesn't come for free, she's a real lady / And as for me' and so on. Such behaviour – even more pronounced in the actions and statements of other girl bands like 'Girls Aloud' (see Munford, 2007, pp. 266–279) or by solo singers such as Rihanna – has been discussed by theorists as a process of 'disarticulation'. This refers to the dismissal of the need to confront patriarchal values by a younger generation of women on the assumption that the feminist battle has been won; previous ideological gains are undermined as women succumb to and become complicit in their own objectification (see McRobbie, 2009, pp. 26–27). Look, for example, at the YouTube clip of Rihanna singing 'Stay' with Mikky Ekko, and ask yourself why the female singer is filmed naked in the bath while the male singer is fully clothed in other interior spaces.

Thus a contemporary understanding of 'post-feminism' recognizes both a problematic step backwards in popular culture and asserts a powerful offensive in performative work by artists such as Annie Sprinkle and Carolee

Schneeman, whose 'sex-positive feminism' uses images from pornography to challenge ideas of objectification, confront complacent attitudes and empower women through sexuality. These artists are esoteric, though; more commonly, images perpetuate the sexualization of the body in magazines, on TV and in pop music, disempowering women as the third wave call for independent self-expression is misrepresented. Thus the behaviours of contemporary (young) women exacerbate objectification by returning to a use of the 'instruments of torture' – high heels, makeup, glamour and cleavage – by choice. What may seem innocuous on television or on a night out in fact risks being the thin end of the wedge, normalizing sexual behaviour among even pre-teen girls and ingraining violent attitudes to women among young men.

Musical theatre: guilty

The commercial musical has done little to challenge such gender politics throughout its history: even in the 1890s, musical theatre sold itself on sexualized images of women from the Gaiety Girls to the Tiller Girls, and in Hollywood in Busby Berkeley's chorines. Years later nothing seems to have changed as the minimalist aesthetic of the long-running revival of *Chicago* (1996) has proved: this production's marketing – iconic black and white images of women in black lingerie and striking makeup – has dominated billboards in London and New York. Despite a narrative that gives the two leading female characters a certain level of power, it is gained by sensationalist manipulation of the media (with the aid of a man, of course) and relies on their looks. This musical reveals a complex power structure in which the women use their looks to achieve their own ends – they end up with power and independence – but the objectification of the female bodies in the production undermines the potential post-feminist reading.

Beyond the imagery, gender politics becomes a more subtle and arguably more ideological game. Female characters have tended to be written as stock types: the virgin, the whore, the witch or the mother; and musical narratives have tended to perpetuate the boy-meets-girl trope, in which the pretty woman melts in the arms of a strong and dominant man before walking down the aisle to embrace happily married bliss. We only have to look at the Rodgers and Hammerstein canon to see the ubiquity of these stereotypes, which reinforce the idea that men are dominant while women are needy (if pretty). The only power women have (we are told) is the sexual power of their body, a commodity that they flaunt to seduce men. Thus women are forever consigned to being supported by men or paid for sex, ideas that are prevalent in the territory of commercial Broadway. Such stereotypes form the backbone of this repertoire, though these have long been established in the operatic canon. One example of this trope is seen in *La Traviata* (1853).

La Traviata (1853)

Music by Giuseppe Verdi

Book by Francesco Maria Piave

Based on a novel (1848) and play (1852) *La Dame aux Camélias* by Alexandre Dumas (the younger)

Featured production: Salzburg Festival (2005) re-staged at The Met, New York, in 2012. Directed by Willy Decker

Synopsis: Violetta is a high-class Parisian prostitute with whom the French nobleman Alfredo falls in love. Alfredo manages to pull Violetta away from the city, but without financial means they slip into poverty, to the family's disgrace. Violetta realizes that to help Alfredo preserve his family dignity she must leave him, throwing Alfredo into romantic and jealous confusion. When he sees Violetta with her previous lover, Baron Douphol, he becomes incensed. He scorns her publicly, throwing money at her feet as payment for her services. But Alfredo's father, Germont – who at first had wished to block their relationship – shows sympathy for Violetta, consoling his son but revealing that she is now dying from consumption. Full of remorse Alfredo rushes to her bedside to comfort her. Violetta is overjoyed, but despite a momentary euphoric state (spes phthisica) that sometimes occurs before death from TB, she succumbs to the disease and dies in his arms.

La Traviata (1853)

La Traviata is typical of mid-nineteenth-century romantic opera, often tragic in tone and driven by deeply sentimental but ultimately doomed relationships. It typifies the move towards opera *verismo*, which dealt with 'real' characters and the harsh reality of life which suffused European culture in general towards the end of the nineteenth century. It also consolidates a particular trope that has become pervasive on the musical stage, the character of the sympathetic whore, elsewhere the basis for Charity in *Sweet Charity* (1966), Fantine in *Les Misérables* (1985) and Satine in *Moulin Rouge* (2001), whose storyline was based on *La Traviata*.

Although Violetta is a prostitute, this is a role whose activities we never see enacted in the opera, she never explicitly sells herself for money. In this sense, the idea that she is a prostitute exists only as a signifier of moral corruption and weakness. Even the common translation of the title, 'The Fallen Woman', reminds us that woman is prone to slip. This rhetoric is familiar from the story of Adam and Eve's banishment from the Garden of Eden (also known as 'The Fall') – for which Eve (the woman) is responsible (emphasizing how religious narratives entrench powerful ideologies). The figure of the prostitute, though, is one that not only identifies women as weak (apt to fall), but also as hardwired to entice and therefore corrupt men. This trope, then, is a double sleight on women, establishing a fundamentally weak character whose only strength lies in her ability to corrupt. Here is a dynamic that in *La Traviata* gets paralleled by the fact that Violetta is suffering from consumption, a debilitating disease (or weakness) with which she can spread illness (corruption) to others.

The way to 'handle' a woman (as King Arthur sings in *Camelot*, 1960) is to neutralize this threat through careful control. Marriage is conventionally seen as the appropriate way to assert this authority. Woven into this narrative is the idea that women crave marriage, or to be more precise, that they crave a strange metaphysical affliction that we call 'love', whose social seal is the marriage vow. For Violetta, this is 'the fever of love', and she bemoans her 'folly', her 'mad delirium' for having fallen for Alfredo, singing: 'Follie! Follie! Delirio vano è questo!' (Folly! Folly! Madness is here in this room!). In contrast to this stereotype in *La Traviata*, the principal male characters represent masculine tropes of heroic love (Alfredo) and paternal authority (Germont) that rhetoricize the opposite. When young, the passion of the character is shown as a 'noble' love: 'Di quell'amor ch' è palpito Dell'universo, Dell'universo intero, Misterioso, Misterioso altero, Croce e, Croce e delizia Croce e delizia, delizia al cor' (I loved you with that love which is the very breath of the universe itself – mysterious and noble, both cross and ecstasy of the heart). As Act 1 concludes Alfredo and Violetta sing, separately, of these two dimensions of love: his 'mysterious and noble' and hers 'folly'.

Women and hysteria

In consolidating the character trope of the 'Fallen Woman' and establishing her as an emotional creature, *La Traviata* helps construct two of the dominant rhetorical statements that culturally support gender ideology: women, we learn, are likely to waver from the straight and narrow unless men rescue them; furthermore, they are perilously emotional creatures, prone to succumbing to hysterical madness.

The mythology of hysteria was something that was forcefully determined in the eighteenth century by the (male) medical establishment. Hysteria was, even in its name, encoded as a female disease, linked etymologically to the womb. It was diagnosed as the symptom of unmanageable emotional excess, brought about by sexual dissatisfaction, ultimately leading to madness, an ideology that strengthened the belief that men were rational and reasonable and therefore more capable as authority figures. The cure for hysteria, it was believed, was to stimulate the clitoris which would lead to a hysterical paroxysm (i.e., an orgasm). Thus male medical practitioners would routinely massage their female patients' genitals as part of the medication for this malady.

While the ethical implications of this treatment are clearly unsettling, it is the more subtle rhetoric of hysteria mythology that seems more invidious. Linking women to states of emotional excess and sexual instability and bestowing upon men the right to control and 'cure' these ailments promoted an obsession with the female body as wayward and gave cultural permission to men to have that body controlled. Thus women's clothing took on a specific nature, at once sexualizing and restricting the gendered differences of the female body. In particular, the corset 'contained and disciplined the feminine body. [...] Through its ambiguity – being both seen (in the shape of its wearer) and unseen (hidden under other garments) – the corset took on erotic overtones, swiftly becoming an object of fetishistic enthusiasm' (Wilson-Kovacs, 2001, pp. 123–125). Thus the hysterization of the female body constructed a medically acceptable idea of what a 'normal' (and therefore 'abnormal') woman's body should look like, based on sexual overtones. The corset prescribed the female ideal as slim at the waist, with busty cleavage and full hips: the sexuality of the body was emphasized in its cultural aesthetic and in its representation in art. Even in situations in which it was not explicitly displayed, the leisure body was framed in clothes that shaped a construct of femininity, hair styled to enhance the curve and flow of a womanly shape, and makeup that promised sexual excess in the enhancement of fulsome lips and exaggerated eyes.

The fact that these developments are nowadays so taken for granted is testament to the way that a particular image expectation has permeated Western culture with regard to female appearance. It is clear though that the establishing of certain shapes, emphases and expectations about the female body is a construct, at least in part controlled by the patriarchal subjugation of women. It is also clear that many of the images in fashion and performance that are ubiquitous, including the emphasis of shapely legs in the Tiller Girls' routines and the particular style of corsetry displayed in the *Chicago* imagery, come from this influence as well as the semi-nudity in high-heeled shoes of many female pop performers. Such construction of gender appearances has been discussed in detail by the theorist Judith Butler, and it is worth considering briefly her thoughts with regard to the way gender is performed.

In her book *Gender Trouble* (1990), Butler argues that gender identity and difference is not a 'natural' or 'normal' thing, but that it is constructed by and in discourse, by the acts that we perform and by the way that we behave socially. Although men and women are distinguished biologically in terms of their *sex*, their *gender* is a social – and socially performative – construct. Butler (1990, p. 23) writes about 'a convincing act of repetition', 'the repeated stylization of the body, a set of repeated acts within a highly rigid regulatory frame' that create gendered difference, and that lead to the sort of social assumptions about men and women that are prevalent in culture: men are strong, powerful, reliable, sensible, authoritative, dominant, athletic, natural leaders; women are soft, gentle, weak, emotional, hysterical, unstable, passive, kind, pretty, smooth, curvy, maternal gossips.

Hysterical Violetta

Not surprisingly, the cultural forms that have arisen in this climate repeatedly impress these ideals through their own aesthetics. Thus as Violetta sings of plunging into the vortex of her feverish love, Verdi offers the singer a flowery (feminine) passage that is riddled with ornamentation, a coloratura cadenza that seems to reflect exactly that skittish and hysterical emotion that has been rhetoricized. And as the couple conclude Act 1 we hear the gendered difference of their emotional love very clearly, as the music associates his (masculine) passion with strong legato phrases ('amor è palpito Dell'universo' [love that's the pulse of the universe]) and her (feminine) passion with frantic flights of coloratura and wayward shrieks ('ah! ah! ah! ah!'). Such gendering of the music offers clear distinctions between male and female which not only reflect but also characterize their passion, encoding gendered signifiers of strength (masculinity) and hysteria (femininity) into our cultural lexicon. The trope of 'mad women' is clearly evidenced for contemporary listeners in Natalie Dessay's recording of *Mad Scenes* (2009), which contains arias sung by five coloratura heroines in operas composed across a period of 120 years: Lucia (*Lucia di Lammermoor*: Donizetti, 1835), Elvira (*I Puritani*: Bellini, 1835), Cunégonde (*Candide*: Bernstein, 1956), Ophélie (*Hamlet*: Thomas,

1868) and Dinorah (*Le Pardon de Ploërmel*: Meyerbeer, 1859).[1] Even at a basic level such gendering is insistent: think of how we refer to endings in music and poetry as masculine or feminine, depending on whether or not they conclude with a strong beat or harmonically strong cadence (see McClary, 1991).

However, the fact that many of these operatic cadenzas provide the singer with moments of virtuoso display and the fact that such virtuoso display itself requires bodily strength and projects a performative power into the acoustic space of the opera house means that, in opera, there is an ambiguous encoding of feminized strength – what Carolyn Abbate (1993, p. 254), in a direct reference to Clément's categorization of character, refers to as an 'envoicing of women': 'Visually, the character singing is the passive object of our gaze. But aurally, she is resonant; her musical speech drowns out everything in range, and we sit as passive objects, battered by the voice'. In short, despite a storyline in *La Traviata* which portrays Violetta in the morally dubious identity of a prostitute and the disempowering state of becoming a victim (to disease), the opera itself presents her as the central focus of attention, and the particular qualities of the art form afford her a powerful and dominant voice.

A glance at the opening sequence in the Salzburg Festival's controversial production of *La Traviata* in 2005 (re-staged at The Met in 2012) reveals this ambiguity. Throughout the overture Violetta (Anna Netrebko) is seen as a tiny figure against a gaping grey cyclorama, a clock serving as the reminder of the short time remaining in her life.[2] She collapses with exhaustion or madness into the patrician arms of Dottore Grenvil (Luigi Roni), a dominant masculine figure who here is a personification of death. Violetta is clearly weak, and dressed in red she mimics the classic image of tubercular affliction: a spluttered droplet of blood on the white handkerchief of the stage as can be seen in Figure 8.1. Yet as the overture comes to an end and the party scene begins, she greets her guests and starts to sing passionately and with energy – as a strong woman who commands the whole stage. Her strength in this particular scene is magnified by the directorial decision to make her appear to be the only female at the party (the female singing chorus are in male attire), and the only character not dressed in black tuxedo and bow tie. This swarm of doting, anonymous admirers raise the bright scarlet Violetta above their heads on a bright scarlet sofa. Despite her illness, and despite the first unnerving image, Violetta is cast as a triumphant, powerful figure. Immediately after the number, however, she collapses from a coughing fit – the first signs of her tuberculosis – and once more she is left alone onstage with the silent authoritarian figure of Dottore Grenvil.

Figure 8.1 Anna Netrebko as Violetta in the opening scene of *La Traviata* (2005). Salzburg Festival Production. Deutsche Grammophon

This sort of ambiguity can be seen in much musical theatre, which often positions women and their voices in situations of strength, even if their storylines cast them as weak or victimized. The fact that they sing bodily and powerfully to us and that we give them our undivided attention for the duration of their stage time means that these female characters and the performers whose bodies they inhabit become icons of power, allowing them to unsettle patriarchal expectations: consider Anita and Maria's duet 'A Boy Like That / I Have a Love' in *West Side Story* (1957), Mama Rose's 'Rose's Turn' in *Gypsy* (1959) or Sally Bowles' 'Cabaret' in *Cabaret* (1966). Elsewhere and particularly on the operatic stage the female voice can empower where plot and narrative often weaken or madden: think of Isolde's final outpouring of grief in the haunting 'Liebestod' (in Wagner's *Tristan und Isolde*, 1865), or Berg's *Lulu* (1937) whose hysterical outbursts show an emaciated and weakened woman but give her a powerful and prominent voice.

It's clear that the musical stage has a very complex relationship with women and gender, in how it presents characters and storylines, and in how the body can be variously objectified and dehumanized. Of course, not all theatre conforms to the same stereotypes but it is interesting to see how often the tropes we have been discussing and their feminizing signifiers – madness in the voice, sexuality in the body – appear.

Reclaiming feminist texts

Perhaps musical theatre was never a likely feminist vehicle, even if shows like *I'm Getting My Act Together and Taking It on the Road* (1978) present a proto-feminist storyline in a vaguely second wave mould; however, although unlikely, the musical has offered a cultural area as rich as any for overturning and undermining patriarchal ideologies. The strategies for doing this are twofold: firstly, to deal with the texts, reclaiming 'feminist' texts or rewriting texts as feminist; and, secondly, to work through criticism, exposing the patriarchy, subverting norms and re-reading texts from a feminist perspective.

Reclaiming feminist texts is more accurately a question of revealing texts written by female authors. Like many arts, musical theatre's canonic legacy is almost exclusively male, so the challenge of this agenda is to find amongst the Monteverdis, Mozarts, Wagners, Gershwins and Sondheims *any* women who have contributed to the repertoire. Of course, there are many but their work has typically been overshadowed by a historiography that has emphasized men and occluded women. Nevertheless, the names of Dorothy Fields, Agnes de Mille, Betty Comden and latterly Susan Stroman, Phyllida Lloyd, Julie Taymor and Lisa Lambert are not so obscure, and a great many other writers, including operatic composer Judith Weir, and musical theatre writers Rida Johnson Young, Dorothy Donnelly, Anne Caldwell and Gretchen Cryer – writer of *I'm Getting My Act Together* mentioned earlier – have been extremely significant in the development of the musical stage (see Peck, 2009; Coleman and Sebesta, 2008).

The challenge to re-write texts as feminist is one that has been embraced by practitioners in non-musical theatre, firstly, 'to demonstrate past oppressions and to give dramatic expression to a feminist plea and urgency not to revisit, not to allow the oppressions of the past a place in future histories', and, secondly, to develop 'a "new" theatre language: a feminist poetics which would challenge the theatrical apparatus, its systems of representation and narrativization that positioned women as Objects and "Others"' (Aston and Harris, 2006, p. 5). The call for a new feminist language is enticing, though it rather flies in the face of the commercial musical idiom, which with its chorus girls, boy-meets-girl plots and self-reflexive narratives remains relentlessly patriarchal; perhaps the answer here is to look to more innovative staging and more avant-garde practices (by, for example, Cathy Berberian, Laurie Anderson or Diamanda Galas) to find the musical theatre equivalent of 'feminine écriture' – the writing style invoked by French feminists Julia Kristeva, Hélène Cixous and Luce Irigaray to give women a voice despite the ubiquity of the dominant (patriarchal) discourse.

In musical theatre, that voice may well remain hidden, though perhaps the other strategy of subverting norms and re-reading texts as feminist is the approach to take. This is something that Mary Ann Smart and Susan McClary are undertaking in opera studies and musicology, while Stacy Wolf has focused on re-reading musical theatre texts in her books, *A Problem Like Maria* (2002) and *Changed for Good* (2011). The first of these sees, in four mid-century stars of musical theatre, performances that disavow the conventional patriarchal inscriptions of gender: these are women whose strength of performance magnifies certain *masculine* qualities in their characters. Specifically, she considers Julie Andrews's performance of Maria in *The Sound of Music* (1959), Barbara Streisand's Fanny Brice in *Funny Girl* (1964), Ethel Merman's Mama Rose in *Gypsy* (1959) and Mary Martin's Peter Pan (screened on telecast in 1960). Although Martin's Peter Pan is slightly different for obvious reasons (she is playing a boy), each of the others plays a woman who shows (masculine) qualities of determination, independence and assertiveness, and though each assumes certain aspects of a woman's social role (wife, mother, lover, carer), their prominence in the narratives and their overshadowing of the men in these narratives turns on its head the gender expectations of both musicals and society. It's true that Wolf reads these performances not only as reclaiming a feminist voice but also a lesbian voice, and her writing is taking on an additional agenda regarding sexuality. However, in drawing attention to these women Wolf reminds us that despite the heteronormative and ideologically ingrained storylines of the musical stage, 'the midcentury American musical is a feminine yet active cultural form that does not locate a woman as a passive, to-be-looked-at object but allows her to take up the position of self-spectacle. Women in musicals', she writes, 'look back' (2002, p. 23).

In her second book, *Changed for Good* (2011), Wolf considers (among other musicals) the more recent *Wicked* (2003) from which the title of the book is derived. The show presents a woman who resists patriarchal values and thus offers another alternative image of women.

Wicked (2003)

Although the show's source material is the 1995 novel by (male) writer Gregory Maguire – a book that politicizes the social setup of Oz prior to Dorothy's visit – its libretto, notably, was written by (female) dramatist Winnie Holzman with music and lyrics by Stephen Schwartz.

Wicked's concentration on the story of Elphaba and Glinda means that the stage becomes a feminized space whose most dominant characters are

---

Wicked (2003)

Music and Lyrics by Stephen Schwartz

Book by Winnie Holzman

Based on Gregory Maguire's novel *Wicked: The Life and Times of the Wicked Witch of the West* (1995), which is a parallel to Frank L. Baum's classic novel *The Wonderful Wizard of Oz* (1900) that was filmed in 1939

Synopsis: *Wicked* features the witches of Oz in their late adolescent/young adult years: Glinda who later becomes the good witch of the North; Nessarose who becomes the wicked witch of the East; and Elphaba, the wicked witch of the West. As the girls take up studies at Shiz University, Elphaba discovers that the animals of Oz are gradually losing their ability to speak. When favourite teacher Doctor Dillamond – a goat – is arrested, she pledges to fight for his cause. Meanwhile, it is discovered that Elphaba has extraordinary magical potential, and she is recruited to work with the Wizard. Introduced to his magical book of spells, Elphaba inadvertently causes a monkey to grow wings. At the same time she realizes that the Wizard is responsible for the crusade to dumb the animals. She rebels and escapes from the palace while the Wizard spreads rumours that she is in fact evil: the Wicked Witch of the West. It becomes Elphaba's mission to free the caged winged monkeys, but in order to prevent her, the Wizard's assistant Madame Morrible conjures up a tornado that brings a small wooden house crashing down to ground on top of Nessarose. As Dorothy's exploits in *The Wizard of Oz* play out in the background, we see Glinda overthrow the Wizard and allow her childhood friend Elphaba to feign her death and escape Oz forever.

---

women with dramatic stories not defined by men, love or marriage. Indeed, when men are staged they often appear emasculated – encased in tin as Boq becomes, or presented as half-animal like Doctor Dillamond (a goat). This re-orients the narrative with which we are familiar, that of *The Wizard of Oz*, whose female central character Dorothy needs the support of three men to seek guidance from the patriarch before she can return home. Other (female) characters also re-orient the expectations of the traditional romance narrative: Boq becomes the Tin Man because Nessarose casts a spell on him to make him lose his heart to her. When the spell goes wrong and his heart shrivels, Elphaba has to save him by turning him into a man with no need of a heart. In this sequence the seduction of the man by the woman is desexualized (it is magic, not prostitution), and the result is a weakening of the man and his rescue by a woman: this is not the damsel in distress rescued by the brave knight but the knight in distress rescued by the brave damsel.

In Elphaba, Schwartz and Holzman create a heroine who easily maps onto many of the first and second wave concerns of feminism, as a political activist fighting for the rights of a silenced demographic (here, the animals). She is unafraid to voice her anger at the status quo and resists defining her identity with the feminizing accoutrements of patriarchal discourse (those 'instruments of torture'), even when Glinda does (in the song 'Popular'). The magnitude of her battle against the patriarch is symbolically associated with a fight against nature in the signature song 'Defying gravity'. Here, in a duet, the two women argue about the different courses their lives are taking: 'I hope you're happy how you hurt your cause forever', sings Glinda; 'I hope you're proud how you would grovel in submission to feed your own ambition', retaliates Elphaba. For her, the independent cause is everything: 'I'm through accepting limits 'cause someone says they're so.' This is 'Girl Power' writ large, and unlike (most) other musical theatre heroines, Elphaba – indeed all the women in *Wicked* – do not need men to guide or support them, and do not need to resort to sexual power or the stripping off of clothes to achieve their goals. In this unusual world, it is a woman who stands up to be counted, whilst at the same time deflecting the male gaze.

Yet these women are very different: Elphaba is clearly a proto-feminist who is resistant to patriarchal influence; Glinda, on the other hand, is modelled as a far more superficial character, a stereotype desperate to be loved and prone to fashion consciousness who decides to conform to patriarchal demands. Stacy Wolf (2008, p. 9) discusses this in *Changed for Good*, noting how the women are constructed in opposites, but emphasizing that these opposites, in a sense, form a couple: 'while in mid-twentieth-century musicals the difference of gender at once undergirds and overdetermines the couple's differences of culture or personality, in *Wicked*, the two women form a couple of both sameness and difference'. In the different behaviours of these women we see how hard it is to fight against an entrenched system and how easily 'normative' behaviour can perpetuate the status quo. While *Wicked* may offer a significant step away from conventions and ingrained assumptions about gender, it will take a great deal more to overturn the sort of entrenched values and expectations that have become ideologically formative.

Further reading – theoretical

Case, Sue-Ellen (2008) *Feminism and Theatre* (reissued edition) [1988] (Basingstoke and New York: Palgrave Macmillan).
McClary, Susan (1991) *Feminine Endings: Music, Gender and Sexuality* (Minneapolis: University of Minnesota Press).

Wolf, Stacy (2002) *A Problem Like Maria: Gender and Sexuality in the American Musical* (Ann Arbor: University of Michigan Press).

Further reading – relating to the examples

Abbate, Claudia and Roger Parker (2012) 'Verdi – Older Still' in *A History of Opera: The Last 400 Years* (London and New York: Allen Lane), 373–382.
Boyd, Michelle (2010) 'Alto on a Broomstick: Voicing the Witch in the Musical Wicked', *American Music* 28(1): 97–118.
Laird, Paul (2011) *Wicked: A Musical Biography* (Lanham, MD: Scarecrow Press).
Rutherford, Susan (2013) *Verdi, Opera, Women* (Cambridge: Cambridge University Press).
Wolf, Stacy (2011) *Changed for Good: A Feminist History of the Broadway Musical* (Oxford and New York: Oxford University Press).

9 'The Bitch of Living': Youth Cultures, Power and Sexuality

If the representation of women in musical theatre has conventionally traded on patriarchal assumptions, the representation of children has been equally complex. Like women in relation to men, children are distinguished from adults on stage both physically and vocally. However, unlike the gender politics between men and women which can only be 'changed for good' with sustained ideological pressure, the identity politics relating to children acknowledges that they will grow, mature and actually change for good into the adults in contrast to whom their identity is often represented. As such, children on stage are often seen either as 'proto'-adults (innocent, young versions of the grown-ups they will become); or 'becoming-adults' (adolescents in a state of transition, negotiating the uncertain journey from child to adult). In terms of musical theatre the various representations of these children are often characterized by the distinctive quality of expression that changes as part of this process (particularly with males): the voice. Linked to this are distinctive physical changes that the bodies on stage undergo as the innocent child grows into a sexually knowing grown-up.

The sound of children's voices, and especially the sound of choristers, has long been associated with ideas of innocence and purity. Boy choristers have sung in church music since the Renaissance; as church music developed from plainsong into polyphony, higher voices were needed to contrast with the male voices, but women were not allowed to sing in church. This led to the development of castrati, about which we say more in the next chapter, and to a tradition that was particularly strong in Britain of training boy church choristers. This practice has extended to girls only in the past 20 or 30 years, and indeed Canterbury Cathedral is introducing girl choristers only now.[1] Boy choristers' voices were generally perceived to be innocent, angelic, 'natural' and, most importantly, powerful because in the church acoustic the overtones of the voice carried and resonated particularly strongly. It was not just in church music that children's voices appeared, however. As Rachel Cowgill notes Handel first used a boy in his opera *Alcina* (Handel and Broschi) in 1735.[2] The character Oberto, played by a 14-year-old performer, William Savage, was an innocent boy searching for his father. In *The Magic Flute* (Mozart and Schikaneder, 1791) three child spirits lead Tamino to Sarastro, linking ideas of purity and innocence to the spirituality practiced by Sarastro. In *Tosca* (Puccini, Illica and Giacosa, 1900) a shepherd boy again reflected a pastoral idyll, and the innocence of boys was contrasted with the experience of men by Leonard Bernstein in his choral work *Chichester Psalms* (1965). Even Elliot Carter's opera *What Next* (1996–1997) contains a young boy who is the only character who remains sane at the end. What these representations share is a view of young people that is idealized, focusing on innocence and purity through the sound of 'natural', 'uncorrupted' voices. This is one way young people are represented.

Some more recent representations have challenged this view of childhood and teenage years. It was during the latter part of the nineteenth century that urbanization and industrialization, alongside the development of regular schooling, meant that a defined period began to be recognized between childhood and adulthood. By about 1944–1995 young people in this interim period began to be known as teenagers (Savage, 2007). As a result of further cultural changes, teenagers, and especially boys, stopped aspiring to be like their parents. Instead young peoples' identities were defined in opposition to the perceived oppression of the adult world; and affiliations to likeminded groups developed which were expressed through shared tastes in dress, language and music (Lewis in Campbell, 2000, 187). As each generation of adolescents becomes adult, the new generation establishes an identity that opposes their predecessors. As such there is a dynamic development of new ideas within the popular culture of youth. The development of rock 'n' roll, for example, was linked to the immediate post-World War II period of youth disaffection in the United Kingdom and United States. A second wave occurred with the development of rock music in the 1960s followed by different types of punk, metal, rap, hip-hop and so on as generations of young people expressed their difference and their alienation creatively.

In this chapter we first consider how this process of alienation and evolution is reflected in the film musical *Dirty Dancing* (1987) using ideas developed in relation to political theory by Antonio Gramsci. *Dirty Dancing* offers a positive and uplifting view of the transition from adolescence to adulthood, which we consider in relation to political theory by Antonio Gramsci. The oppression and alienation of young people is less optimistically presented in the stage works *The Turn of the Screw* (1954) and *Spring Awakening* (2006), which we discuss in relation to the power structures of society explored by Michel Foucault. What we discover in these representations is that dynamic evolution initiated by young people can be extremely destructive, and yet can also be a powerful motor for creative cultural and societal development.

Youth cultures

> *Antonio Gramsci*
>
> Antonio Gramsci, who developed most of his ideas while imprisoned in Italy in the early twentieth century, was interested in Marx's ideas about the economic exploitation of the working-class and questioned why the working-class didn't simply revolt. He proposed the theories of *hegemony* (the dominance of one social class) and *consent* (the consent to be dominated) to explain this anomaly. While the political class might rule by force using the police and army to put down revolution, civil society – the bourgeoisie – manufactured consent within the workforce through control of ideas and ideology and thus created a cultural hegemony. Education, the unions, religious institutions, the family and the media promulgate ways of thinking to the extent that ideas, including the power structures of capitalism, seem 'natural' or 'common sense'. If revolution is to be achieved, Gramsci suggested, the ideas, understanding and knowledge of the working-class majority has to change first so that the consensus or hegemony is challenged. And when hegemony is challenged the power of the state tends to be revealed through its forceful and repressive actions. Gramsci also understood that ideas are not static, but that there is a continuous evolutionary process; as ideas are challenged, new ideas become dominant and in turn are replaced in a dynamic process of evolution.

In popular musicology Gramsci's theory of hegemony and consent is used to examine the ways in which teenagers offer a challenge to dominant society, questioning the status quo and rebelling against restrictions – that is, refusing consent. This has resulted in the development of gang culture and music-focused sub-cultures as young people resist the cultural hegemony established by their parents' generation, a rebellion that has led to new forms of popular music becoming established. In the main there is a gradual process of evolution as new cultural forms become accepted. Older forms decline as the teenagers who supported these new forms grow into adulthood and promote the new consensus.

In musical theatre and film, that rebellion takes the form of challenging society's limitations on the forms of music or dance that are acceptable; engaging with new forms of dance or music represents the alienation of youth, and resistance to the cultural hegemony is enacted in teenage support for the new musical or dance craze. There is quite a large group of theatre and film musicals that essentially follows a very similar narrative structure, including *Grease* (a 1972 musical set in 1959), *Hairspray* (a

1988 film followed by a 2002 musical and a 2007 musical film set in 1962), *Footloose* (a 1998 musical based on a film from 1984) and *We Will Rock You* (a 2002 musical using songs by Queen and set in a dystopian future). All of these shows see young people engaging with new forms of music or dance in a rebellion against conservative culture or the withdrawal of consent. By the end of the musical the new dance form is successfully incorporated, consent is re-established and the young people move into adulthood. We focus here on *Dirty Dancing* (a 1987 film followed by a stage show in 2004) that also follows this pattern.

Dirty Dancing (1987)

Screenplay by Eleanor Bergstein

Direction by Emile Ardolino

Music supervisor Jimmy Lenner compiled a film soundtrack of songs by The Ronettes, Frankie Valli and the Four Seasons, Otis Redding, The Drifters, The Shirelles and others

Original music for the film was by John Morris and Erich Bulling, while the theme song and other original songs were written by Franke Previte (lyrics), John DeNicola and Don Markowitz (music)

Synopsis: Set in the early 1960s against the backdrop of civil rights activism, Baby (whose full name is Frances Houseman) goes with her family to Kellerman's summer holiday camp in the Catskill Mountains. There she meets dancer Johnny Castle, leader of the working-class youngsters employed at the camp. As a result of a botched abortion undergone by his dance partner, Baby agrees to dance with Johnny at a demonstration event. Dancing together leads to their sexual relationship; learning to dance with the sensuality required by Johnny, and achieving the trust for a difficult overhead lift mirror Baby's sexual awakening. This is also mirrored in the abandonment of her childhood nickname, Baby, for her given name Frances. Both Johnny and Baby/Frances learn from each other and grow into adulthood transformed.

There are two types of music and dance in *Dirty Dancing*. The working-class youngsters dance their rebellion and difference to contemporary (1960s) rock 'n' roll in their own lodgings, in opposition to the ballroom dance Johnny has to teach and demonstrate to the middle-class families and older guests staying at the camp. The leader in this case is the owner and manager of Kellerman's who imposes a style of dance and behaviour on the guests and workers at the camp based on what he perceives to be respectable middle-class culture and morality: the cultural hegemony. Thus his strenuous aversion to new styles of dance and music is seen to result from his resistance to change; he wants to conserve the traditions of the camp since he perceives that his clientele desires continuity – in this argument cultural conservatism is linked to economic security, and the power to control these resides in the older generation that promotes the consensus. The dominant dance style is ballroom and the musical language derives from the 1940s and 1950s. By contrast, in the group of huts inhabited by the young people who need to work for their economic security, a different musical and physical language is enacted. Here, as we see in Figure 9.1, rebellion is danced to rock 'n' roll and the dress reflects the alluring sexuality and rebellious mood of the late 1950s films. Johnny Castle's black jeans and t-shirt, his leather jacket, his appearance in sleeveless undershirt, his hair style and his boots all demonstrate an inheritance from James Dean and Marlon Brando. The sensuality and sexuality of rock 'n' roll and the rebellion of urban youth are present in the scenes of dancing within the young community – a community that challenges and resists the normative requirements of the dominant group. Johnny repeatedly asks permission to dance a different dance to contemporary music for the paying guests, but it is only within their own space that the young people can dance their dance to the music that represents them. It is only in the final scene, after Johnny has been thrown out of the camp and Baby has been ostracized by her family, that Johnny returns and the two dance together combining the new and the old styles in one dance.

Figure 9.1   Baby/Frances (Jennifer Grey) and Johnny (Patrick Swayze) dance to rock'n'roll in *Dirty Dancing* (1987). Columbia Tristar Entertainment

The young people join the dance and gradually so do the middle-aged residents of the camp, accepting the excitement and sensuality embodied in the dance, and so the cultural hegemony shifts.

This process of development and renewal corresponds to Gramsci's concept of 'passive revolution' that features regeneration and evolution. *Dirty Dancing* represents this passive revolution that continues in popular music as new groups of young people create new styles that represent their response to their own contemporary societies. Thus music and popular culture is dynamic and continually evolving – and this feature of cultural hegemonic process is documented in a host of popular musical shows and films in which young people are the catalysts for change and creativity, leading the older generation and becoming dominant.

Michel Foucault challenges Gramsci's ideas by questioning the extent to which individuals can cause change. In effect the optimism of the utopian ending in *Dirty Dancing* would be questioned from a Foucauldian perspective; each character that has experienced the change at Kellerman's would have to go out into the world, which would not have changed at all. According to Foucault a combination of surveillance and the internal repression it produces creates a power structure, but that structure is not an externally policed state; rather it is an internalized repression within individuals, families and the whole of society. This idea is similar to Gramsci's idea of consent in that it is enacted within the whole of society, but the way it functions is different. Foucault argues that any person might try to make changes in society through their own personal resistance, but the possibility of achieving fundamental change remains remote because of the web-like layers of power structures and ideology that operate throughout society. So although the music and dance style has evolved in the final scene of *Dirty Dancing* we might question whether society has actually changed; whether Frances and Johnny will form a permanent and successful relationship given their different backgrounds and goals in life. They have made a successful transition to adulthood and have transformed music and dance in that community through their cultural resistance, but the question Foucault might ask is whether this cultural transformation will lead to wider political change.

Power and resistance

We saw in Chapters 3 and 4 that Marxist theory proposed a binary relationship between those in power and the oppressed masses. Foucault conceptualized power relations differently. Alongside the web described above, Foucault developed the image of the Panopticon described in *Discipline and Punish* (1977) and seen in Figure 9.2 to exemplify the way disciplinary structures function. The Panopticon is an architectural arrangement described in the eighteenth century in which a prison is arranged in a circular formation (like a doughnut with a hole) around a central guard tower. The result is that all the inmates can be observed while the observer in the guard tower cannot be seen. This architectural arrangement creates the opportunity for surveillance and supervision that imposes discipline – the inmates discipline themselves because they are not certain whether or not they are seen. In this way discipline imposed by the prison warden becomes internalized by the inmates. Whether or not there is actually a guard present there is the sense of being observed that alters the actions of those being observed and imposes

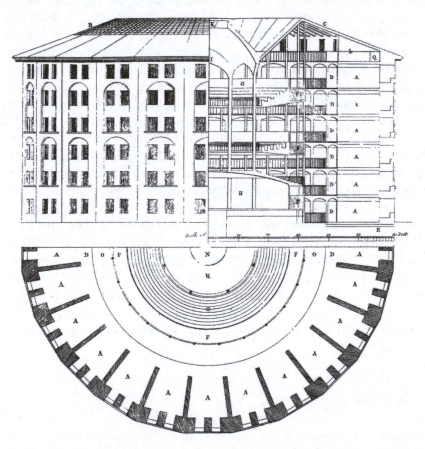

Figure 9.2 Elevation and Plan of Jeremy Bentham's design for the Panopticon penitentiary (1791)

a power relationship. CCTV cameras in our cities have a similar effect. Their presence and the knowledge that we can be observed are sufficient to deter petty crime and alter behaviour. This is a hierarchical structure that imposes a form of behaviour on us whether or not the observer/oppressor is present. It is created and reinforced consistently through the moral codes taught to us in families, schools, churches and so on. In this way our actions can be shaped and altered by an external power that becomes internalized to the extent that we discipline ourselves and pass on that ideology to others.

However, the most important element in Foucault's thinking about power is that he argues that power structures (governments, states, armies and wars) are largely unsuccessful in achieving domination over individuals. Like Gramsci, he realized that empowerment isn't a static relationship between people and institutions (as Marx had proposed) but that it is performed or enacted between individuals through relationships spread throughout society that are constantly in flux. This means that individuals are not recipients of oppression, but make choices about how power is enacted on them or resisted by them – something we have seen already in the narrative of *Dirty Dancing* where Johnny and Frances resisted the structures imposed on them. Instead of simply accepting hegemonic institutions and ideas as 'natural' or 'necessary' Foucault proposed that individuals should analyse the networks of power within which they live – which we are doing here by analysing the way power structures are reflected in our popular culture. Baby didn't only learn to dance and enact her sexual awakening, she questioned her father's (and implicitly society's) prejudices about abortion and class politics, and she enacted a civil rights agenda through attempting to treat everyone equally. Moreover, it is from her position that the film is told, and it is the male character even more than the female who is transformed, thus breaking with 'the patriarchal viewpoint that structures Hollywood cinema' (Tzioumakis and Lincoln, 2013, p. 7). *Dirty Dancing* is an 'atypical American film that firmly stands its ground when it comes to privileging a female perspective' (ibid.). What this suggests is that the makers of the film as much as the characters within it were challenging the cultural hegemony both in the content of the narrative and in the position from which it was filmed, perceiving young people as the dynamic friction that instigates change in society. Gramsci and Foucault challenge us all to be aware of the hegemonic power structures of our society and to take responsibility for its social, historical and cultural values – to discover what we are, and perhaps to change who we are.

The Turn of the Screw (1954)

Music by Benjamin Britten

Libretto by Myfanwy Piper

Based on a Victorian gothic novella by Henry James (1898), it has been adapted into films both under its own title and as *The Innocents*

Synopsis: The prologue introduces a narrator who tells the story of a new governess who arrives at an isolated country house to educate two children, Miles and Flora. They are currently being cared for by the housekeeper Mrs Grose at Bly House, but are in the guardianship of an unseen uncle who is busy in London. The contract described in the prologue is that the governess must not contact him, ask about Bly House or abandon the children. She agrees. At night she hears footsteps and sees a face at the window and is told of Peter Quint and the former governess Miss Jessel who had a sexual relationship; it is also implied that their relationships with the children were somewhat close and 'unnatural'. Both these adults are now dead but seem to exert power over the house and the children.

Several different adaptations of the story have different viewpoints about whether the children, the governess or the ghosts are the source of evil that destroys them – or whether there is evil at work at all – and the brilliance of the work is the way in which this confusion and uncertainty is maintained for the reader/viewer. In the opera, the ghosts appear, making themselves present for the audience, so that interpretation focuses on the psychology of power relations between the characters rather than the metaphysics of ghostly presence. At the end Flora has become maddened and is about to be sent away with the housekeeper when Miles, abandoned by the ghost of Peter Quint, drops down dead. The work explores what we believe about evil and innocence through the haunting and corruption of the children in relation to the morality of the young governess.

At the start of the opera *The Turn of the Screw* the children appear angelic. They wait to greet the governess on her arrival and dance about asking her questions. They practice bows and curtsies and chatter in an innocent and endearing fashion before taking the governess on a tour of the house. All the time, however, there are intimations that something is not right. In scene 3 a letter is received which says that Miles has been expelled from his school, and the governess and housekeeper are so enamoured of the delightful children that they believe it must be a malicious fraud. But at play the children recite the lurid tale of 'Tom the Piper's Son', and later, in a Latin lesson, Miles sings the verse 'Malo' (I am bad), while Flora, gazing at the lake where Miss Jessel drowned, refers to it as the Dead Sea. These hints always suggest evil undertones to the watching governess. Later in Act 2, scene 2 the children first chant a hymn and then sit on a tomb. Opinions begin to vary between the housekeeper and the governess as to whether the children are innocent or whether 'they are talking horrors'.

When challenged, Miles addresses the governess as 'My dear', an archaism that is entirely inappropriate from a boy to his governess, making him seem much older and more experienced than his years. Figure 9.3 shows him touching her face in a patronizing and paternalistic gesture. He challenges her to tell his uncle of her suspicions, but when she writes to the guardian, Miles – prompted by the ghost Peter Quint – steals the letter. In Act 2, scene 7 Flora follows the ghost of Miss Jessel to the lake and when challenged becomes spiteful, angry and distraught. Although all the actions could have logical and innocent explanations the hysteria of the situation is such that Flora is considered mad for talking in her sleep and so preparations are made to send her to London. Meanwhile in Act 2, scene 8 the governess confronts Miles and asks him to reveal Quint's influence. He says the words 'Peter Quint, you devil!' before screaming and dying in the governess' arms as Quint too disappears. It is always uncertain whether Peter Quint or the governess is the 'devil' he refers to, and whether he longs for or hates Peter Quint or even whether Quint is simply a figment of the imagination that he conjures up in the fanciful minds of the others.

Figure 9.3 Miles and the Governess in *The Turn of the Screw* at the Glyndebourne Festival (2011). Photo: Alastair Muir. Courtesy of Glyndebourne Productions Ltd

In the opera the audience ostensibly sees the transformation of the children from angelic youngsters to haunted and maddened evil monsters, but the audience is seeing the children through the eyes of the governess. Although there is always a presentiment of evil in the music, the set and the slightly offbeat images, the children's language and the situations in which the children are found, these might all be reflections of the internal repression in the mind of the governess/narrator. Is the morality and fear projected onto the children really hers? The result of this complexity is that the children could be seen as innocent *and* corrupt, so that the audience is forced to examine society's expectations of childhood innocence. The opera questions whether childhood is, in fact, a time of innocence at all, or whether it is a time of confusion and impressionability that reflects the ideologies and fears of adults. Through the relationships of the children with the adults we also see Victorian morality as oppressive. In this way the opera constantly questions the nature of morality in our own society, as well as the perception of childhood innocence and its alienation.

The events of the opera explore where power lies in the relationship between the children and the two sets of adults – Quint and Jessel, house-keeper and governess – especially as the children become alienated from the moral Christian values of the governess. The governess and the house-keeper are ultimately revealed to be powerless as the children are increasingly empowered by their fantasy world. This could be seen as an allegorical tale of the development of alienation as the children move into their teenage years and resist the ideology being presented by adults and educationalists, or it could reflect the fact that power operates through consent and when consent is withdrawn, as the children withdraw it, the governess is powerless.

In terms of the power structures of surveillance, the governess is always working at the behest of the unseen guardian, even though she is instructed never to contact him. The morality she imposes on the children thus derives from her internalized understanding of the structures imposed on her by the unseen guardian as well as from the internalized societal and religious institutions that restrict her. Equally, the house, the children and increasingly the governess perceive themselves to be under surveillance by the ghosts, Quint and Jessel – whether or not they are actually there. The sexual freedom implied by the ghosts is a challenge to the first set of internalized restrictions the governess feels – and so she attempts to resist the ghosts. This conflict is the source of her psychological uneasiness and fear.

The children, too, are at the mercy of the ghosts of Quint and Jessel as the children remember them in life and as they perceive them as ghosts. So the power of Quint and Jessel has become internalized for the children but is challenged by the power of the guardian, the power structures of education and home and the new morality the governess imposes. They are torn between these competing ideologies and never become empowered except through madness and death.[3] The extent to which the children attempt to resist these hegemonic structures varies in the details of different productions, but it is the children's negotiation of these dramatically different power structures that can be seen as a source of their alienation and turmoil. In the end, the work raises questions about children's empowerment, subjectivity, resistance, surveillance and the ideologies underpinning morality and good behaviour.

Youth and sexuality

Spring Awakening (2006)

Music by Duncan Sheik

Book and lyrics by Steven Sater

Based on the play *Spring Awakening* by Frank Wedekind (1891)

The play was not performed until 1906 (in a production by Max Reinhardt at the Kammerspiele in Berlin) because its depictions of youth sexuality and suicide were too ideologically sensitive.

Synopsis: Wedekind's play is an angry polemic against a German establishment that failed to offer its young people any guidance. The story is a violent and tragic experience of sexual awakening among a group of school friends. They have no information from their parents about sexuality or love, a situation that is laid at the door of the parents and the teachers. The young peoples' ignorance results in one suicide and one death through a botched abortion following an unknowing and innocent sexual encounter. There is also incest, homosexual sex/love and lots of masturbation as the youngsters attempt to understand what is happening to them without any guidance or care. As Michael Billington remarked, 'What gives it continuing vitality is Wedekind's extraordinary understanding of the adolescent mind: not merely the fascination with sex but the fixation with death' (Wedekind, 1980, back cover).

The young people in *Spring Awakening* are perhaps the most innocent – or lacking in knowledge – of all those discussed so far, though they are not the youngest. Jon Savage (2007, p. 22) notes that youth suicide was a major social problem in 1890s Germany caused, according to psychiatrists of the time, by the stresses and strains of industrial civilization. The fact that the young generation of the most advanced country were killing themselves was startling in the context of the increasing militarism of that society:

> The young often reflect the dominant values of society back at adults, and these pubescent suicides revealed the presentiments of collapse that lay under the bullish surface of 1890s Europe. [...] the great empires were beset by fears about the new mass age, and the consequent devolution of human society. (p. 22)

Jon Savage refers to a study conducted by sociologist Emile Durkheim in France, Italy and Germany that revealed that the highest rates of suicide among 16- to 20-year-olds were in Saxony and Prussia. It was assumed that the day gymnasium system in Germany – with its academic hot-housing and strict discipline – produced angst-ridden pupils in response to its hypocritical authoritarianism (Savage, 2007, p. 103) – a hypocritical authoritarianism that is revealed in *Spring Awakening*. A repressed society that keeps its children ignorant of life and sexuality and that attempts to perpetuate the hegemonic power structure and its moral values and ideologies is revealed. The young people are caned for giving the wrong answers in an excessively repressive education system. In this system the clever Melchior survives and stands up for his friend in a show of resistance, but Moritz flounders and his resistance is ultimately futile.

The 2006 musical reveals the alienation of its youthful protagonists most clearly in the contradiction between its late-twentieth-century musical styles and instrumentation and its dramatic setting and actions. As Steven Sater (2007) writes in the Preface to the libretto of the musical version, Wedekind's play (subtitled 'A Children's Tragedy') 'is full of the unheard, anguished cries of young people. It struck me that pop music – rock music – is the exact place that adolescents for the last few generations have found release from, and expression of, that same mute pain' (pp. vii–viii). Sater created a separate world of song that was distinct from the spoken world and that reflected the interior world of the characters, 'as confession [...], as denial [...] or admission [...]. Songs as cri-de-coeur' (p. ix). The time shifting use of contemporary music and electronic technology attaches the themes in the work and the alienation of the young people to contemporary society. The characters live in the shadow of social convention, but their alienation from society is revealed in the alternative rock and power ballads of their songs. These violent, electronically accompanied, loud evocations of alienation express resistance to a repressed and bleak world within which their creativity and optimism have no outlet. The music thus represents the resistance of the young people to their society and by extension draws attention to the need for resistance in our own world.

The young people overtly conform to what is expected of them; Melchior is successful at school, Wendla goes to her sister's wedding and celebrates the arrival of her sister's baby. However, when they question ideology or challenge conformity, tragedy occurs; Wendla asks her mother where children come from in an attempt to understand her own body and what the future holds for her. She is rebuffed so that the institutionalized repression of girls is maintained, but this ultimately leads to her death. At the same time we see the loyalty of the group as they attempt to understand the world in opposition to their parents and teachers, but in this case they turn in on themselves. They respond to the surveillance by their parents and teachers with depression and anxiety and find release in musical explosions and through the exploration and expression of their sexuality. In this way sexuality is seen as a resistance to the hegemony as well as a representation of their adolescent transformatory potential.

Foucault's *History of Sexuality* describes how society's views of sexuality change at different times by documenting practices since the Ancient Greeks. The classical world embraced the notion of 'Aphrodisia', engaging openly in diverse sexual acts, some of which confront our contemporary moral sensibilities. Ancient Greeks were assumed to be attracted to both men and women: same-sex pederasty – the love between an older man and a younger boy – was openly accepted and heterosexual paedophilia – the sexual relationship between an older man and a teenage girl – was normal. Many societies repress or restrict sexuality and types of sexual practice, especially in relation to children and young people. For example, Foucault contrasts the seventeenth-century openness to discussion and awareness of sexuality with the prudery of the Victorian era. He records that in the seventeenth century there was freedom for children and adults to discuss sex and sexual matters, and that some types of 'perverse sexuality' were quite normal. This freedom was lost in the nineteenth century as repressive moves were introduced to limit the sexuality of children and to prevent male children masturbating. This can be seen in the architecture of schools and the new discourses that came into being. Masturbation was seen as an epidemic to be eradicated. The effect of this was, Foucault argued, to bring it to light and make it the subject of endless discussion, revealing the workings of power – and the fact that unpredictable effects can ensue.

The effect was to increase the desirability of breaking taboos:

If sex is repressed, that is condemned to prohibition, non-existence and silence, then the mere fact that one is speaking about it has the appearance of a deliberate transgression. A person who holds forth in such language places himself to a certain extent outside the reach of power; he upsets established law; he somehow anticipates the coming freedom. (p. 85)

Foucault demonstrates that rather than closing down forms of sexuality, eighteenth- and nineteenth-century taboos had the effect of categorizing forms of sexuality, promoting rules and recommendations. More importantly for the discussion of youth here, there was a focus on the sexuality of children, madmen and women, and criminals. These were all the 'others' of society – those who were not white men – the alienated whose voices were not heard. 'It was the time for all these figures scarcely noticed in the past, to step forward and speak, to make the difficult confession of what they were' (p. 86).

This process was linked with the Christian church's practice of confession, 'to say everything in order to efface everything, to formulate even the least faults in an uninterrupted, desperate, exhaustive murmuring, from which nothing must escape' (p. 86). Foucault's analysis reveals that children's sexuality and especially boys' masturbation was brought to light and discussed endlessly in a reversal of the expectations of the repressive authorities. The result of the energized awareness of sexual behaviour was moral self-judgement. In the same way that the Panopticon encouraged individuals to internalize power structures, the awareness of taboos and transgression heightened their desirability and intensity. Instead of conforming to these power structures, Foucault asks us to analyse the ways we categorize sexual acts and deviancy.

The overt sexuality in *Spring Awakening* represents a desire for girls to attain social and sexual equality, while for boys there was a desire for an identity other than the soldier/athlete binary (Savage, 2007, p. 104). In the period after *Spring Awakening* was originally written (and perhaps in response to the types of passions the work reveals, though not causally linked) prolonged group hikes in youth groups were introduced in imperial Germany as an attempt to create a world for young people away from the excessive discipline of school.

The musical version encourages audiences to identify with the young people who are disturbed by their sexual awakening. The adults, who represent the hegemony, with the exception of Frau Gabor (Melchior's mother) range from thoughtless to downright cruel. The teachers manipulate Moritz's school results so that he will leave school, his parents call him a failure because of this, and in desperation at this failure and the 'sin' of masturbation that has been keeping him awake at night and causing a highly emotional state, he shoots himself.

Melchior and Wendla make love without her understanding what is happening to her emotions or what the consequences of the act might be, and she becomes pregnant. Meanwhile, Melchior has attempted to enlighten Moritz by writing a pamphlet explaining sexual intercourse, and this falls into his parents' hands. As a result, and despite being aware of Wendla's condition, they send him away to a reformatory. Wendla meanwhile is taken by her mother for a backstreet abortion and she dies.

Ilse is abused by her father until when she is old enough to refuse his sexual advances, she is thrown out onto the street. She goes to live in an artists' commune where she is forced into prostitution. Martha is also sexually abused by her father and beaten if she 'doesn't do as he likes' (Act 1, scene 7). The boys all masturbate energetically but fear that it is sinful and will make them blind, while in their midst a homosexual relationship begins between Ernst and Hänschen which is the most successful, if illicit, relationship in the work. The whole atmosphere reverberates with the energy and misery of sexual knowing and unknowing and the fearful perception of being sinful for becoming emotionally and physically close to another person. The hypocrisy and blindness of the adults to what is happening is mirrored by the suggestion that the young people will be blinded by masturbation and by the attempt to keep them, and especially the girls, ignorant of sexuality or 'in the dark'.

Clearly, Foucault's power structures are revealed in this work. The young people resist or refuse to consent to their parents' and teachers' attempts to discipline them in various ways and with vastly different consequences. But as they resist, they take power, Moritz by choosing death and Melchior by choosing life and promising the ghosts of Moritz and Wendla that it will be a different life. 'The stars, too, they tell of spring returning – And summer with another wind that no one yet has known' (p. 91). And in a final reflexive statement he vows that 'one day all will know' (p. 92) predicting the increased awareness of the difficulties of youth made public in performance. Finally, Ilse sings the Coda, asking the audience to 'Listen to what's in the heart of a child' as it works its way through sadness, doubt, loss and grief to 'A time of hope through the land' (p. 93) before the company joins her singing of 'the wonder / Of purple summer' (p. 94).

All these works reveal an exploration of the awakening of sexuality in young people as part of their transformation into adulthood beyond the shadow of their parents. Moving away from the perceived innocence of the boy choristers, the representation of young peoples' alienation from and resistance to the cultural hegemony is expressed through music, song and dance, mirroring the ways in which contemporary young people express their alienation and group allegiance through adherence to alternative and rebellious music and dance forms. But we have to wonder about the relationship between the present and these performances of past moments. In all three performances an alienated stage of life is revealed, a time when developing sexuality adds to the feeling of powerlessness, fear, frustration and disaffection. However, all three works finish with some sense of moving forward into a new world that has been changed by the strength and resistance of young people. Thus, ultimately, all three reveal the creative strength and evolutionary dynamic that can result from the refusal of consent. Though not all musicals represent young people so coherently or so carefully, these works demonstrate the radical potential young people can represent on the musical stage.

Further reading – theoretical

Jones, Steve (2006) *Gramsci* (London and New York: Routledge).
Mills, Sara, (2003) *Michel Foucault* (London and New York: Routledge).
Nayak, Anoop and Mary Jane Kehily (2008) *Gender, Youth and Culture: Young Masculinities and Femininities* (Basingstoke: Palgrave Macmillan).

Further reading – relating to the examples

Brett, Philip (2006) *Music and Sexuality in Britten: Selected Essays* (Berkeley and Los Angeles: University of California Press).
Howard, Patricia (1985) *The Turn of the Screw* (Cambridge Opera Handbooks) (Cambridge: Cambridge University Press).
Tzioumakis, Yannis and Sian Lincoln (eds) (2013) *The Time of Our Lives: Dirty Dancing and Popular Culture* (Detroit, MI: Wayne State University Press).

10   'I Am What I Am': Sexuality and Queer Theory

One of the most popular songs in *Avenue Q* (2003) is 'If You Were Gay', which Nicky (a green puppet) sings to his uptight roommate, Wall Street banker Rod (a blue puppet). Nicky suspects that Rod might be gay, and he wants to reassure his friend: 'If you were gay, / That'd be OK', he sings. Of course, Rod is gay, but he is also in the closet, since his sexuality threatens many of the values he holds: as a Wall Street banker he works in a world of macho testosterone; and as a Republican (in one interview he even talks of his friendship with the then president George Bush[1]) his views tend towards the conservative. To convince friends he is straight, Rod invents a fictitious girlfriend living in Canada, but as we learn in the song 'Fantasies Come True', he actually has a desperate crush on Nicky. We are not surprised: the dead giveaway was his passion for Broadway musicals.

This chapter explores sexuality: both hetero- and homosexuality and gender identities. Our gender is a fundamental part of our identity, and we all perform it and self-identify with it in obvious and subtle ways. Importantly, the whole discussion surrounding gender and sexuality is about inclusion and exclusion and relates to earlier discussions of the ways in which the world is viewed from the perspective of a white heterosexual Western male, leaving other – marginalized – viewpoints to be variously described as 'queered' or 'othered'. This is particularly evident if we consider language that highlights gender or sexuality. Some of this is extremely offensive and has been used to create prejudice or to marginalize people who don't behave exactly like us ('dyke', 'poof', 'slapper'); some is used as a sort of euphemistic disguise by which we either protect our own identity or cast aspersions on someone else's ('one of the lads' has a very different connotation to 'one of them', for example); some may have further associations with religious, clinical or even non-human overtones. Either way, the use of language in relation to sexuality is complex: think how the term 'gay' has changed over the years from meaning 'happy' to 'homosexual', and more recently, to 'rubbish'.

If we try to define sexuality, we might put it something like this: our sexuality is the extent to which – and the reasons behind why – we conform to or subvert conventional expressions of identity in regard to our gender or sexual preference.

169

As we have already seen, the study of sexuality is dominated by the work of Michel Foucault, whose *History of Sexuality* – as it relates to young people and power – was introduced in the last chapter. In this chapter we're interested in the way Foucault explored the classification of sexuality, the way we represent it culturally and – perhaps most significantly – the way we control it. This focus on sexuality brings into play many of the concerns that we have explored in previous chapters: that identity, and especially gender identity, is a construct, a performative identity that is both created and confirmed by repeated behaviours. As such, we behave in ways that are socially recognized and labelled as 'camp', 'extrovert', 'butch' or 'queer'; we make identity statements in the clothes we wear or the hair style, tattoos or piercings we sport; and we affiliate ourselves to things like football, cheerleading or musical theatre partly as expressions of our gender identity and sexuality.[2]

Some of the shows that engage audiences with sexuality are ostensibly 'gay' shows (*Falsettos*, *Bare*); however, other shows like *Little Shop of Horrors* (1982) present nothing but straight relationships and conventionally heteronormative lifestyles, reminding us that sexuality is not an exclusively gay domain. In this chapter we focus on three shows – all of them musicals from the past 40 or so years – that explore sexuality explicitly but in very different ways, thereby revealing some of the complex manifestations of sexuality in culture.

Foucault's *History of Sexuality* (1976–1984)

As we have seen in Chapter 9, one of Michel Foucault's starting points is to consider how sexuality has been classified, represented and controlled from the time of the Ancient Greeks. To puritans, sexual expression was the sign of corruption, and carnal lust was a sin, even if sex within marriage for procreation was permitted. Sexually transmitted diseases such as syphilis were seen as punishments from God, and promiscuous women were often charged with witchcraft.

As times changed Enlightenment sensibilities brought about a fascination in the erotic, with eighteenth-century European art openly displaying fulsome, sexual bodies. In this period, 'sexual practices had little need of secrecy', reports Foucault; 'codes regulating the coarse, the obscene, and the indecent were quite lax [...] it was a time of direct gestures, shameless discourse, and open transgressions, when anatomies were shown and intermingled at will' (in Rabinow, 1986, p. 292). It seems something of a surprise, then, that in the twentieth century we seem to have reverted to shyness about sex and the body, viewing promiscuity, nudity and eroticism as manifestations of the perverse, and restricting legitimized sexual behaviour to the intimacy of the bedroom.

Foucault's study of sexuality reveals four ways in which this attitude was formulated by Victorian perspectives on sexuality: firstly, as we saw in Chapter 8, science promoted the idea of the female body as a site of hysteria. Secondly, as we saw in Chapter 9, Foucault notes how the teaching of sexual rights and wrongs consolidates ingrained ideologies and – rather worryingly – sexualizes what Laura Mulvey calls the 'to-be-looked-at-ness' of girls, whilst bestowing on boys a predatory 'male gaze'. Thirdly, Foucault sees society controlling the construction of attitudes to sexuality in the socialization of procreative behaviour. Society emphasizes the virtue of certain behaviours, in particular heterosexuality and the promotion of monogamy through marriage. The dominance of this particular ideology can still be seen in the obsession of politicians with 'family values' and the privileging of marriage. As a corollary to this promotion of virtuous behaviours, the state has, in some places, outlawed non-normative sexual behaviours: non-normative desire is wrong (but curable), prostitution is sinful and illegal, homosexuality (until even very recently) is aberrant and seen as an illness (queer), and transsexuality is seen as monstrous (freakish). The strength of the repressive and ideological apparatuses in dealing with these variances from 'the norm' is such that a dominant and extremely powerful narrative has arisen according to which any marginal or minority behaviour is considered – literally – 'abnormal'. Accordingly, the fourth strategy for controlling the expression of sexuality is in institutionalizing the practices of perverse pleasure into the brothel and the mental hospital. 'Everywhere else', suggests Foucault, 'modern puritanism imposed its triple edict of taboo, nonexistence, and silence' (p. 293).

Socializing heteronormativity

In the mid-twentieth century America took the lead in defining *normative* sexuality according to the organizational unit of *the family* and the behavioural codes of *heterosexuality*. With powerful images, the media projected the ideal 'nuclear family', an aspirational domestic arrangement reinforcing the already-powerful rhetoric of the 'American Dream'. Wholesome images of happy families appeared everywhere, with mother baking and cleaning at home while father went off to work. The ideal 1950s man was the provider, protector and boss of the house, while the ideal modern woman was expected 'to combine in her one ladylike person the functions of wife, mother, interior decorator, registered nurse, child psychologist, landscape gardener, participator in public affairs, scintillating hostess, director of budgets and general good sport [...], counted on nightly to dish up savory ragouts, casseroles, crepes and sauces' (McGinley and Benchley, 1959, p. 155). The threat to this model existence came from media images of unashamedly sexualized pinup girls: Jayne Mansfield, Bettie Page and most of all, Marilyn Monroe, whose nude photoset graced the centrefold of *Playboy*'s first edition (1953). Here was a projection of sexuality – the confident and wilful woman – that directly confronted the chasteness of the family, tempting men and confirming women as sexual objects. Fuel was added to the fire by the publication of Alfred Kinsey's *Sexual Behavior in the Human Male* (1948) and *Sexual Behavior in the Human Female* (1953). According to Kinsey, and in contrast to the image of respectability championed by the government, the nation as a whole was rampantly engaged in clandestine sexual activity, illicit adultery and casual sex. As the allure of sexualized images increased, commentators roundly condemned the report 'as an assault on the family as a basic unit of society, as a negation of moral law, as a celebration of licentiousness and as a bad influence generally' (Wickware, 1948, p. 87). To 1950s America, then, the threat of sexuality was not just a homophobia; it was a fear of any behaviour outside the nuclear model.

Little Shop of Horrors (1982)

In order to discuss this, we are going to start with a show that images 1950s American life and its fear of another outside threat: *Little Shop of Horrors* (1982) plays out the threat of alien invasion in an update of the 1960s B-movie of the same name.

If this narrative of alien invasion seems to have departed from a consideration of sexuality, it is worth recollecting how these themes are linked in American ideology through an affirmation of what sexual behaviour is normative and what is 'queered' or 'other'. *Little Shop of Horrors* establishes both the normative and the 'other' as part of its narrative, and it pastiches and therefore undermines the period in which these ideologies were entrenched. Its hero and heroine, for example, are cast as a small-town American couple (even though they are in New York) whose only aspiration is to live the American Dream, which they sing about in 'Somewhere that's green'. This song is littered with cultural references such as 'we snuggle watching Lucy' – referencing *I Love Lucy* (1951–1960), and 'I'm his December bride' which refers to *December Bride* (1954–1959). 'He's father, he knows best' reminds us of *Father Knows Best* (1954–1958). These and many other references in this song and throughout the show to TV shows and other media of the 1950s, all of which portrayed stereotypical images

Little Shop of Horrors (1982)

Music by Howard Ashman

Lyrics by Alan Menken

Based on the Hollywood B-movie of the same name

Synopsis: Seymour Krelborn is a young no-hoper who works in Mr Mushnik's downtown flower shop and who is desperately in love with beautiful blonde Audrey. Business is bad, but one day Seymour stumbles on a strange plant which he brings to the shop and christens Audrey II. The plant not only sings but also demands to be fed on human blood. Seymour reluctantly assists the plant, leading to a killing spree in which he feeds first Audrey's sadistic boyfriend Orin to the plant, and then Mr Mushnik. Finally, by accident, Audrey gets eaten, and as Seymour vows to avenge her death he leaps into the jaws of Audrey II with a machete, only to be swallowed himself. The show concludes with the plant getting bigger and more powerful than ever – a 'mean, green mother from outer space' – and with its cuttings sent across America to repeat the events and take over the world.

of the normative (straight, white, married) American household, create a picture of the society to which Audrey and Seymour aspire, as shown in Figure 10.1.

Figure 10.1   The home Audrey and Seymour dream of in 'Somewhere that's Green' from *Little Shop of Horrors* (1986). Warner Brothers

By way of contextualizing the (alien) 'other' as a perceived threat within American society, *Little Shop* voices the dangerous plant with a quintessential black identity (Levi Stubbs, Jr. from Motown band The Four Tops), a particular sound (black, voracious, dangerous funk) and an orality that combines sucking and eating in a lascivious sexualized display. The imagery conflates sexualized and racialized tropes but the message is clear: don't feed the plant/don't depart from the norm.

In this we can see that the expression of sexuality is not simply an expression of our orientation, nor something defined by the way in which we flaunt or conceal our bodies; it is also something that co-opts other expressive forces into its control of what is normative and acceptable and what is threatening and 'queer'.

La Cage aux Folles (1983)

Music and lyrics by Jerry Herman

Book by Harvey Fierstein

Based on a French play of the same name by Jean Poiret (1973)

The play was filmed as *The Birdcage* (1996) directed by Mike Nichols

Synopsis: The musical explores the relationship of a gay couple, Georges and Albin, who run the *La Cage aux Folles* nightclub in Paris. Georges is the proprietor, while Albin performs as popular drag artiste Zaza Napoli. The couple's relationship is tested when Georges' straight son introduces them to his extremely conservative future parents-in-law. As the heteronormative world of conservative Paris disturbs the insular world of the gay club, Albin in particular goes through a steep learning curve to conform to heterosexual behaviours.

The sexualized voice

We have seen in Chapter 8 how female operatic characters have been defined as unstable, emotionally extreme or mad; and we have seen how compositional techniques have created musical patterns for sopranos that embed this emotional instability into the representation of femininity. The same principle has been applied to the representation of other voices as we saw in Chapter 2. But even as other patterns become ingrained there is an insistence on certain timbres as signifying a 'normal sexuality' within defined musical styles. When drag queen Albin's behaviour threatens to expose the gay relationship at the heart of *La Cage aux Folles* his voice becomes a key signifying feature in adapting to become more masculine (normalizing himself), being advised to 'Grunt like an ape, and growl like a tiger... / Try making it rough and gruff and low' (Herman and Fierstein, 1983).

Such awareness of identity is clearly present in the unusual vocal play of transgender singer Antony Hegarty with Antony and the Johnsons. Just as Hegarty's identity evades categorization within the conventional classifying system of male/female (though he self-identifies as a man), his voice and vocal style slip between expected norms, creating idiosyncratic and beguiling music. If this is a response to the heteronormative sound palette of conventional popular music, both of these examples underline the degree to which normalizing conventions can marginalize individuals or communities whose identity resides outside the 'norm'. To express oneself in such a way and thereby announce an 'other' identity can itself be a marginalizing act; on the other hand, it can be a powerful act of assertion with significant political and ideological value.

Because the voice is produced by the body and is therefore biologically gendered, it carries with it the implication of sexuality. Sometimes, that sexuality can be confirmed when the sound of the voice matches qualities that are ideologically gendered: think of the strength and virility (masculinity in excess) of the Russian bass that Barthes so evocatively describes in 'The Grain of the Voice', for example; or the flirtatious fragility (femininity in excess) of Marilyn Monroe's voice as she sings 'Happy Birthday' to JFK. These are examples of the vocal aesthetic supporting and even magnifying the sexuality of the characters who are performing. But because its sound is a part of that musical aesthetic, any stylistic manipulation of the voice will inevitably de-normalize (queer) its expression of sexuality; one only has to consider the use of falsetto (by figures such as Prince, Michael Jackson or a band such as The Darkness) to see how queerings of identity are transcribed in part through the voice.

By far the most significant example of the voice's aesthetic queering the biological body is in the tradition of the castrato that is discussed in Chapter 13. Similar resonances are layered into the voices of black identity whose first threatening sounds began to overwhelm the values of conservative white music with ragtime, jazz and blues, articulations that were not only coded racially but also and explicitly as statements of sexuality. The purity, control and decorum of a classical European sound was subverted with an informal, bodily and – one might even say – *wayward* sound, carrying implications of how American (white) values might be threatened. The terms 'jazz' and 'rock 'n' roll' were euphemisms for sex, and their sound has been intrinsically linked with dynamic and metaphorical thrusts of the body. Part of the attraction (and danger) of Elvis Presley was the way in which his thrusting groin was seen to fascinate young women, and throughout the history of rock, various performance props like the guitar (Jimi Hendrix) or the microphone stand (Freddie Mercury) have been appropriated to symbolize the power of the phallus. As such, popular music serves as an accompaniment and even a determinant of sexuality, and it is in part for this reason that even white popular music and pop stars were seen as such a threat to American stand- ards. Cultural expressions of sexuality are adaptable, though, and the dif- ference in sexuality between the performative characters of Jimi Hendrix and Freddie Mercury – who struts his virile masculinity around the stage whilst self-consciously styling himself as a 'Queen' – attests to this.

Drag and sexuality

The notion of cross-dressing has also been a feature of the musical stage that is worth exploring because what appears to be a queer manoeuvre in fact builds on a number of character types. The trouser-role (a male char- acter played by a mezzo-soprano) was popular throughout the eighteenth and nineteenth centuries, from Cherubino in Mozart's *The Marriage of Figaro* (1786) to Prince Orlofsky in Strauss's *Die Fledermaus* (1874); the Pantomime Dame (an older female character played by a man) has featured in stage productions from Widow Simone in *La Fille Mal Gardee* (1789) to the still current traditions of British pantomime; and both male and female imper- sonators became extremely popular during the British music hall period, in which Vesta Tilley was celebrated as 'Burlington Bertie' (1900). Nevertheless, despite the gender disguise, these characters remain sexually innocuous, because they don't actually attempt to disguise the gendered identity, but to reveal it. Since that time, two main outlets for drag have become prom- inent. The first presents the drag queen as graceful and elegant, mimicking qualities of luxury and affluence that pervade feminine fashion. Drag stars such as Danny La Rue, Lily Savage, Lady Chablis, Dame Edna Everage and RuPaul offer safe, unthreatening subversions of feminine sexuality, some- times tinged with mild innuendo but typically fairly respectable. By contrast, many major cities now bubble with drag as an outrageous and often explicit performance culture centred within the gay community. In queering male sexuality, this culture finds its voice in the expression of feminine sexual- ized excess: the clothing still signifies glamour and affluence, but in this environment it is generally more revealing, tapping into signifiers of sexual availability and promiscuity and emphasizing the sexualized body.

Interestingly, such drag performers typically include song in their acts, usually miming to recordings of female torch singers or gay icons (Judy

Garland, Barbara Streisand, Gloria Gaynor). Like their costumes, the mime is not an attempt to deceive or convince the audience of any veracity; these performances are self-conscious statements of artifice, which thereby make deliberate and bold comments on the performative construct of sexuality in general. In one particularly interesting example of mainstream drag performance, the stage version of *Priscilla, Queen of the Desert* involves drag (male) characters miming to the real (live) vocals of real (female) singers, thereby deliberately revealing the artifice. In a fascinating cycle of references, the overt vocal and physical performances of female sexuality by groups like The Weather Girls ('It's Raining Men') become stable cultural documents whose excess is then parodied in further performances of both male and female sexuality by the onstage performers. As such, this articulation of drag performance is not so much a gay expression as an expression of *excess*, of *openness* and of *difference*. The musical stage – with its vocal and physical embodiments of identity, and with its awareness of excess and artifice – is the ideal location for issues of sexuality to be played out.

La Cage aux Folles (1983)

A number of songs in *La Cage aux Folles* explicitly discuss sexuality ('I Am What I Am') and drag ('A Little More Mascara'), the latter emphasizing how, for Albin, putting on his makeup is a conscious act of camouflaging his own biological identity in order to take on the persona of a woman. However, it is the underlying dramatic narrative of the show that produces the most comedic and performative exploration of sexuality, and in the course of the unfolding drama, Albin's excessive display is stripped away so that we see the real person and the real relationship beneath.

Georges's son Jean-Michel is engaged to the daughter of Edouard Dindon, a leading conservative politician whose campaign policies hinge on a stringently anti-gay agenda. Jean-Michel wants to marry Anne Dindon; clearly it will not be possible to introduce Georges and Albin as a couple, so Jean-Michel at first asks Albin to make himself scarce. Albin is extremely hurt by this, and they decide he should meet the prospective family – first as Uncle Albin and then, when Jean-Michel's mother fails to arrive, as the mother herself. The various roles Albin is forced to adopt in the course of this subterfuge require him to learn different gender identities. Already fluent in the two different personalities Albin and Zaza, both of which are overtly feminized in the performative vocabulary of gay identity, Albin must first take on a masculine attitude for Uncle Al and a different type of feminized persona for Jean-Michel's mother. These subtle (and not-so-subtle) gradations of gender performance throughout the show reveal all identity to be just 'A Little More Mascara'.

In 'Masculinity' Georges tries to teach Albin to become more masculine; first encouraging him to slouch and round his shoulders, then to stop holding in his stomach, and spread his legs when sitting. All of these instructions contradict Albin's learned feminine postural traits, drawing our attention to some of the subtle ways in which feminized behaviour is culturally restrictive. In performance this sequence allows the performer playing Albin to explore masculine and feminine distinctions in physicality, and to introduce gay sexual humour into the mix. Albin struggles, and it is only when Georges reminds him that he is a great performer with an impressive track record and that 'playing simple Uncle Al is beyond your range!', Albin manages to adopt a masculine gait.

At the 1983 Tony Awards ceremony, where the musical won a number of awards, George Hearn was asked to sing the hit of the show, 'I Am What I Am'. Although this number is sung on stage in drag as a celebration of non-normative identity, Hearn was requested to perform it at the ceremony in dinner jacket and bow tie: as a man. This was a strikingly heteronormative instruction that highlighted the institutional conservatism of the organizers while at the same time – in its irony – magnifying the identity rhetoric of the show. This event, years after the gay liberation riots outside the Stonewall bar in Greenwich Village, shows how extremely heteronormative American society was even in the mid-1980s (and arguably still is). We might consider it surprising that, as recently as this, such stigma could be attached to prominent displays of non-normative sexuality.

In pre-war America, the occasional attempt to showcase risqué sexuality on stage was often met with hostility: Mae West's production *Sex* (1927) led to her incarceration for ten days as a pornographer. In the United Kingdom, the taboo on sexuality was also enshrined in law. When censorship was repealed in 1968 the first show to appear in London's West End was *Hair*, with its famous nude scene. Despite this expression of liberal sexuality the male characters in the show lead the action, which is underpinned by female desire for heteronormative relationships. Thereafter, a slew of adult musicals on both sides of the Atlantic revelled in the new-found freedom to express sexuality on stage (see Wollman, 2006). But more significant than any of these was a show that was to become a cult classic, exploring issues of normativity, gender and sexuality, and featuring drag, excess, openness and difference. This – perhaps the most non-normative of musicals – was in no way a gay show (though it has a healthy following in gay and straight communities alike); it surfaced, as such musicals often do, in the seemingly most innocent and unlikely of places.

The Rocky Horror Show (1973)

Music, book and lyrics by Richard O'Brien

Produced and directed by Jim Sharman at the Royal Court Theatre, London

Filmed as *The Rocky Horror Picture Show* (1975)

Based on the novel Frankenstein (1818) by Mary Shelley, and a tradition of science fiction horror B movies.

Synopsis: All-American couple Brad and Janet break down outside a mysterious castle and find themselves invited into a hedonistic party thrown by the alien transvestite Dr Frank N. Furter. Frank is a scientist who, in a ground-breaking biological experiment, has managed to create a man. But Rocky is just a sexual plaything for a doctor who turns out to be sadistic, emotionally unhinged and bent on power. It falls to his butler and chambermaid Riff Raff and Magenta to bring an end to Frank N. Furter's unstable reign over the house, and – now rather more worldly wise – Brad and Janet are released.

The Rocky Horror Show (1973)/The Rocky Horror Picture Show (1975)

Richard O'Brien's *The Rocky Horror Picture Show* (1975) – the film version of a show originally staged at London's Royal Court Theatre – begins with all-American couple Brad and Janet driving home from their friends' wedding. The scenario could not be more conventional. Brad and Janet are subtly mocked as figures of stability: he the provider, masculine but weak; she the virginal fiancée, pathetic and weaker. As rain pelts down outside the car and as doomed President Richard Nixon speaks on the radio, the car has a blow-out (puncture) and the couple are forced to seek help at a decidedly gothic castle, where they are greeted by the butler Riff Raff and the maid Magenta. Once inside, they discover a host of unconventional convention-ists and a world in which all the normative codes of gender and sexuality are completely undermined. Presiding over the hedonistic world inside the castle is Dr Frank N. Furter, a biologist who, like his near namesake, has been making a man in his laboratory. In the course of the evening Frank seduces both Brad and Janet, releasing Janet's inhibitions to the extent that she seduces Frank's new plaything, Rocky. The party atmosphere continues until, after a risqué floorshow, all the main characters end up in a free-for-all orgy in the pool.

 This is a domain where – sexually – anything goes. Despite Frank's trans-vestism, and despite the homo-eroticism of his relationship with Rocky, Frank is overcoded as unquestionably masculine, a sexuality enforced by the pumping glam rock of his opening number ('Sweet Transvestite'). Although at other points his behaviour borrows feminized tropes – the delicate satin-draped opening of 'I'm Going Home', for instance, or the maternal, even matronly surgical dress and string of pearls he wears whilst 'giving birth' to Rocky – Tim Curry's performance actually subverts sexuality through reconfiguring the normative signifiers of the basque, stockings and stilettos rather than his gender behaviour. In fact, the character of Frank is authoritative, assertive and butch; in most respects extremely masculine. In this context, though, subverting normative codes is not just a playful or provocative act of shock, but a clever commentary on American paranoia. For Frank and his entourage are not just unconventional hedonists (whose presence in itself is a threat to the moral fibre of the country); they are also aliens from the planet of Transsexual in the galaxy of Transylvania, and thus they represent the non-normative outsider in social as well as sexual terms. There have been clues to this throughout the movie, not least in the opening number 'Science Fiction Double Feature', in which an androgynous pair of singing lips references dozens of 1950s B movies – *The Day the Earth Stood Still* (1951), *It Came from Outer Space* (1953), *Forbidden Planet* (1956) – those very films that articulated America's fears about experiment and invasion in the first place. But even more intrinsically than this, Frank is a pastiche of both Mary Shelley's Dr Frankenstein (1819) and Bram Stoker's Dracula (1897) – earlier characters whose stories rehearse fears about scientific research and monsters in our midst; as Frank tries to escape from being cornered he references another cultural monster figure, emulating King Kong (1933) as he climbs a mock-up of the RKO mast to escape. Eventually Riff and Magenta decide that their consort has gone far enough, and with space guns drawn they take Frank prisoner to return to their own galaxy of Transylvania.

But if *The Rocky Horror Show* comments on American paranoia through its overt sexuality, this is made to stand out against its referencing of other normalizing American images: the heteronormativity of Brad and Janet, references to college proms and reunions, the opening wedding scene. And in the movie the use of Grant Wood's 'American Gothic' (1930) appears, a painting in which a stern American couple pose in the yard of a small-town church. He holds a pitchfork and has clearly been interrupted from his manual labour; she wears an apron and gazes up at his authoritarian figure. The gabled roof of the church-house frames the space between them, its arched window a clear sign of the value system governing this world. This well-known image is renowned for its comment on middle America and particularly the way in which domestic labour roles have been divided in the family (Saunders, 1987, p. 6). In *The Rocky Horror Picture Show* this image is reframed with the characters Riff Raff and Magenta appearing as the husband and wife as can be seen in Figure 10.2 where they appear behind Brad and Janet while they are singing 'Dammit Janet'. With this commentary the movie announces that the gender sub-version for which it is notorious is intrinsically commenting on normative American ideology.

If *The Rocky Horror Show* is a celebration of liberal expression and non-conformity, it highlights the fact that anything non-normative can easily be essentialized as abnormal. In many ways, this seems like an inescapable trap. In adopting alternatives to the masculine signifiers of straight sexual identity, drag performers typically embrace feminine signifiers that are ultra-feminized, drawing attention to their excess and artifice. *Priscilla, Queen of the Desert* (2006, adapted from the 1994 film) not only delights in and highlights excess and artifice but also – in the characterizing of Adam/Felicia – stages lifestyle behaviours common in the gay community (risk, promiscuity, provocation) that deliberately position individuals as the 'other' to society's heteronormative majority. Given this, it is sometimes difficult to see alternative sexuality as anything but excessive, extreme or 'queer'. One strategy for doing this is to disrupt the assumption that 'non-normative' means 'abnormal'.

Figure 10.2 Riff Raff and Magenta mirroring the American couple in Grant Wood's 'American Gothic' in *The Rocky Horror Picture Show* (1975). 20th Century Fox

---

Hedwig and the Angry Inch (1998)

Music and lyrics by Stephen Trask

Book by John Cameron Mitchell

Productions: Jane Street Theatre off Broadway. A film adaptation was made in 2000

Synopsis: The show is ostensibly a performance by a young East German émigré Hansel and the rock band s/he fronts, The Angry Inch, during which Hansel/Hedwig tells his/her story. Born with ambiguous genital organs, Hansel undergoes a botched sex-change operation and now lives with his own 'angry inch', struggling to find an identity in a world that does not accommodate the transgender community. Now known as Hedwig, s/he adopts the persona of a bleach blonde pinup girl, and shares an intimate relationship with fellow transgender band member Yitshak. But the band is destined to failure, performing in two-bit bars next to the giant rock venues in which Hansel's ex Tommy Gnosis has made himself a star. Hansel is unsure whether to reveal Johnny's secret, a revelation that will exploit the public horror of transgender identity, destroying Tommy's stardom but forever casting Hedwig as a freak.

Hedwig and the Angry Inch (1998)

Just as *La Cage aux Folles* presents as its anthem the paean to acceptance 'I Am What I Am', *Hedwig*'s 'The Origin of Love' mounts a persuasive argument for accepting all genders and sexualities, and calls on classical philosophy to support it. 'The Origin of Love' vocalizes Aristophanes's thoughts on sexuality, originally set forth in Plato's *Symposium*. According to Aristophanes, the original human beings were creatures with four arms, four legs and two heads: two people rolled into one. The Children of the Sun resembled two men bound together, the Children of the Earth two women and the Children of the Moon a man and a woman. But in order to control the Earth's defiant mortals, Zeus decided to punish them by splitting them all in half, creating a human race of incomplete people with just two arms and two legs. From that point, all humans have roamed the earth in search of their other half, and when two halves meet they hug tightly to try to squeeze themselves back into their original form. This is an inclusive mythology that caters for all sexual orientations and reminds us of how different attitudes to sexuality were in the classical period. It also normalizes Hansel/Hedwig, who – despite being coded as 'other' in dress and gender – is revealed to share 'universal' desires for love and monogamous companionship: 'It's clear that I must find my other half', she mutters. 'But is it a he or a she?' And then poignantly, 'Does he have what I don't?'

Just as the film challenges the hegemony of normalized gender and sexuality in mainstream culture by foregrounding non-normative characters, it also 'identifies and critiques the violences of heteronormative national belonging' according to Sandell (2010, p. 231). Hansel's botched sex-change surgery, which left behind the mutilated 'angry inch', was carried out so that he could marry an American G.I. and escape to the West from behind the iron curtain of East Berlin. The sacrifice Hansel makes to find his freedom literally scars him physically and emotionally for the rest of his life, now as Hedwig. But this event, which leaves Hansel/Hedwig forever an outsider to any normative personal identity group, also causes his G.I. to flee, leaving Hansel/Hedwig caught in between his identities of national belonging and alienated from any determined citizenship. His later relationship with Yitshak connects him to another dispossessed community (Jewish). In this way the identity politics of individuals are linked with the wider narratives of communal identity or its lack. If the sexuality of *Rocky Horror* makes pointed references to the ideologies of American identity rhetoric, the sexuality of *Hedwig and the Angry Inch* draws similar parallels to issues of citizenship and belonging, other control mechanisms that normalize and entrench identity. This reverses the lens, so to speak, to present the outsider's perspective, and to present American culture as the alienating force.

Where *The Rocky Horror Show* portrays outsiders as freaks both *La Cage aux Folles* and *Hedwig and the Angry Inch* humanize their alienated characters. Yet, ironically, the performative codes of both of these shows work against that normalizing dynamic to essentialize their narratives as 'queer'. Unfortunately, one of the inevitable imbalances of heteronormativity is that its very cultural prominence makes everything else a minority expression. So although a handful of recent musicals have explored non-normative sexualities in non-sensational ways, shows like William Finn's *In Trousers* (1985), *March of the Falsettos* (1981) and *Falsettoland* (1990) or John Hartmere and Damon Intrabartolo's *Bare* (2000) nevertheless remain essentialized as gay shows (the same can be said of any number of 'black' musicals). For Sandell (2010, p. 231), this is a problem that reaches beyond the surface discussion of sexuality in *Hedwig*: 'It becomes apparent that the film's popular reception frequently erases the transnational and imperial histories that undergird and produce sexual identities and identification'. Audiences, in other words – presumably those who are already alienated – engage with this film *because* it is counter-cultural and an expression of their own (normalizing) resistance to convention. Kinkade and Katovich

(1992, p. 192) say something similar about *Rocky Horror*: 'Cult films are a type of social criticism, yet often validate and can be read as surface affirmations of society'. The equally unconventional characters in a show like *Rent* become ciphers of non-conformity and not only lose any resonance in countering heteronormative assumptions but actually consolidate mainstream values: we don't relate to the most transgressive character Angel because s/he is so extreme; and any value in the expression of Maureen's performance art is negated when she encourages everyone to moo like a cow. In terms of normalizing sexuality, many of these texts work against their own intentions.

Further reading – theoretical

Butler, Judith (1993) *Bodies That Matter: On the Discursive Limits of Sex* (London: Routledge).
Foucault, Michel (1985) *The History of Sexuality, Vol. II: The Use of Pleasure*, trans. Robert Hurley (Harmondsworth: Penguin).
Garber, Marjorie (1997) *Vested Interests: Cross-Dressing and Cultural Anxiety* (second edition) (New York and London: Routledge).

Further reading – relating to the examples

Taylor, Millie (2010) 'Experiencing Live Musical Theatre Performance: *La Cage aux Folles* and *Priscilla, Queen of the Desert*', *Popular Entertainment Studies* 1(1): 44–58.
Wollman, Elizabeth L. (2006) *The Theater Will Rock: A History of the Rock Musical, from* Hair *to* Hedwig (Ann Arbor: University of Michigan Press).
—— (2012) *Hard Times: The Adult Musical in 1970s New York City* (Oxford: Oxford University Press).

PART IV
Rethinking Relationships

11 'It's the Last Midnight': Playing with Time and Space

'It's the last midnight' is a song from *Into the Woods* that explores the situation towards the end of the story when the characters appear to have run out of options: 'Now, before it's past midnight, I'm leaving you my last curse', sings the Witch. And she reminds us that this is a story told in song: 'It's the last midnight, It's the last verse.' She anticipates what might happen: 'Coming at you fast, midnight – soon you'll see the sky fall', and she recasts from her cynical perspective events that have already occurred: 'Told a little lie, Stole a little gold, Broke a little vow, Did you?' The Witch is about to disappear and leave the characters to their fate, but first she reminds the audience that every thought and action is created and perceived within a particular context that gives it perspective.

Layered against that internal dynamic of time-awareness is the temporal logic of how the story might be told and consumed; and layered against that – as if these layers are palimpsests giving multiple perspectives to the texture – is another. She reminds us that decisions and choices – often made in the moment – have consequences, creating a connection between past and future; in this the dynamic of time is revealed as crucial to our understanding of drama. In the musical in particular, where moments are often magnified as reflection in song, or where time is expanded or contracted in a musical gesture, the notion of time as a dramatic device becomes even more resonant. Thus layers accrue, and it is often in the recognition of the difference or *space* between each that resonances emerge, creating as it were the impression of dimensionality.

This final part of this book explores the way all meaning and interpretation is founded on relationships of difference, or *différance* – first in this chapter in relation to space and time, then in Chapter 12 in relation to the performance text and the external world in the deferral or deconstruction of meanings. In Chapter 13 we think about the relationships between voices, bodies and audiences in an extension of reception theory from Chapter 3, and finally in Chapter 14 we expand on ideas introduced in Chapter 4 as we explore relationships between musical theatre and human experience.

The three works we explore in this chapter are *The Marriage of Figaro* (1786), *The Mikado* (1885) and *Into the Woods* (1987). These appeared at almost exactly the same point in three different centuries, the mid-1980s, and so provide three moments, like the three midnights in the woods, that can be drawn into synchrony (another 'time' word derived from the Greek *chrono*). This momentary synchrony is used to explore issues of time and space in narrative, theatre and music.

In this chapter, then, we explore narration, which you've already been introduced to in Chapter 1, and the disruption of linear time, as well as changes of pace and place. But, first, let's establish how commonly we use dynamics of time and space by considering how we are using them now. We started this paragraph, for example, by looking forward and predicting what will come later: 'In this chapter...we explore narration.' This is a technique from classical rhetoric known as *prolepsis* or flash-forward. It suggests the authors' omniscience narrating and guiding you through the book. The words 'which you've already been introduced to' do something else; they look back, using *analepsis* or flashback. The sentence continues by referring to 'anachronism', which is another 'time' word meaning a disturbance or error in chronology. The anachronism of speech and especially musical theatre confirms that our understanding of stories and music is not really based on a linear chronology at all. The final part of the sentence speaks of 'changes of pace and place'. Here 'pace' signifies a different understanding of time, an understanding of how time is perceived rather than how it is measured by a clock. And, finally, 'place' suggests that all these temporal anomalies might be the result of different contexts, different readings that create different understandings.

By now you must be aware that language isn't simple; it is an accumulation of ideas and references that exist in time and that refer to other times, places and experiences. More importantly, you already know all this, and were introduced to an important theorist of this way of thinking in Part I – Roland Barthes. Writers of words and music explore and play with the possibilities that the synchronous presentation of ideas opens up to create tension, understanding, comedy and irony, and so 'Into the woods, but mind the past. Into the woods, but mind the future'.

Looking back and looking forward

The narratologist Gérard Genette has analysed the ways in which certain features appear in fiction. One such feature is the way time interacts with events in the presentation of a story. We've already seen, in Chapter 1, that narrative consists of events and their ordering in a particular version of a story. Genette discovered that within the narrative some events are predicted thematically, a type of flash-forward that he called 'prolepsis', and other events occur as flashback, what he called 'analepsis'. He also discovered that there were sometimes gaps in the time between the events presented, an 'ellipsis'. These ideas apply very interestingly to a discussion of musical theatre, not only in the structure and words, but also in the music.

An analepsis or flashback allows new information to be revealed about plot or characters' histories at an appropriate moment. This can take the form of a character narrating events from a different time or place, and in musical theatre this often occurs in song. In the 'Opening Part III' of *Into the Woods* the Witch recounts the history of her relationship with the Baker's parents and her casting of the spell that underpins the plot. This narrated flashback creates an imagined time and place that feeds into the onstage world. There are also several such moments in *The Mikado*: Ko-Ko recounts his personal history in 'Taken from the County Jail'; Nanki-Poo recalls his in 'A Wand'ring Minstrel I'; and Ko-Ko fabricates the story of a little bird in 'Tit-willow'. All of these extend the performance world by creating imagined moments in extended time and space, and all of these examples are woven in song.

Le Nozze di Figaro (The Marriage of Figaro) (1786)

Music by Wolfgang Amadeus Mozart

Book by Lorenzo Da Ponte

Based on a play by Beaumarchais, *La Folle Journée, où le mariage de Figaro* (1784) whose characters derive from the *Commedia dell'arte* tradition

Opened at the Burgtheater, Vienna

Synopsis: Figaro is engaged to Susanna, but their employer, Count Almaviva, is also pursuing Susanna, wanting to enjoy the 'droit de seigneur' (the right of the master to bed the young virgin before her marriage). The count's wife isn't pleased about this, though the situation is complicated as she is also being pursued by a young page, Cherubino. A number of farcical situations arise, including the revelation that the old woman Marcellina, who has been pursuing Figaro, is in fact his long lost mother – he had been stolen at birth. Disguises are assumed: Cherubino – a boy played by a woman – dresses as a girl; the Countess and Susanna swap clothes to fool the Count. Eventually all is revealed and the happy ending ensues.

One such moment in *Figaro* is instigated by the production of a contract
by Marcellino and Bartolo that will prevent the wedding of Figaro and
Susanna. Figaro must marry Marcellina as a result of a promise revealed
in the contract (see Figure 11.1). But then, in a recitative, Figaro describes
the circumstances of his birth; he was stolen as a baby and can produce the
jewels and garments that prove his highborn status. These, and a birthmark
on his arm, allow his mother to recognize him. So it is revealed that Bartolo
and Marcellina are, in fact, Figaro's parents. This narration is compressed
into a brief recitative, but it serves two purposes. It provides a very speedy
opportunity to transform the characters' relationships and the forthcoming
plot events, and opens up a vast imagined history for all three characters.
The revelation occurs at the moment in the story when most tension can
be created. Had that information been revealed at the start there would
have been no tension in the relationships and half of the story would not
have happened.

It is not only stories that are filled in through flashback or forward, but
themes or leitmotifs (that you were introduced to in Chapter 2) which
appear early on and then gradually coalesce into a significant song or
idea. Equally, the recurrence of songs or motifs marks moments of change
because they act as reminders that new situations or contexts surround
something that is ostensibly the same. If you play the same piece of music
repeatedly you will be aware that a shift in your mood or emotion will

**Figure 11.1   Marcellina insists that the contract should be fulfilled and
Figaro should marry her in *The Marriage of Figaro* at the Glyndebourne
Festival (1994). Glyndebourne Productions Ltd**

Into the Woods (1987)

Music and lyrics by Stephen Sondheim
Book by James Lapine (who also directed the first production)

Synopsis: *Into the Woods* combines four fairytales: *Cinderella, Little Red Riding Hood, Jack and the Beanstalk* and *Rapunzel*. In Act 1 all the characters set off into the woods on some sort of quest. A fifth fairytale narrative (this one an original invention) is used as a device to link these stories: the quest of the Baker and his Wife, to lift the curse of barrenness from their family, requires them to acquire items from characters in the other stories. At the end of Act 1 all have achieved their 'happy ever after', but all have had to cheat or lie a little, and this has consequences in Act 2 when a giant appears in the woods. The characters make a second journey into the woods ostensibly to kill the giant, but also because they have more to learn, and because their 'happy ever after' has not been as happy as they had hoped. Some are killed, including the narrator, before the surviving characters re-emerge to a more muted happy ending.

---

lead to your interpreting it differently based on the changed context. It is this feature of repetition – its ability to draw attention to context and difference – that is important in this chapter.

A key theme in *Into the Woods* is the issue of time, with constant reference to 'midnight', 'time' and 'moments': in the opening scene alone are references to 'Once upon a time', 'How many times must I tell you?', 'We've no time' and 'It's time to go'. There are also reflections on the pace of time passing: the Witch's 'The Last Midnight' announces a deadline in the quest narrative of the main characters, whilst 'Moments in the Woods', sung by the Baker's Wife, reflects on how fleeting experiences can carry great personal significance and therefore appear to last longer than they really do. Musically, the opening song 'Into the Woods' is adapted and repeated at intervals throughout the show, including at the beginning and ending of each act, providing a frame for the performance as well as continually reinforcing the awareness of this theme. The theme is finally played out in four songs at the end of Act 2: 'Moments in the Woods', 'Last Midnight', 'No More' and 'No One Is Alone.' Some of the motifs of Little Red Riding Hood, Jack, Cinderella and the Baker's Wife are also linked through musical references. This serves to convey the thematic similarity between their journeys of self-discovery. Repetition in plot, words, phrases, motifs and musical accompaniment all help to unify the score, but it also means that themes and character types are prefigured and character development is conveyed through awareness of change.

Cinderella sings two versions of 'On the Steps of the Palace'; the second is longer and more developed, built out of the earlier material. The first acts as a flash-forward for the later occurrence. Both contain musically and lyrically similar material; the starting point, 'He's a Very Nice Prince' in the first prefigures 'He's a Very Smart Prince' in the reprise, both sung using the same melodic motif and accompaniment vamp, and both occurring at a similar dramatic point in the story – Cinderella has been dancing with the Prince on each occasion. The song is distinctive at its first appearance, and, given the fact that the story is known, there is a sense of its importance to the plot that heightens awareness further. So since the song is immediately distinctive the musical and lyrical repetition is easily noticed, as is the difference between a 'nice' and a 'smart' prince as Cinderella's knowledge of him develops. When the reprise arrives audiences can make the connection and notice the changes that have occurred in the interim, while also being already familiar with the phrasing and melodic motifs.

'Agony' is also sung at two different points in the narrative. In Act 1 the two Princes compare their feelings about the unavailability of Cinderella and Rapunzel. In the second act, now married to Cinderella and Rapunzel, they speak of the agony of having fallen for Snow White and Sleeping Beauty. Their particular agony is always to want what is out of reach. The similarity of the two versions draws attention to the detailed differences between the statement and the reprise – between who the Princes want and don't want – so that audiences can discover information about the characters not through what they say about themselves, but through the differences or gaps between the iterations of the song. Repetition also draws together the two moments in time so that the hopefulness and anticipation of the first act clash with the events of the more cynical second act. So understanding for the audience results from the relationships between moments in time.

The third time feature Genette identified is the ellipsis – when time passes but the events in it are not told or shown. This happens between Acts 1 and 2 of *Into the Woods* when the initial happiness concluding the first act has begun to pall. The reason for the ellipsis in this case is that the important events and themes are those that mirror each other, not those in between – so the themes can be articulated more effectively as a result of the omission. Again, what we discover is that ideas are understood through their relationships. Meanings are constantly deferred as new contexts, gaps or provocations challenge the stability of assumed understanding. This idea is identified by Jacques Derrida as 'différance', meaning both difference and deferral.

Différance

This term, developed by Jacques Derrida (and first referred to in Chapter 2), is ambiguous – an ambiguity that derives partly from the untranslatability of the term from French to English. It illustrates the difference between written and spoken language since the two French terms différance and différence which are indistinguishable in speech mean different things; to defer or delay, and to differ or be different from. In Derrida's analysis, the term (which is always used in French so that both meanings are encapsulated) indicates that meaning is constantly deferred since each word or phrase adds to the sum of knowledge, constantly destabilizing or transforming anticipated meaning. In this way a text is perceived as an endless sequence of signs and signification that has no single or stable meaning.

Changing the pace and the context

Already, in this discussion of the ways in which musical theatre refers backwards and forwards and musical material is reprised or restated, it is obvious that musical theatre has consistently resisted a 'realistic' aesthetic. When a character starts singing there is a break with 'realistic' speech and an awareness of a different technical facility, a change in the mode of performance caused by the introduction of music – what Scott McMillin (2006, p. 2) calls the 'crackle of difference' between narrative and number. 'Book time' – when the story is enacted without singing – can be understood within a framework of dramatic 'realism' in which characters speak in dialogue, and events proceed in a linear fashion. Once a song begins, the musical moves into what McMillin calls 'lyric time' in which repetition of music and/or lyrics is common.

McMillin applies the separation of 'lyric time' and 'book time' to twentieth-century musical theatre, but the disjunction that occurs between plot developments and the transition to reflective song is much older. In *Le Nozze di Figaro* there is no spoken text, but, as was common at the time, Mozart used recitative with simple chordal accompaniment for moments of plot development. The end of a recitative is clearly signalled by a musical cadence before the re-entry of the orchestra for the aria – this is significant because it marks the end of one form of address (recitative) and the start of a new form (aria). The time frame of these two sections is different: the recitative moves forward at almost the pace of speech, and conversations and actions progress in a linear fashion, while arias contain numerous musical and lyrical repetitions and provide opportunities for reflection on an idea or theme.

For example, in the first act Bartolo and Marcellina have a conversation about the contract Marcellina holds. She hopes to use it to force Figaro to marry her and not Susanna. Bartolo, the lawyer, agrees to help since he also wants vengeance on Figaro for another slight. The pace of the recitative allows the action to progress almost at a realistic pace, and there is no repetition of ideas or phrases. There is a cadence to mark the change of musical language and then the aria 'La vendetta' (I'll have vengeance) begins in which Bartolo elaborates on his intentions. Within the aria each line is sung at least twice, sometimes more often. The emotion is conveyed through melodic flourishes and accompanying phrases. The pace of action is no longer realistic and the repetitions mean that the plot's time frame has now become static, while the melodic invention progresses.

This disjunction between time moving forward during recitative and pausing for emotional and musical elaboration is particularly noticeable in Act 3 when both the Count and Countess have extended opportunities to express their emotions. In fact the act as a whole contains relatively little action and revolves around two opportunities for emotional outpouring, first with the Count's 'Vedrò, mentr'io sospiro' (Shall I in sorrow languish?), and then with the Countess singing 'Dove sono' (Flown for ever). These characters become more than stereotypes through the orchestral and melodic invention and the emotion that is portrayed through that music.

The Mikado, or The Town of Titipu (1885)

Music by Arthur Sullivan

Book and lyrics by William Schwenk Gilbert

Synopsis: The story of *The Mikado* is set in a mythical combination of England and Japan that satirizes English decorum, bureaucracy and class through the faux-exoticism of Japan. No one has been executed in the town of Titipu despite the demands of the Mikado (equivalent to an emperor). Nanki-Poo, the Mikado's son, has fled from his betrothal to the domineering Katisha and appears incognito in Titipu where he has fallen in love with Yum-Yum. There, he agrees to be executed to appease the Mikado's orders and help the town's bureaucrats on the condition that he can marry Yum-Yum first. Of course, none of the townspeople knows that he is the Mikado's son, and that they would be executed for executing him. Yum-Yum is also somewhat wary when she discovers that wives are executed with their husbands. Katisha and the Mikado eventually arrive, all is revealed and all is resolved with Ko-Ko (the Lord High Executioner) condemned to marry Katisha, thus releasing Nanki-Poo to reveal his happy marriage to Yum-Yum.

Leaping ahead a century, Gilbert and Sullivan use recitative very occasionally in *The Mikado*. At Nanki-Poo's first entrance he sings a short recitative interacting with the nobles before the aria begins in which he introduces himself. The second moment of recitative is an exchange between Nanki-Poo and Pooh-Bah in which Nanki-Poo's hopes of marrying Yum-Yum are dashed. There is the opportunity for high-flown poetic language in Katisha's recitatives 'Your revels cease!' and later 'I claim my perjured lover, Nanki-Poo!' The final occurrence of recitative occurs in Act 2 when Katisha sets the scene for the aria that follows ('Alone, and yet alive!'). These recitatives offer the opportunity for melodramatic language and style accompanied by a deliberately formal and archaic musical language. The action continues almost at the pace of speech, but there is a different sense of poetry, drama and formality than is possible in the spoken scenes. What is also apparent is that the different contexts in which these works were written has led to different uses of the recitative. Unlike in *Figaro* recitative is used here as a comic formal device, because it is now outdated. It is not only within the narrative, but also in our understanding of the functioning of genre that we become aware of the importance of contextual understanding and the passing of time.

In the rest of the opera there is little pretence of continuity between speech and song. For example, Act 2 opens in Ko-Ko's garden where Yum-Yum's maids are dressing her hair singing 'Braid the Raven Hair'. They leave, and Yum-Yum ruminates on her own beauty in a speech that is both reflexive and ironic: 'Yes, I am indeed beautiful! Sometimes I sit and wonder, in my artless Japanese way, why it is that I am so much more attractive than anybody else in the whole world'. This is followed by her aria 'The sun whose rays' which is pure musical interlude, and to be enjoyed as such. There is no plot development, no action. Instead, in a static moment of book time, a bubble of lyric time is opened up in which the delights of song, with its poetic lyrics, melodic similarities and sequences, and instrumental and harmonic repetitions, can be enjoyed.

The juxtaposition between lyric and book time is potentially disruptive, causing a sort of dramatic disturbance between a moment of reflection and a moment of action. In *The Mikado* there is an absolute delight in such moments of disparity between the action of the scene, its progress in time and the musical and lyrical explosion into joyful irrelevance.

A century later in *Into the Woods* there is no recitative, but instead a greater use of underscore linking scenes and songs with unifying musical motifs. This technique developed in the 'integrated' musical as a means of moderating the discrepancy between speech and song, serving as a way of smoothing the passage from one expressive medium to another. However, there are still moments of disjunction between speech and song as action gives way to reflection, and in any case, our reading of integration might seem to be just as outmoded as recitative in another hundred years.

As discussed earlier, Cinderella stops on the steps of the Palace in the middle of the post-midnight chase and sings 'On the Steps of the Palace'. The song has a tighter link to action than some of the examples discussed earlier, since Cinderella's lyrics articulate her indecision about what to do next, but it is still a moment out of time and an occasion for musical elaboration. In the end she decides to leave the prince a shoe.

In *Figaro* the beautiful duet between the Countess and Susanna, 'Sull'aria' (When the Western Breeze is Dying), offers a similar opportunity for reflection, the extension of time perception and the interruption of momentum. The first verse reflects the dictation of a letter, and the second verse the re-reading of the letter, giving the opportunity for musical ornamentation. The song feeds the action but also allows a breathing space in the action as descriptive passages can do in novels, a time for audiences to take stock while enjoying a moment of empathetic connection to these two characters. Repetitive verses are also a reminder of song form, though, so this song also has the effect of reflexively reminding listeners of the operatic fiction.

The appearance of reflexivity through repetitive verses is much more apparent in *The Mikado* where it is used to comic effect. In fact in the work of Gilbert and Sullivan verse structures are often highlighted by choral interjections of repeated lines or phrases that draw even more attention to the artificiality of song form.

All these examples focus on moments when the development of action is interrupted or delayed for musical elaboration that might allow for character exposition or exploration of a situation. Progress of the plot is deferred while understanding is altered through the insertion of new information that expands and destabilizes meaning. The linear development of plot in spoken or underscored scenes and recitatives contrasts with the deferred quality of repetition and musical elaboration in aria and song. So the crackle of difference between book time and lyric time has been used in slightly different ways in these examples, but in all of them it has contributed to the changes of texture and extension of potential readings of the work.

Musical time and space

Musical space is a conceptual idea, but it relates to different perceptions of time. The harmonic and dynamic structures of music exist within a time and space that is different from, but interacts with, the fictional world of plot and characters and the real world of the audience. Yum-Yum, in *The Mikado*, sings 'The Sun Whose Rays' as described earlier. Its function in the plot is to allow her to reflect on her own beauty before her wedding, but it doesn't move the plot forward. As such it exists in a moment outside book time. This suggests that it is a moment of narrative stasis, but musically it is not static, and for audiences time is passing in enjoyment of the song. The song itself consists of two identical verses, each returning to the musical phrase first presented in the introduction, which gives a sense of peaceful circularity that creates an appropriate reflective atmosphere. But circularity is not necessarily static, for within each verse there is a harmonic direction, a gradual ascent to, and a falling away from, the climax. The harmony modulates from G major, through D major to A minor and back to G, before rising to C major for the climax and returning once again to G major. This accompanies a melodic pattern that gradually rises and falls in a series of waves before arriving at the high point an octave above the starting note and falling back to the same pitch it started on.

The volume of the verse follows the same pattern of slowly rising to the climax and falling back, a pattern reiterated in the second verse. The musical shape of this song consists of two large waves (each verse) that are themselves made up of smaller movements forward and then falling back. So even though the song is a reflective moment out of time in terms of the plot, it can be conceptualized as having a circular harmonic structure and a wave-like pitch and dynamic shape that take the place of the linear movement of the plot. This allows the perception of a moment of stasis, outside the time of the plot, but the song itself remains dynamic in its musical structure. Thus music can occupy an aural space that is sometimes foregrounded, as in this soliloquy. Sometimes the space the music occupies is much more limited and becomes almost entirely subservient to plot and characters, as, for example, in patter songs like Ko-Ko's list song.

There are examples in the act finales of each of these works in which multiple voices are singing, and which exemplify the interaction between musical time and space and book time. At moments of high energy and choral excess, music fills the aural space and surrounds the listeners creating sensations caused by volume and energy and vibration and acoustics. Also at moments of soliloquy, the repetition of words allows attention to shift from lyric and book to musical space, harmonic and dynamic structure and melodic ornamentation.

The Act 1 finale of *The Mikado* contains a series of moments of choral joy and energy. The first of these is the chorus 'Then let the throng'. This joyful, loud and vibrant chorus moves beyond plot to a musical space of high energy before being interrupted by Katisha. The effect of her arrival and interjection is not only to interrupt the singing, but also to draw attention back from the musical expansiveness to the plot. A sequence follows using recitative and choral interjections, before Katisha's aria 'Oh fool, that flee'st my hallow'd joys'. Like Yum-Yum's aria discussed earlier, the narrative exposition extends beyond explanation to a musical, emotional and poetic tour de force. There is still momentum in the musical structure and the force of the emotions, but not in the plot. Here is a moment in which the audience enjoys the sound and poetry before returning to the linear plot.

The finale proceeds with moments of recitative, solo song and choral interjection before the act closes with everyone singing at full volume with full orchestral accompaniment and in conflict with one another. Katisha sings 'My wrongs with vengeance shall be crowned' while the chorus sings 'For joy reigns everywhere around'. The difference between the two sentiments contributes to the heightening of tension as the gaps between the conflicting meanings are revealed. The plot provides the excuse for enjoyment of a purely musical sensation, and the excitement is created not only by the volume and excess of the musical space, but also by the frequent transitions between the time and space of the book and the musical time and space of orchestral and vocal energy. There are always plot and character reasons out of which songs develop, but excess occurs in a fictional musical space.

The Act 2 ensemble finale of *Figaro* contains a similar variety of times and spaces. Plot moments follow each other with great speed interrupted by vocal elaborations in a kind of compressed time as characters express their feelings simultaneously. In the first section of the finale the Count insists that the Countess hands over the key to her dressing room where he believes Cherubino is hiding. The duet between the two continues for over 100 bars of accusation, resistance and submission before he opens the door. No action other than the handing over of the key occurs, but the emotional relationship between the characters constantly alters. Musical and verbal phrases are repeated in an extended moment of musical time and space before, to everyone's surprise, Susanna appears from the dressing room.

A few words from Susanna are followed by a trio: Susanna comments on the Count's vexation, the Countess is overjoyed that it is Susanna who has appeared, the Count expresses his wonder and then decides to search further. So despite the repetitions in the trio, there is a compression of time as three emotions are presented simultaneously. There is also musical excess in the interactions of the vocal lines and musical accompaniment;

the harmonic and orchestral development moves beyond plot to a musical space.

Various other exchanges follow between the three characters that move fluidly between plot development and musical time and space. Then Figaro enters and begins the fabrication that it was he who jumped from the window. Now the interchange is between four characters. When Antonio enters, it continues between five characters. A series of discussions and debates leads to a quartet, 'Se mi salvo de questa tempesta' (If I weather this tempest). All appears resolved when Bartolo, Basilio and Marcellina enter. They sing a trio asking for justice. Another short series of discussions and debates follows before the final tutti section of the finale, which builds in pace and volume as all the characters articulate their own positions repeatedly. The whole finale involves a gradual increase in the complexity of the plot alongside an increase in vocal forces, pace and volume. So while the plot is progressed through a series of events followed by multi-voiced commentary, the musical space can be conceptualized as a gradual increase of voices and pace interrupted by moments of recitative.

Like the Act 1 finale of *The Mikado*, this finale proceeds in a series of sections that moves the plot along briskly, but are then interrupted by choral/tutti emotional statement or commentary. Audiences might read this combination either as musical development with plot events as interruption, or as action and commentary. In either case the end result has textural and acoustic variety. Energy is created through the excess of tutti singing and through interruptions and alterations as the texture, and more importantly for this discussion, the perception of time shifts between the pace of action and the tempo of music.

Showing and telling

In Chapter 1 we introduced the concept of narration – who is speaking and how the story is being told. Genette uses the term diegesis to depict the narration of events, in opposition to mimesis, which is the enactment of events. Clearly, in the musical finales, each performer is enacting the actions of a character – mimesis – but there are moments of narration too. Diegesis can create the sense of a moment out of time, an embedded narrative, or the appearance of a separate imaginary space, but it can also interact with the mimetic or enacted events. This is most obvious in *Into the Woods* which contains a non-singing character, the Narrator, who begins the performance diegetically. In between sung phrases, mimetically represented by other characters, the Narrator introduces characters, scenes and situations with the impression that he exists in a theatrical space close to the real world of the audience; the action he narrates is mimetically enacted by the characters in a more distant fictional space.

Act 2 opens in a similar way, but during scene 2, in the middle of a moment of philosophizing about the predicament of the characters, the Narrator realizes they are looking at him and the narration becomes intrusive. The Narrator speaks directly to the characters for the first time, explaining that he tells the story and is not part of it, that he has been relating the story diegetically. The characters object to the way he has been telling it and the argument itself becomes part of the mimesis. The Witch pushes the Narrator into the Giant's reach and offstage we hear the Giant pick him up and drop him with a thud. The Narrator is dead. Thus the previously separate narrative space and fictional world, diegesis and mimesis, are conflated and the audience is suddenly drawn into a new, closer relationship with the characters.

This is an unusual event in a work that is particularly deconstructive of the theatrical frames, but it demonstrates the ways in which imaginary spaces can be layered. The theatre stage can be both the place where the narrator tells the story, *and* the fictional space where the action is imagined, played or replayed. The barriers between such layers are permeable, and liminal moments occur as they are transected or exposed. Moreover, the offstage imaginary world of the Giant also extends the fictional/mimetic world of the performance. The audience doesn't see the Giant killing the Narrator, but it is implied by the sound of his voice, dialogue between the characters and their responses to events that have disrupted their world. Combining these effects creates a mimetic representation in the audience's imagination. These ideas of voice and narration relate to moments of narrated flashback and we're back at the start of a discussion about anachronism and the playful interruptions of time and space.

Further reading – theoretical

Abbate, Carolyn, (1991) *Unsung Voices: Opera and Musical Narrative in the Nineteenth Century* (Princeton: Princeton University Press).
Barry, Peter, (2002) *Beginning Theory*, second edition (Manchester: Manchester University Press).
McMillin, Scott (2006) *The Musical as Drama* (Princeton: Princeton University Press).

Further reading – relating to the examples

Eden, David and Meinhard Saremba (eds) (2009) *The Cambridge Companion to Gilbert and Sullivan* (Cambridge: Cambridge University Press).

Goodhart, Sandor (ed.) (2000) *Reading Stephen Sondheim* (New York and London: Garland).

Hunter, Mary (2008) *Mozart's Operas: A Companion* (New Haven and London: Yale University Press).

12 'I'm Just a Broadway Baby': Intertextuality in Music and Lyrics

We saw in the first part of this book how musical theatre texts signify for audiences, and in the last chapter we discussed the way understanding relies on relationships. In this chapter we build on that understanding and on your wider awareness of the world – an awareness we all utilize in order to understand the way texts interact. In any performance, since there are so many layers of signification, the layering of potential references can be incredibly complex. In musical theatre the addition of singing voices, dancing bodies and musical accompaniment increases that complexity – and, as we learnt in Chapter 2, each of these layers signifies through its relationship with other experiences. For example, the song 'Broadway Baby' from *Follies* (1971) contains many references to the home of New York's theatre district – Broadway – and to the historical revue the Ziegfeld Follies. Such references, rather than focusing the mind of the audience member on the text being performed, connect the experience of performance to the experience of life as relationships are constantly discovered and rediscovered in the playful interactions of the intertext. This challenges any assumption that texts and their meanings are stable and unified; that all audiences will discover a single meaning generated by the author and communicated to a monolithic audience. This idea of the stability of meaning was challenged in literary theory during the 1960s and 1970s and led to a theory of intertextuality, a term first coined by Julia Kristeva in the 1960s.

The death of the author

Roland Barthes recognized that we tended to understand texts by referring to what the author intended. In an important essay from 1967, 'The Death of the Author', Barthes contested the conventional view that an author defines the meaning of a text. Paradoxically, he suggested that this view actually restricted the possibilities for interpretation. 'To give a text an Author is to impose a limit on that text', he wrote; 'to furnish it with a final signified, to close the writing'. Instead, the possibilities for interpreting a text should be more fluid and open.

Intertextuality suggests that each text and each instance of reading a text is open to interpretation by active, individual and empowered readers. In this chapter we focus on three works that exemplify the idea of a text as a tissue of quotations that blend and clash – *La Cenerentola* (Cinderella) (1817), *Follies* (1971) and *Jerry Springer, The Opera* (2003).

Post-structuralism

As we discovered in Chapter 2, Saussure developed the concept of the linguistic sign in his *Course in General Linguistics* (1915). A word represents an object through an arbitrary system that everyone using the same language accepts. But during the 1960s theorists started to question the idea of language as stable. 'The death of the author' didn't mean that there was no author, but that theorizing how a text works had moved from analysing its production to considering the variability of its interpretation. As we saw in the last chapter Jacques Derrida developed the idea that all meaning is relative; there is no fixed centre, but a free play of ideas that are constantly in motion.

Putting words together in sentences or ideas into stories using grammatical structures combines signs in a 'syntagmatic' axis – so their relationships develop as more words are added to the sentence. The choice of particular words from a selection ('speech' rather than 'talk', 'prattle' or 'recitation') uses a 'paradigmatic' axis that is particularly important for intertextuality since it reveals that meaning also operates through a relationship of difference – 'tree' is not 'tea', 'sea' or 'bee'; nor is it 'bush' or 'shrub'. Words and meanings are produced, therefore, not simply by the operation of signs, but by the relations between combinations of words and their associations within the language. Words are combined within sentences the relations of which produce part of the sense, but those words and sentences are understood further through their relations with objects, processes and experiences in the world. They are also understood in the context of a contemporary moment and in the awareness of what they are not. What all this implies is that the reader does not simply read the text, but *produces* it by deconstructing ideas and interpreting them within their own experience and context.

In reading, you may anticipate that a sentence will take you in one direction. As you are given more information with each successive word, your reading is either confirmed or challenged. Options open up to reveal more possibilities or unexpected imaginings – lots of jokes work by setting up one expectation and then undercutting it in the punch line. This type of comedy plays on the way meaning is constructed in a progressive and open interaction. Barthes (1977, p. 146) is very often quoted (and we quoted him in Chapter 2 too as well) as saying, 'We now know that the text is not a line of words releasing a single "theological" meaning (the "message" of the Author-God) but a multi-dimensional space in which a variety of writings, none of them original, blend and clash. The text is a tissue of quotations drawn from innumerable centres of culture'.

If we apply these ideas to your reading of this chapter we have to consider that the words on the page are ones you understand, they are familiar to you and you have read most of them before. The combination of words and the ideas they generate may be less familiar but they create images and ideas that you can apply in your own way. They will trigger possibilities for how you negotiate the world. Moreover, you may not have begun this book at the beginning, but you might instead be dipping into it, skimming some sections, reading about particular theories or works. Your understanding of this book then becomes something you construct through your interpretation of the symbols and ideas we have placed here. You have an active role in the way meaning is constructed from this text.

La Cenerentola (Cinderella) (1817)

Music by Gioachino Rossini

Libretto by Jacopo Ferretti

Based on Charles Perrault's version of *Cendrillon*

Synopsis: *La Cenerentola* is an operatic version of Cinderella, but since there is no Ur-text (an originating or authorized text) of Cinderella it is necessary to be more precise. Cinderella (whose real name in this version is Angelina) is treated as an unpaid servant by her two stepsisters, Clorinda and Tisbe, daughters of her thoughtless and uncaring stepfather, Don Magnifico, Baron of Montefiascone. Together they live in a rundown mansion and are very short of money. The prince's tutor, Alidoro, visits the house dressed as a beggar, and despite her sisters' wishes, Cinderella gives him bread and something to drink. Her goodness is communicated to the prince, Don Ramiro, who wants to meet her. Don Ramiro and his valet, Dandini, exchange clothes and roles so that the prince has the opportunity to arrive unannounced. He meets and falls in love with Cinderella, while the stepsisters throw themselves at Dandini. All are invited to a ball where the prince will choose a bride, but Cinderella is left behind by her family. Alidoro reveals his real position and arranges for her to go to the ball. At the ball the prince identifies himself to Cinderella when they realize they love one another. Before leaving she gives him one of a pair of bracelets, entreating him to find her. The prince sets out with his men and, after his carriage overturns nearby, returns to Don Magnifico's family home. Cinderella and he are reunited. After their marriage, as apology for his behaviour, Cinderella asks only for her stepfather to acknowledge her, and when he does so the prince and Cinderella forgive him and her stepsisters and all ends happily.

Let's take the title of the opera *La Cenerentola* as an example. If you know Italian you will already be aware of its connection with the fairy story we, in the English-speaking world, call 'Cinderella'. Perhaps you know the story through Perrault's version which you read as a child; maybe you've heard the more bloodthirsty Grimm Brothers' version; perhaps your knowledge derives from the Disney film, or from the adaptation of the story into the film *Pretty Woman*; you might have seen the Rodgers and Hammerstein television musical or its 1997 version, or even the 2013 live Broadway production of that show. There are many different versions of the story – in the Chinese version written down in AD 850–860, Yeh-hsien is befriended by a golden fish and after the wicked stepmother kills and eats the fish, Yeh-hsien is told by an enchanter to hide the bones in her room. They create an enchantment that leads to the happy ending. In this version the heroine has golden shoes and the wicked stepmother and sister are stoned to death (Warner, 1995, pp. 202–203). In the Grimms' *Aschenputtel* it is a hazel sapling on her mother's grave that becomes a powerful wishing tree, and at the end the doves, which have helped Aschenputtel sort lentils and peas from cinders earlier in the story, peck out her wicked sisters' eyes.

These different versions draw attention to the differences between your expectations of the story and the version being described to you. When we described *La Cenerentola* earlier in this chapter, we prioritized the meeting of Cinderella and the beggar who is revealed to be Alidoro, the prince's tutor, not because it is necessarily significant, but because he replaces the fairy godmother who appears in the Disney version. We mentioned the bracelets Cinderella wears and by which she is recognized because they are *not* a glass slipper. Most importantly in *La Cenerentola* the heroine is not assisted through magic but through knowledge and investigation by the tutor and the prince. What this reveals is the way the word 'Cinderella' carries resonances, characters, stories and emotions that are likely to be reasonably common within a culture but are subtly different for each of us. Those differences become apparent when we are made aware of our own expectations.

Let's consider *Follies* in the same way. Think about the word – it might remind you of the Ziegfeld Follies of the early twentieth century, or perhaps the Folies Bergère in Paris. Whichever image you have is based on your personal experience, though we have a shared understanding of the representation of showgirls and perhaps an idea of a grand staircase and a Las Vegas-style costume and head dress. But the word might also denote moments of madness or silliness, which we might also apply to this work given that each of the principals experiences moments of madness and despair during the reunion. A folly is also a small building in a large (probably eighteenth-century) garden that has no particular use, built as

Follies (1971)

Music and lyrics by Stephen Sondheim

Book by James Goldman

Original production directed by Harold Prince and Michael Bennett

Other productions: The show has been continually adapted since the first Broadway production. The first London production (1987) was regarded as slightly softer and more optimistic. New material and songs have been added and replaced in each subsequent production.

Synopsis: *Follies* is set in 1970 at the final reunion of the pre-World War II Weissman Follies before the Weissman theatre is torn down to make way for a parking lot. Attending the event are Phyllis and Sally (erstwhile Follies show-girls) with their husbands, Ben and Buddy. Some of the other ex-performers have cameo moments, many of which have become extremely well-known outside the show, including 'Ah, Paree!' and 'Broadway Baby'. However, the main thrust of the story concerns the two couples whose memories are re-en-acted by their younger selves. The result of their memories of youth is that they realize how shallow and unsatisfactory their marriages have become. Each of them has the opportunity to exorcize their pasts, reliving other loves and paths they didn't take. They become upset or disillusioned as they remember the exuberance and optimism of their younger selves. At the end of the evening they leave, and the audience is left to decide how or whether they rebuild their lives.

a romantic ruin or as the end point of a vista. Perhaps this has a bearing as the derelict theatre is also a romantic ruin and visual point of focus. Certainly, it could feature in some peoples' interpretation of the multiple clashing meanings of the term and may feature in your interpretation of this musical.

Jerry Springer: The Opera reminds us of the television show and the person on whom the work is based. But this title also explores and challenges our understanding of the term 'opera'. This is a work in which the music is in a mix of styles, some of which might be characterized as 'operatic', but operatic styles from different eras and with a mix of popular styles too. The work contains very little dialogue and the tessitura of some of the voices is operatic – but why is it not thought of as an almost through-sung musical like *Rent* or *Les Misérables*? What is the term 'opera' denoting here, and how is it feeding into your individual expectations of the work? Perhaps what it does is to set up expectations that are continuously and playfully deconstructed as the work progresses, first by the coarse language, then by the stories and characters involved in the show. But it may be that the

---

Jerry Springer:The Opera (2003)

Music and lyrics by Richard Thomas and Stewart Lee

Based on the television show *The Jerry Springer Show*

Synopsis: The first act of *Jerry Springer: The Opera* appears to present an episode of the Jerry Springer television show as a stage musical performance. Each of the guests tells his/her story: Dwight is cheating on Peaches with Zandra, and with a transsexual, Tremont. Montel likes to dress as a baby and is cheating on his partner with a girl who likes to dress as Baby Jane. The third guest Shawntel wants to be a stripper, and her husband, Chucky, who doesn't approve, is revealed as a hypocritical strip club patron and a Ku Klux Klan member. In the chaos as the klan mount the stage, Montel is given a gun and he accidentally shoots Jerry. The second act is in purgatory where Jerry meets ghostly replicas of his guests, before discovering that his warm-up man is actually Satan. Satan is asked to spare Jerry's soul, but in exchange Jerry must conduct an episode of his show in hell. Each of the guests appears as a biblical character: Montel is Jesus; Chucky and Shawntel are Adam and Eve; Shawntel's mother Irene is Mary. As the chaos deepens, Jerry prays for a miracle, which is answered as God and the angels appear, asking him to do a show in heaven. As he is suspended between heaven and hell Jerry finally makes an honest statement and is returned to earth. However, he is back in his body, mortally injured by the gun shot, and he dies in the arms of his security guard, Steve.

---

inclusion of Jerry's inner Valkyrie and the fantastical trips to heaven and hell are less unexpected in an opera than a musical. Just by analysing the way our expectations are provoked by the title and the synopsis we can see that our reading is based on what we understand something to be as well as on what it reveals it is not.

Intertextuality

Building on these ideas Julia Kristeva tried to capture the sense of language as something always in the moment of production. Each *utterance* stems from and is filled with all the previous meanings and resonances of the words or signs used within it, as they are perceived by the listener or reader. You might read this book now and find references in it that resonate with you today; but returning to it on another occasion might reveal different resonances, influenced by experiences you have had in the meantime, or new performances you have seen. Rather than perceiving a *work* as a finished and complete object, Kristeva preferred to envisage a continually evolving *text* that is transformed at each moment of articulation and interpretation. She attacked the idea that words or sentences have stable meanings, suggesting instead that an utterance by an individual can be *heteroglossic* (containing clashing meanings that create friction within or between characters or even within sentences, phrases or ideas).

There is a difference in the functioning of language that communicates factual instructions and poetic language. Factual instructions need to be communicated clearly and directly, while poetic language intends that words and images stimulate chains of signifiers and generate multiple associations for the reader, thus opening up interpretation and allowing dialogical possibilities to emerge. Kristeva went even further with her arguments about intertextuality when she related the conscious and the unconscious to these ideas. She argued that the subject (a person) is split between reason and desire, rational and irrational thought and behaviour, and that language is split between communicable, rational ideas and the incommunicable (those ideas and concepts that poetic language seeks to explore).

She developed two more terms – the symbolic and the semiotic (used differently here than in Chapter 2 where they related to the functioning of signs). The symbolic communicates conscious thoughts on a realistic plane, which she referred to in language as the *phenotext*. The semiotic relates to the instinctive drives, the irrational and the poetic which she designated the *genotext*. In the end, she concluded that all language contains both features. Without the ability to communicate clearly, the abstract desires and drives of the semiotic become chaotic, so the semiotic is communicated within the structures of the symbolic, while the symbolic rational thought relies on the semiotic for imagery, passion and effect. A theory of intertextuality exists in the realm of the semiotic *and* the symbolic, just as the combination of phenotext and genotext generate the plurality of meanings within a text and the discourses, ideas and images that derive or spin out from it.

These ideas can be applied to musical theatre by thinking about the difference between scene and song. As we have seen in previous chapters, there has been a debate about whether these are two separate types of communication, and the attempt to make communication consistent between them underpins theories of integration. The scene, or the recitative in opera, contains the action of the plot and communicates in the language of the everyday world, while the song or operatic aria is the opportunity for poetic excess. But it is clear in Kristeva's argument that it cannot be so simple. All language operates through a play of signifiers, so all language has the potential to be dialogical, all dramatic writing can be heteroglossic. A scene can open up intertextual associations as much as a song. In fact Brecht employed this idea by writing internal contradictions for his characters and revealing ideological constructions through his direction of actors, thus deliberately creating a heteroglossic or dialogical text. A song lyric is perhaps more likely to employ a poetic turn of phrase and through its use of musical imagery might focus more fully on the semiotic, but a song still requires a functioning symbolic framework in words, music, voice and genre. The principal difference between speech and song is that sung communication employs mul-tiple languages simultaneously (the melody, the harmony, the words, the voice), enabling more potential for dialogical meanings to emerge from a paradoxical play of signification, in the paradigmatic axis as well as the syntagmatic.

Marvin Carlson (2001) explored many other ways a theatre text can be intertextual in *The Haunted Stage: The Theatre as Memory Machine*. As he notes, 'The relationships between theatre and cultural memory are deep and complex' (p. 2). First a theatre performance attempts to enact a slice of life and so is already to some extent a play with memory, but it uses languages that are endlessly replayed in the ways Kristeva has argued. It employs performers whom audiences may have seen in previous roles, and reinterprets works that audiences have seen in previous productions, stories that they have seen in different media. In Chapter 3 we discussed the importance of pre-performance expectations to understanding genre, and to the ways in which stylistic markers of genre can be recognized. All these rely on the relationship of memory and text, and production teams and authors can choose to activate more or fewer of such associations by the directness with which they draw attention to cultural associations in performances.

In the Houston Grand Opera production of *La Cenerentola* (developed first in Bologna, Italy) Cecilia Bartoli plays the role of Angelina. Bartoli's name is at the top of the advertising, her picture on the cover of the DVD. She is well-known for her interpretations of the coloratura mezzo-soprano roles of Mozart and Handel, Rossini and Puccini, so the inclusion of her name in the publicity, and awareness of her performances in a host of related roles feeds into an audience's reading of this production as they listen to her sing. Moreover the arias have been sung by many other singers and are known through recordings and concert performances in different interpretations. Bartoli's interpretation of these arias is therefore understood in the context of other performances. Thirdly, the image of her first seen in this production is archetypical of productions of Cinderella – she carries a broom, sits at a fireside, her clothes look dowdy in beiges and browns and in an eighteenth-century European style. The wigs and costumes of many characters and servants also refer to fairytale pictures and to Disney versions of Cinderella as well as to actual eighteenth-century dress. The coach that carries the prince is the same construction as those used in British pantomime performances, versions of Rodgers and Hammerstein's *Cinderella* and even ceremonial wedding processions. These three examples, of the performer, the song and the performance design, demonstrate interactions between the work and the wider world, which create a text that is subject to individual interpretation in a complex interplay of ideas and references.

Follies is replete with references to the history of American revues with their grand staircases, lavish costumes and 'Beautiful Girls'. It also offered opportunities for well-known female performers to create roles which resonated for audiences. In the 1971 production Carlotta (who sings 'I'm Still Here') was played by Yvonne de Carlo, a veteran of the vaudeville stage, then a starlet at Paramount and Universal Studios in the 1940s and 1950s before, most famously, playing Lily in *The Munsters* on television.[1] Her presence would have evoked a series of associations for audiences as she sang 'I've gotten through "Hey, lady, aren't you whoozis? Wow! What a looker you were".' Ethel Shutta created the role of Hattie Walker (who sings 'Broadway Baby' in *Follies*). Shutta was 74 years old when she returned to Broadway for this production, at a theatre where she had first performed for the Shuberts in 1922. As Hattie, she sang 'Some day maybe, If I stick it long enough, I can get to strut my stuff working for a nice man like a Ziegfeld or a Weissman.' Audiences roared if they knew that she had actually worked for Florenz Ziegfeld. Other performers in this role have included Elaine Stritch, while Elaine Paige (star of Andrew Lloyd Webber's early musicals) played Carlotta in the 2011 Broadway production, singing 'Good times and bum times, I've seen 'em all and, my dear, I'm still here'. The idea of the Follies star is thus evoked not only through the writing of the work, but also the casting of performers who bring a history that feeds into the way the work interacts with life to create intertextual resonance.

While *Jerry Springer: The Opera* also employed well-known performers, especially in the non-singing role of Jerry, the most comprehensive resonance comes from the references to *The Jerry Springer Show* on television and to the Bible. Particular excitement was generated on the occasions that Jerry Springer attended the show in London as the real and the theatrical were juxtaposed. The set, the costumes and the questions asked of guests on the 'show' were derived from the television show, but the performance of those guests in song altered and extended the melodrama of the television show. Characters from the Bible featured in the second and third acts, creating interactions with the Christian tradition. The spectacle and fantasy were amplified as the design depicted the fiery furnace of hell and the descent of angels in white robes and wings. In the final moments of the show Steve holds Springer in his arms in a Piéta-like image reminiscent of many religious sculptures (see Figure 12.1). Think, for a moment, of the myriad resonances that derive from the use of this image in relation to that television show at this moment in the musical.

However, it was the content of the second half of the show during which Jerry appears in hell and purgatory in interactions with characters from the Bible that led to enormous controversy and attempts to ban the show in the United Kingdom. The first protests began over a television broadcast of the show in 2005 and continued as it toured the country in 2006–2007. The *Christian Voice* regarded the show as blasphemous, but this was rejected repeatedly in several courts of law. Nonetheless protesters (many of whom hadn't seen the show) picketing outside tour venues made life very difficult for the performers. In a sense the scandal offstage mirrored the scandals depicted in the show, but the scandals onstage were ridiculous, outrageous and melodramatic objects for television to glorify. The scandal offstage was a challenge to freedom of speech that, while unsuccessful in the courts, may have had an effect on theatres' subsequent willingness to perform the work. The layers of intertextuality that resonated for audiences at performances resulting from the combination of the onstage references and the

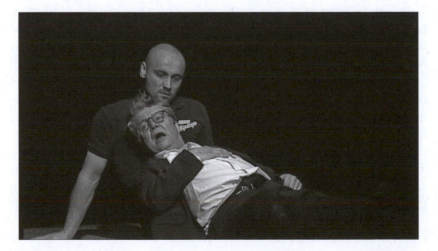

Figure 12.1   David Soul playing Jerry Springer in a pose reminiscent of Michelangelo's *Pieta* in *Jerry Springer the Opera* at the Royal National Theatre (2003). Broadcast on BBC Television, 2005

external events is impossible to imagine. Perhaps this work most fully exemplifies the idea of the text as a tissue of quotations that resonate outwards, and of a text as unstable and dependent on its contexts and relationships for meaning.

Pleasure and bliss

The playfulness of language with its intertextual associations allows readers to perceive multiple meanings within a text. Certain types of language – such as poetry – stimulate a response that is more open to complex or diverse readings, while others – detective fiction– offer less opportunity for an open reading. A detective story, a James Bond film, or an action thriller are all likely to encourage a linear reading based on the cause and effect of 'whodunnit'; these are 'readerly' texts, inviting audiences simply to read what has been prescribed. On the other hand, as discussed earlier, a poem or a modernist novel, or films like *The Matrix* or *Eternal Sunshine of the Spotless Mind* can encourage a dialogical understanding through repeatedly challenging perceptions; these are 'writerly' texts, which invite the audience to contribute to meaning through their different interpretations. Although Kristeva argued that all writing uses language intertextually, the way that a text constructs meaning for its audiences still needs to be questioned. These two (the readerly and the writerly text) are related in Barthes's work to two concepts he introduced in *The Pleasure of the Text* (1975): *plaisir* and *jouissance*. The text of pleasure is that which contents because of the easy understanding for the reader, while the text of *jouissance* is blissful because of the gaps it opens up for the reader to experience the playful interaction of signifiers and to be lost in a state of desire.

La Cenerentola contains a linear narrative. The intertextual associations of the written work relate to the many versions of the story and its adaptation into different media. Then, the intertextual associations of this performance text add to the range of those experiences and images in the interpretation of the viewer. Nonetheless, one might experience it as a 'readerly' text, the sort of text that can deliver an uncomplicated representation for the reader. Cause has an effect; the prince and Cinderella meet, her goodness and his good looks lead them to fall in love, they marry, all live happily ever after. Despite the poetry and excessive vocal ornamentation of the arias that interrupt and elaborate on a moment of emotion or experience, and despite the ghosting of the performance text by the appearance of well-known performers, there is a sense for audiences of a contenting narrative form that has a linear sequence of cause and effect.

This might be Barthes's text of pleasure – and it is not surprising that it is associated with a story that is often seen as a children's fable.

Follies is rather more complicated. The linear narrative of the reunion of the Follies stars provides a basic structure, but the musical offers audiences a potentially more open text to explore. The married couples are ghosted through the evening by the onstage presence of their younger selves so that a complex set of circumstances and experiences emerges that fills in moments of their histories, and simultaneously opens questions about the present. The work as written never establishes with certainty what the outcome of the evening will be for the married couples. The experience of youth and age are juxtaposed so that the marriages of the couples are questioned, but no solution is offered; the dialogical text has opened a gap for audiences to interpret.

But we have discovered another layer that feeds into the reading of this narrative. The presence of older star performers reveals their age and their difference in appearance from previous leading roles. The mutability of time, the decay and evolution of performance, performers and memory are all figured into the narrative and encoded in a performance text which audiences explore as multiple. The relationship between theatrical success, as defined in the song 'I'm Still Here', is rather more nuanced and complicated than the happy ending of many musical theatre love stories. Perhaps what the juxtaposition of cameos of theatre success and marriage success reveals is that longevity in a theatrical career, and singing 'I'm Still Here' at the end, is read into the experience of marriage. Buddy, Ben, Sally and Phyllis are 'still here'.

The aspect of an apparently 'readerly' text that allows meanings to escape from the linear, consecutive order is connotation. There is a story, a series of events that provides a catalyst for Buddy and Ben, Sally and Phyllis to re-evaluate their relationships, but what is revealed for audiences can become the 'writerly' text in which audiences must take an active part in the process of creating meaning. The show within a show, the reflexivity, the continual revisions and adaptations of the work, the narrative of ghostly links between eras opens a space so that the text offers opportunities for audiences to engage with the bliss of intertextual associations and playfulness. And since film imagery is for many the only memory of the actual Ziegfeld Follies, and of some of the stars performing onstage, the work might be described as intermedial (between media) as well as intertextual.

Jerry Springer: The Opera is the most complex of these texts in its narrative structure, since Acts 2 and 3 are retrospectively revealed to be hallucinations, but there is a linear narrative, albeit a chaotic and sometimes indecipherable one. This work is also diverse in its web of signifiers, its tissue of quotations and its deliberate reflexivity and excess. It is almost entirely sung through (only Jerry and Steve speak); all the 'guests' on the 'show' sing, and in doing so reveal themselves to be different from the showmakers who only speak. It is clear that they are different from Jerry and different from the audience; they are onstage, outrageous, excessive and they sing. The chaotic disintegration of the show and its even more bizarre recurrence in hell creates gaps and awkward contradictions or juxtapositions that force audiences to analyse media representations, talk shows and religious iconography.

There are other issues that arise from the context in which this work was performed. It was developed through a theatre fringe system first at Battersea Arts Centre and then at the Edinburgh Fringe Festival before arriving at Britain's Royal National Theatre, a subsidized high-profile venue and the home of British theatre. The theatre has staged revivals of musicals and has a well-developed music department, but this was the first 'opera' it presented. How, then, might the audience understand the idea of opera, and how would their expectations of opera be challenged? The show opens with a chorus of audience members at the television show whose music and vocal range is operatic, but whose language is coarse. This type of challenge to expectations continues throughout the work, and its presence in the home of British theatre is perhaps another example of this deliberate play with expectations. Then there is the question of how audiences might read their own society through the discomfort of the participants at talk shows, the hypocritical values revealed in the characters, and the place of the media in glamorizing pain.

This bizarre combination of characters, performers, references and contexts leaves audiences with a wealth of ideas and images related to the world around them, but no clear sense of what they are to make of them. This is the writerly text that encourages an active, potentially blissful response to the dialogical playfulness of images and ideas.

Finally, Barthes also explored the paradoxical relationship between speech and writing, questioning which has priority, which comes first and which has power. Ultimately, he argues that the *work* is the material object – the book, which offers the potential for interpretation but is fixed in print – while the *text* is the play of signifiers within the work as they are unleashed within reading and interpretation. Bruce Kirle applied these arguments to musical theatre in *Unfinished Show Business* (2005). Musical theatre works, he suggests, are incomplete as written librettos or scores and are transformed in complex and unpredictable ways as they are transferred to the stage in diverse contexts and, importantly, productions. In the process they become performance texts and much more open to interpretation. The performance text operates through the creative teams and performers who realize a new production and the audiences who deconstruct the text as the product of a particular cultural moment and historical context. Thus the performance text is not only an infinitely fluid event from night to night, but also a work revised and recreated by production teams and audiences who are themselves influenced by their historical and cultural background. A spiral is unleashed in which the performance is created for and by the audience and every performance experience adds to the sum of cultural knowledge from which new performances are created.

Many of the arguments about musical theatre focus on whether the text is integrated or not. Integration in musical theatre has been defined in many ways, but implies that songs and dances further the plot. However, as we have discovered in this chapter, intertextuality introduces a way of thinking about a text as unstable, messy, diverse and excessive, such that it relies on the three 'r's; references, relationships and resonance through which audiences playfully interpret the imagery and web of quotations that create meaning for them. Perhaps the text of pleasure most clearly relates to the 'integrated' musical with its linear narrative, and the text of jouissance to those musicals that challenge a linear understanding of narrative; but even this is too simple. Poetic excess requires structure to communicate and vice versa; song and scene each incorporate both of these attributes. So perhaps through the theory of intertextuality we reveal something about the diversity and the potential for dialogical and heteroglossic communication that is inherent in the mixing of theatre and music.

Further reading – theoretical

Allen, Graham (2011) *Intertextuality*, second edition (London and New York: Routledge).
Carlson, Marvin (2001) *The Haunted Stage: The Theatre as Memory Machine* (Ann Arbor: University of Michigan Press).
Kirle, Bruce (2005) *Unfinished Show Business* (Carbondale: Southern Illinois University Press).
McAfee, Noëlle (2004) *Julia Kristeva* (New York and London: Routledge).

Further reading – relating to the examples

Senici, Emanuele (ed.) (2004) *The Cambridge Companion to Rossini* (Cambridge: Cambridge University Press).

Swayne, Stephen (2005) *How Sondheim Found His Sound* (Ann Arbor: University of Michigan Press).

Symonds, Dominic (2007) 'The Resistible Rise of Jerry Springer: How an Opera Revived the Polemical Stage', in Chris Westgate (ed.), *Brecht, Broadway and United States Theater* (Newcastle: Cambridge Scholars), 146–165.

13 'Dreamgirls Will Make You Happy': The Pleasures of Voice and Body

Before mobile phones allowed us to see the name of the person calling us, and choose whether or not to answer, it was possible to answer the telephone and within a word or two identify the speaker (if they were known to us) without them giving their names. The voice and the speaking patterns, the style of articulation, the pitch and tone of individuals are so unique that they become a marker of identity and they make a person identifiable through the combination of voice and speech patterns. That persona can be changed by consciously altering the way we perform our identity, changing our accent, tone or the pitch of our voices to fit into new contexts. But despite any alteration we make in the way we perform our identity, the voice remains somehow distinctive. Former British prime minister Margaret Thatcher was still identifiable by her voice even after she moderated her pitch and tone; US president Barack Obama's measured deliberate articulation is easily recognizable. The voice is produced from the body of the speaker – its physiology and its cultural development – and when we speak we perform our identity and communicate our emotions and desires not only in words but through our voices, which is why both utterances can be understood when we say one thing and mean another.

John Potter extends this idea into the way song reflects the singer; his argument is that the voice not only signals the identity of the person speaking or singing, but also – through its longer phrases, greater pitch and dynamic range, and more energetic reliance on the breath and body of the singer – reveals and communicates much more than identity. It communicates the inner emotion of the singer; indeed we might say it reveals the emotional vulnerability of the performer as much as the eyes (which are often regarded as the windows of the soul). Not surprisingly, audiences develop an attachment to singers and songs, often feeling as though the singer is speaking for them and expressing their emotions. This chapter explores the ways in which we recognize, interpret and are moved by voices, and the way voices signify and embody characters for audiences in specific historical and cultural contexts. The relationships this chapter

explores are those between performers and audiences that become established through the performance of sung character and vocal practice.

Underpinning the way we think about voices in musical theatre and opera
are two theories. One sees the voice as a distinct object that becomes separated from the singer at climactic moments of excessive musicality, while the
second theorizes the voice as inherently soulful and embodied. These theories
of voice are applied to performance, so we begin our discussion by reviewing
the layering of character and performer articulated in performance theory.
These ideas are then applied to two case studies: the opera *Giulio Cesare* (1725)
and the musical *Dreamgirls* (1981), both important works that contain excessively emotional uses of voice in totally different cultural languages.

Performance theory

Richard Schechner's theory of performance, which we encountered in
Chapter 3, derived from his work in ethnography. Schechner realized performance happens not only onstage, but that people perform throughout
their everyday lives. However, he separated those experiences of performing
along a continuum from behaviour in a job or in social circumstances,
through sports performances to performing arts, ritual and trance. Defining
how and when different types of performances occur is (among other
things) the area covered by performance studies.

In performance studies an individual is perceived as performing through
a combination of 'being' (existing), 'doing' (activity) and 'showing doing'
(pointing to what one is doing) (Schechner, 2006, p. 22). Some contemporary
performances such as Happenings, Installations, Durational performances and
Live Art may incorporate 'being' and 'doing', but the types of performance
in musical theatre and narrative theatre more widely are predominantly in
the realm of 'showing doing'. In 'showing doing' there is a consciousness
about the act of performing, about the preparation and rehearsal for that
performance and about the layered state of performance (encompassing performer and character or persona) when the audience is present.

The performer shows the audience the character she has constructed
through rehearsal by re-constructing it in performance, and the singer
demonstrates both practiced technique and rehearsed performance when
singing. To describe this process Schechner coined the term 'restored
behaviour' or 'twice-behaved behaviour'. It applies to actions that have
been rehearsed or prepared, and though it includes many routines or activities undertaken in life, it applies particularly to the preparation for and
presentation of theatre and concert performances.

One of the most important features in any discussion of musical theatre is the negotiation between the actor/singer and the character, especially as the character uses the heightened language of song, and the performer maintains the technical prowess required for singing. This differs from the performance of 'naturalistic' theatre in the sense that the expression is markedly heightened (into song) and the technique is self-conscious. In naturalistic or 'method' acting, the performer is intended to be subsumed into the role to the extent that the audience becomes unaware of the actor as a separate entity. Famous method actors include Marlon Brando and Daniel Day Lewis, but no matter how much they submerge themselves into a character, since the work is rehearsed and prepared, these performers are still using restored behaviour and 'showing doing'; their heightened expression and self-conscious technique are not as pronounced as performers in other forms, but they are still present. There are other moments in a performance, or indeed entire forms of popular entertainment such as stand-up comedy and concert performances, during which the performer is perceived to address the audience directly. Stand-up comedians appear to be 'themselves' (though, as we have seen, one feature of performance theory is that it questions the extent to which each person has a single stable identity); a comedian onstage, then, is also performing an identity or a persona and using restored behaviour.

Bert O. States has categorized three modes to describe these relationships between actors and audiences. In the 'self-expressive mode' the body of the performer in the theatre playing a character is what the audience perceives; the performer, a technically proficient actor, is revealed alongside the character being played. For performers who are simultaneously maintaining their vocal technique and performing character, this may sometimes be the mode of communication.

In the 'collaborative mode' the distance between audience and performer is broken down as the character addresses the audience directly or enfolds them in the world of the performance. This effect is epitomized by the comic aside and the epilogues and prologues of classical drama. It applies, too, to the sung soliloquy, songs which are not directly addressed to the audience as such, but which reveal the inner thoughts of characters to the only people present – the audience. The audience has inner information about the character and is drawn into their worldview – they are enfolded within the character's position.

Third is the 'representational mode' in which the performer is subsumed within the character and the audiences 'look in objectively on a "drama" with a beginning, middle, and end that is "occurring" before our eyes' (States, 1995, p. 35). 'Integration' in musical theatre is the attempt to maintain this representational mode by smoothing the separation of singing and dialogue. It is more likely, however, even in through-sung works, that the representational mode occurs at times for some audience members, but that the mode constantly changes. For example, while Effie describes her attempt to move on with her life in 'I Am Changing' from *Dreamgirls*, the song is also staged as a diegetic performance as shown in Figure 13.1. Audiences look on from outside, empathizing with her pain, hope and determination, in the conflated diegetic and non-diegetic performance. But they can't fail also to be impressed by the beauty of Jennifer Hudson's voice and the remarkable control she exerts over the ornaments, thus moving between the representational and the self-expressive. In addition, the fact that she is singing directly to the audience using the pronoun 'I' suggests collaboration between Effie, Hudson and the audience, thus also drawing in the collaborative mode. In essence, the mode of representation blurs all of the above during this song, though it could be any. Part of the audience's pleasure is that this is open to interpretation, and one of the features of that open interpretation is that the performance of character is the product of a blend of these modes.

These modes co-exist throughout performance, allowing audiences to read its textural density, to perceive the characters through the bodies of the performers. However, when a performer stands on the stage the audience engages with that person's body; the body onstage represents the character being portrayed, but it is also the body of the performer. The more the performer and character seem identical the more there is the appearance of 'iconic identity'. Iconic identity is subverted or challenged (and the self-expressive mode more fully revealed), when, for example, Johnny Depp is playing Sweeney Todd, or Russell Crowe is playing Javert. Simultaneously, the audience is aware of the body of the (star) performer and the body of the character. Whether or not the performer is a star, there are times in a theatre performance when audiences can become more or less aware of these layers of representation, seeing the body sometimes as that of the performer and sometimes that of the character, but mostly moving between and blending these positions. Certain types of performance deliberately draw attention to the discrepancy between the actor and the performer, such as Brechtian epic theatre, which aims to reveal the 'showing doing' or self-expressive mode of the performer. Equally, certain theatrical codes such as cross-dressing fall into this category, since audiences are not drawn so easily into empathetic identity because the *performance* is highlighted.

One of the issues with integration in musical theatre studies is that it's hard to perceive the character in the representational mode when the character breaks into song, even though it remains the body of the performer/

character that is singing. The actor is showing the audience a performance of character, doing a performance of song and being present at the same time. Even in so-called integrated musicals the combined experience of the self-expressive and collaborative modes can be particularly strong, often one of the reasons why some people don't like musicals – the characters who break into song don't seem 'real'. We explore this idea here by looking at some devices that accentuate the experience of 'showing doing' and distancing. Towards the end of the chapter we discuss a particularly repetitive musical form, the da capo aria, that challenges the continuity of integration, but first let us look at cross-dressing and one of its predecessors, the use of castrati in opera.

Giulio Cesare in Egitto (Julius Caesar in Egypt) (1724)

Music by George Frideric Handel

Libretto by Nicola Francesco Haym

Based on an earlier libretto by Giacomo Francesco Bussani

The work is an Opera Seria written for the Royal Academy of Music, London

Production: The performance referred to here is the 2005 Glyndebourne Festival production directed by David McVicar.

Synopsis: The story centres on the consequences of the arrival in Egypt of Caesar, who has just defeated Pompey. Tolomeo and his sister Cleopatra are the joint rulers of Egypt, but also rivals for absolute power. Cleopatra uses her beauty to seduce Caesar, while Tolomeo attempts to seduce Pompey's widow Cornelia. Ultimately, Caesar assists Cleopatra to defeat Tolomeo, and he places her on the throne of Egypt.

The performance of body

Castrati had been used in the Eastern church since the twelfth century, but moved to Western Europe only in the sixteenth century. From then onwards many Italian boys with promising treble voices were castrated and trained for a musical career, especially in the church where women were banned. There was prestige and a safe income to be gained by being such a musician. Monteverdi wrote three small parts for a castrato in *L'Orfeo* (1607), and by the time the comic opera split from the Italian serious opera (about 1700) the castrato vocal range and performance had become so popular that castrati were often used for the juvenile leads, heroes or lovers (Rosselli, 2000, p. 89). The sound of the castrato is difficult to imagine, since the practice of castration became outlawed before recording technology emerged and only one example has been archived. However, accounts suggest that the adult castrato voice, whilst having the range of a soprano, was a unique sound, differing in quality and tone from the female equivalent.

Castrati were much less common in comic opera which relied on 'everyday' situations and commedia character stereotypes. In these perform-ances there was a greater desire for iconic identity between performer and character – audiences were perceived to want to see and hear a body that they could imagine as the character in comic opera, whereas at that time in opera seria it was more important that heroic performances were sig-nalled by the device of astonishing vocal virtuosity. Gradually this would change, so by the latter part of the eighteenth century the preference for iconic identity between performer and character spread even into opera seria; tenors, who had been playing fathers or rulers, began to replace cas-trati as heroes (Rosselli, 2000, p. 92).

In the first performance of *Giulio Cesare* (1724), Caesar was sung by an alto castrato, Senesino, and Cleopatra by the soprano Francesca Cuzzoni, with a second alto castrato playing her brother Tolomeo. Sesto, the son of Pompey, was sung by a soprano, while Nireno, the servant of Cleopatra and Tolomeo, was sung by a third alto castrato. It is difficult to imagine the effect of this selection of voices; musically there would be a particular sound (one that nowadays we could only approximate); but dramatically, the distance between performer and character in some of these perform-ances would have been extreme. Here, qualities of manliness and signifiers of masculinity in the characters of Caesar, Tolomeo, Sesto and Nireno are evidently symbolic – artificial, theatrical and stylized.

The performance and reception of *Giulio Cesare* in 1724 when several roles were sung by castrati was clearly very different from its performance and reception in Glyndebourne's 2005 production, in which Caesar and Sesto were played by women as trouser roles, and Tolomeo and Nireno by counter-tenors. The story is the same, and the vocal ranges are those written by Handel, but the way the audience understood it cannot possibly be the same; the intersections between society and its ideologies have changed to the extent that it would be impossible to guess how one might have responded to the performers and characters in 1724. However, the pres-ence of cross-dressed characters is a constant reminder to a contemporary audience of the theatrical nature of performance – the self-expressive and collaborative modes and the technique of singing are highlighted for audi-ences above a sense of 'reality' in the characterization.

The bodies of Sarah Connolly and Angelika Kirschschlager do not have iconic identity with the roles they play (Caesar and Sesto) so that, however well represented the characters are, there is always a level of distance for audiences between identification with character and performer. That's not to say that the performances are not effective, or that audiences don't identify with the emotions of the performers as well as the beauty of the voices. It is this ability of song to connect audiences to performances even without integration of scene and song or iconic identity between performer and character that is discussed in the later part of the chapter – but first we introduce two theories of voice that might account for the acceptance of these apparently incongruous voices.

The performance of voice

The first idea suggests that at moments of ecstatic climax the voice soars and is perceived to become separate from narrative and singer as a voice object. The second theory suggests that through its articulation in one body and reception through the vibrations in another body, the voice can only be perceived as embodied; that it connects the bodies of listeners and singers.

The first theory uses a psychoanalytic approach to the voice that developed in opera studies. At moments of musical climax the listener is assumed to be so overcome by vocal and musical display, technique, beauty and the ineffable experience of sound that she forgets or loses touch with both present reality and the operatic plot. Michel Poizat has expounded this theory to explain the passion of operagoers and the emotional response they have to musical excess. In this theory the listener's experience is likened to a moment of *jouissance* – a sensual experience of bliss.[1]

In his book *The Angel's Cry* (1992), Poizat describes moments when spectators are moved to tears even when there is no narrative reason for the emotional excess. He describes this as a 'collapse of the visual order' (p. 33) as listeners close their eyes to hear the soaring vocal artistry better. This argument draws us back to the employment of castrati in the seventeenth century, and the relative unimportance of the dramatic action in favour of the soaring power of the voice: opera seria was designed for vocal and visual artistry rather than verisimilitude. It also reminds us of the difference between audiences (who hear) and spectators (who see) discussed in Chapter 3.

This argument as it relates to voice developed from Jacques Lacan after Freud: as a babe in arms we understand the mother's voice, which communicates atmosphere and emotion beyond words. Affective response to the sound of the voice is related to the sense of attachment to the mother as well as to the understanding of the mood and atmosphere it communicates. Since the attachment to the mother is broken at weaning, that attachment is always to some extent an object of desire (an *object a*), a lost object, and something the individual wants to regain. The mother's voice of comfort and the sounds the baby makes are transitional phenomena that help the infant to move from attachment to the mother to separation and the establishing of identity. The need for solace to replace this lost oneness with the mother continues throughout life and can lead to an attachment to other objects. In this case the vocal 'cry' in song is a reminder of that lost attachment to the mother.

Pleasure arises from the attempt to regain the attachment, not from its achievement. The listener's objective is to maintain the relationship with the object of desire – the singing voice – but never to satisfy the desire, as that would remove the pleasure of the continuing attempt to attain oneness. It relates to a continual search for wholeness and a repetitive compulsion towards death. The most important feature of this theoretical concept is that the moments when this sense of *jouissance* or bliss occurs are those climactic points when linguistic meaning is lost to the 'cry' of the voice – that is, the voice of the performer above the voice of the character. This is not to deny the signifying function of the voice and language but to suggest that there are moments of vocal excess that have a further effect on listeners and that can produce emotional effects for the listener even in anticipation. So a listener will seek to revisit emotions achieved as a result of previous experiences in anticipation of similar moments of ecstasy.

Opera Seria

Opera Seria developed at the height of the Baroque period and generally told stories of historical or mythological events accompanied by scenic and vocal extravagance. The baroque combined ornamentation and superficial artifice with a humanist interest in relationships and emotions expressed through rhetorical flourishes and metaphorical poetry. The operas were a combination of dynamic recitativo secco (during which the narrative progressed) and aria (the opportunity for reflection on the emotions engendered by the action). The recitative is at the pitch and pace of speech and accompanied by a continuo player (usually a harpsichord). The player is given only the vocal line and the bass notes, sometimes figured and uses her/his discretion both in the voicing and the timing of the accompaniment. The aria is an extended song accompanied by full orchestra in a notated arrangement often with opportunities for ornamentation or embellishment. The relationship between these two is the equivalent of the change of pace that occurs between speech and song in musical theatre.

The da capo aria

This anticipation of such a climax can be built into the structure of song, and a prominent example from the eighteenth century – the da capo aria – plays on that sense of anticipation in its very form. With an opening A section that forecasts the vocal climaxes that are to come, and a B section that delays their appearance, the aria indulges our emotional connection with the voice before eventually returning to the A.

The da capo aria

Many of the arias of the baroque period used the da capo form. It consists of three stages, ABA: an emotional idea is presented in the first A section; new ideas or thoughts, often contrasting with the A section and in a different key, are presented in a B section; this is followed by a restatement of the A section with elaborate ornamentation improvised by the singer. Dramatically, the B section gives the character a new perspective, so that when he/she sings the reprise of A he/she may be in a new emotional position and so the ornamented and altered reprise has a dramatic function. However, the requirement for repetition of the opening A section has led to a contemporary perception that the da capo aria is essentially undramatic, and opera seria disappeared for almost 200 years before being revived in the twentieth century in historical reconstructions.

'Svegliatevi nel core' (Awaken in my heart) is a da capo aria sung by Sesto in Act 1, scene 4 of Giulio Cesare.[2] Coupled with the fact that it is sung by a woman playing a boy, any pretence to verisimilitude – to the stylistic norms we tend to expect today – is just that: a pretence. In the aria Sesto swears to avenge his father's murder by Tolomeo, who has sent Pompey's head in a box to Cesare as a sign of his loyalty and support. The first A section is fast and furious as Sesto's anger explodes. The voice sings short angular phrases characterized by leaps, with few sustained notes or phrases, while the string accompaniment is agitated and fast moving. The words of the first section are repeated continually, with special attention given to the word 'Svegliatevi' (awaken), whose repetitions are punctuated by agitated string phrases, while the longest and highest notes articulate the word 'traditor' (traitor).

The B section changes the mood completely with long sustained notes and phrases as Sesto remembers his father. The accompaniment is marked by continuo and wind instruments in answering phrases with the strings, and these phrases are lower in pitch and slower than those of the first section. The mood is more reflective and fearful as Sesto attempts to build courage. The A section returns, preceded by its furious introduction. Because of the pace and angularity there is not much room for ornamentation, but some of the vocal lines are altered and the range extended, leading to a final cadenza that expresses Sesto's determination. This is what we have been waiting for. The knowledge that the repeated structure will take us back to the climactic expression we desire is central to the emotional connection we have from the experience.

As noted in Chapter 11, moments of emotional reflection when no physical action takes place are not necessarily musically static, and as Carolyn Abbate and Roger Parker (2012) argue in relation to the ornamentation of repetitive musical structures, 'it was that surplus, the unpredictable and virtuosic addition to something already heard, that lent high drama and suspense to the event' (p. 83). Exponents of the psychological theory of voice would argue that the experience of bliss arises from the technical agility and extended range of the voice as it moves to its climax, and the listening subject's separateness dissolves in the vocal excess. What the audience is listening to is predominantly the self-expressive mode as the performer is 'showing doing' the character through the performance of virtuosity, mixed with the collaborative mode through direct address to the audience.

Reading the aria from a dramatic perspective, though, one might suggest that the introduction of the reflective B section explains the driving force of Sesto's determination; his father, who he remembers with pride and affection, would expect Sesto to extract vengeance. The extension of the voice to its limits affords listeners the experience of jouissance, while the articulation of the relationship with his father in words and music explains Sesto's transition from furious rage to deep-rooted determination. Performer and character are overlaid as the listener enjoys the performer's vocal dexterity *and* the character's exploration of emotion. Even though there is no iconic identity between performer and character, even though the performer is 'showing doing', and even though the musical structure challenges ideas of linear narrative and integration, this theory of voice accounts for why audiences are moved when they hear this song in the opera. That this emotional response can be mapped onto the dramatic, narrative reasoning of the character is an additional attraction, though one which in this idiom becomes secondary to the allure of the voice. The repeated form of the da capo aria, in which we anticipate a return to the vocal excess (and jouissance) of the A section's climax is a structure that indulges our desire; because of the very artificiality of the subject, we are enabled to connect emotionally to song.

Dreamgirls (1981)

Music by Henry Krieger

Book and lyrics by Tom Eyen

Performers: Jennifer Holliday played the part of Effie in the original cast. In the film version Effie was played by Jennifer Hudson

Synopsis: The show records the story of a young black female singing group called 'The Dreams'. The best vocalist, Effie, is replaced as lead singer by a prettier but less able singer, her best friend, Deena. Effie feels betrayed but at first continues with the group and her affair with the manager, Curtis. She becomes increasingly difficult and unpredictable as she suspects that Deena is also having an affair with Curtis. When the group is about to leave to headline at Las Vegas her behaviour is such that she is removed from the group completely. Effie returns to Chicago to bring up her daughter alone. As she moves away from the influence of Curtis and learns to be more professional she achieves individuality and recognition and is finally reunited with her friends just as the group breaks up.

It is not only opera singers who have this effect on audiences; there are similarly distancing musical structures in musical theatre. 'I Am Changing' from *Dreamgirls* is a twentieth-century version of the da capo aria, even if the reprise of the A section is more substantially altered than in the historical form. After the two opening phrases the main theme of the song is introduced: 'I am changing, / tryin' ev'ry way I can.' In the second half of the A section Effie asks for understanding and help in phrases that become more ornamented and higher, but the musical line keeps returning to the chord sequence Cmaj7 C6 beneath the same melodic articulation of the words 'I Am Changing'. By the end of the 19-bar sequence, as Effie sings 'But I need you, I need a hand', the climax of this first section has arrived on her longest, highest sustained note so far (D5) and the music has transposed to A (the key moves subtly between major and minor in jazz-inflected harmonies).

A nine-bar, much more rhythmic and attacking B section, follows as Effie remembers the foolishness of her earlier life and culminates in the repetition of the note E5 in the melody before the phrase descends and the phrase 'I Am Changing' reappears at its usual pitch and harmony. However, unlike the da capo aria, this A1 section is developed harmonically as well as melodically. Half way through the restatement of A there is a modulation up a semitone to D flat. The section is extended to 26 bars and concludes with a spectacular climax that rises to F5 in the written version (higher in some interpretations). The final vocal note is a long sustained full belt on D flat5 unaccompanied at first before being completed by the orchestra in a rising optimistic phrase.

The psychological theory of voice suggests that the da capo aria can be enormously dramatic but that attention focuses on the performance of voice at climactic moments, even while the sentiments expressed are a forceful restatement of determination. When listening to these songs we are aware of the vocal excess of ornamentation, and read the performer/character's emotion as expressed through it. But what of the second theory of voice?

The performance of voice and body

Roland Barthes's (1977) article 'The Grain of the Voice' has been fundamental in the development of the idea of voice as embodied. A voice has a quality that is expressive of the body that produced it through the cultural and technical production of timbre and the physical creation of resonance and is therefore always individual. Two ideas have been developed from his theorizing. One is that a voice reveals its cultural background to the listener, a sentiment revealed in the often quoted phrase 'The "grain" is that: the materiality of the body speaking its mother tongue' (p. 182). A singer may sing in many musical genres and alter the vocal production so that the delivery of that genre is appropriate within context, but the listener very often recognizes the voice of a familiar singer or speaker and often the cultural background and training of the singer too. To some extent this idea is challenged in speech by comic impressionists and tribute artists, but for singers there is usually some sort of vocal fingerprint within a performance that identifies their sound.

The second idea is that even when the body of the speaker or singer is not visible the listener perceives an imagined body. In describing the voice of a Russian cantor, Barthes suggests,

> the voice is not personal: it expresses nothing of the cantor, of his soul; it is not original (all Russian cantors have roughly the same voice), and at the same time it is individual: it has us hear a body which has no civil identity, no 'personality', but which is nevertheless a separate body.

Steven Connor has extended the debate to discuss the disembodied voices of ventriloquists, telephones and recording technologies. He argues that all these voices are perceived to have an imaginary *vocalic* body whose sinews and muscles produce sounds and emotions that are understood and felt by the listener. In film theory, the separation of the audio track from the visual has further been explored using the idea of castration anxiety (stemming from Freud), thereby conceptualizing the voice as free-floating but desperate to return to its corporeal source (see Joe, 2013).

Wayne Koestenbaum uses queer theory to extend this relationship of voice and body by proposing that the voice of the singer, through its vibrations, enters into the listener's body. The singer's voice (or indeed the amplification or recording device that recreates the sound) produces sound waves that are transmitted through the air. These are picked up as vibrations in the inner ear. The signals are transmitted to the brain and converted back into sounds. There is always, therefore, an argument that sound is actually perceived as embodied within the listener. With louder sounds this effect is amplified; we all have the experience of rock concerts that are felt as physical vibrations in the listening body. Thus the listener, rather than desiring an absent object, experiences the sensations of the character through the vibrations of the voice of the singer within her own inner ear, within her nervous system, within her body.

What is astonishing about the way Jennifer Hudson performs 'And I Am Telling You I'm Not Going' (Figure 13.1) in the film version of *Dreamgirls* (and even more astonishing in the performance by Jennifer Holliday available on YouTube from the Tony Awards ceremony in 1982)[3] is the way in which she sings within the genre of African American soul and gospel but complements that with harsh, shouted or growled vocal timbres. The context is that she has been replaced in the singing group, and her anger, despair and frustration bubble up to transform the gospel/soul vocal sounds into expressions of deep-felt emotion. The soul growls become the excessive growls of the character's rage, the gospel shouts transform into desperate articulations of pain and hurt. Holliday's performance extends the understanding of this musical genre by exceeding the restrictions of genre, while using the techniques and patterns of its excessively ornamented style – we hear Holliday or Hudson performing Effie through these ornamental excesses that occur predominantly in the repeated section of the da capo form. But interestingly the emotional excess is most extreme during the stage show – this can be seen by comparing the film or show version with a concert performance of the same song by the same singer.[4] The emotional excess of character and drama are replaced by a more controlled expressivity that suits the situation. What can be perceived in this performance is the normative framework of gospel/soul ornamentation and timbre alongside the transgressive excess of the overlaid emotion of

Figure 13.1   Jennifer Hudson as Effie sings 'And I Am Telling You' from *Dreamgirls* **(2006). Dreamworks**

the performance of character. But the emotion is not separate from the vocal performance and is embodied in a formal musical structure often regarded as distancing and undramatic. The demonstration of petulance, tenderness, anger and sobbing all feed into the expression of character at a dramatic moment, even as the moment of climax causes an emotional complicity in the body of the listener. In this musical genre this type of excessive display is appropriate, and the technical production of vocal excess reveals the 'showing doing' of character, which is not present in the concert performances, and causes affect through the self-expressive and collaborative modes. The embodied voice is perceived as having a direct effect on the listener through the physical response to the vocal vibrations produced by the performer especially at the climactic moments.

'Se Pietà di me non senti' (If you feel no pity for me) is sung by Cleopatra in Act 2, scene 8 of *Giulio Cesare*.[5] Cleopatra has been flirting with Cesare and leading him on so that she will be favoured and win the throne over her brother Tolomeo, but when Cesare rushes out to fight her brother she realizes she loves him. After a short recitative she sings the A section, 'Se Pietà di me non senti, / giusto ciel, io morirò' (If you feel no pity for me / Just heaven, I will die), followed by a B section, 'Tu da pace a' miei tormenti, / o quest'alma spirerò' (Grant me peace from my torment / Or this soul will expire). The whole song takes nine minutes,[6] during which the singer explores the depth of her feelings for Cesare using only these few words. This performance is aesthetically different from the performance of lost love in *Dreamgirls* as it conforms to the genre conventions of opera. Nonetheless the performer expresses the emotions of the character through voice and music, through the extended range of the voice, through variations in tone colour and dynamic expression, and with the involvement of breath patterns and phrasing. The 'showing doing' here requires a completely different style of performance because of the cultural expectations of the genre, but nonetheless leads audiences to an emotional climax, if by very different means.

What we have, then, are two explanations for the extreme feelings generated by experiencing climactic vocal moments in musical theatre and opera even when sung by cross-dressed characters and using the da capo form. One theory suggests that excessive emotions are the result of a Freudian-inspired sense of separation from the mother and derive from the experience of loss. The other suggests that these same emotions result from the feeling of the performer's voice/body in the body of the listener. When this is overlaid with an awareness of the authenticity required by different genres of performance, and the layers of 'being', 'doing' and 'showing doing' in the performance the whole performance becomes ever more complex. It is not surprising, therefore, that there is no agreement on how audiences experience sung performance, though some neuroscientific explanations for audience responses are proposed in Chapter 14. However, just as it is possible to understand when someone says something and means something else, we can interpret these layers of performance, recognizing singer, song, interpretation and character through the vocal expression of words and melody and the theories of performance studies. We, as listeners, are expert at blending all these layers of performance and enjoying the climactic emotional excesses they produce even when they are theatrical rather than realistic. What these arguments give us is a sense of the scale and complexity of the emotional impact that can be encountered as a result of being in the audience at performances of musical theatre or opera, and an awareness of how they might be theorized in contemporary discourse.

Further reading – theoretical

Barthes, Roland (1977) 'The Grain of the Voice', in *Image, Music, Text* (London: Fontana Press), 179–190.

Morris, Mitchell and Raymond Knapp (2011) 'Singing', in Raymond Knapp, Mitchell Morris and Stacy Wolf (eds), *The Oxford Handbook of the American Musical* (Oxford and New York: Oxford University Press), 320–334.

Poizat, Michel (1992) *The Angel's Cry: Beyond the Pleasure Principle in Opera*, trans. Arthur Denner (Ithaca and London: Cornell University Press).

Further reading – relating to the examples

Dean, Winton and John Merrill Knapp (1995) *Handel's Operas 1704–26* (Oxford: Clarendon Press).

Dinero, Dan (2012) 'A Big Black Lady Stops the Show: Black Women, Performances of Excess and the Power of Saying No', *Studies in Musical Theatre* 6(1): 29–41.

Hadlock, Heather (2000) 'The Career of Cherubino, or the Trouser Role Grows Up', in Mary Ann Smart (ed.), *Siren Songs* (Princeton and Oxford: Princeton University Press), 67–92.

Woll, Allen (1989) 'Epilogue: Into the 1980s', in *Black Musical Theatre: From* Coontown *to* Dreamgirls (Baton Rouge: Louisiana State University Press), 274–278.

14 'Make 'em Laugh': The Politics of Entertainment

The greatest challenge for performers and practitioners of musical theatre is to entertain, and on Broadway and in the West End, to entertain an audience of theatregoing tourists from all over the world. Although the audience for musical theatre is predominantly a white, middle-aged, middle-class audience with a preponderance of women and gay men, musical theatre performances entertain across a wide constituency. But what do we mean when we speak about entertainment? Different audiences have been entertained by different things at different times in history. So 'the clown, with his pants falling down' may work for one audience, while 'the dance that's a dream of romance, Or the scene where the villain is mean' may be much more successful in another time and place. Expectation plays a part in entertainment as audiences choose to go to a particular type of show based on pre-performance information, and are more likely to understand the show and be entertained by it if they understand its genre and it meets their expectations. 'The plot can be hot, simply teeming with sex / A gay divorcee who is after her "ex". / It can be Oedipus Rex / where a chap kills his father and causes a lot of bother.' The point is that entertainment can be derived from lots of theatrical forms, so how is it possible to categorize or theorize entertainment?

Well, we can begin by analysing the word: 'entertainment' derives from the French 'entretenir' – to draw in. So one of the ways we can think about entertainment is to analyse how it draws its audience in; how it engages and speaks to its audiences. But the French have another word for entertainment: 'divertissement.' A divertissement is an entertainment that diverts, that turns one's mind away, perhaps it helps one escape from the pressing concerns of life. We might wonder whether these are really so different – doesn't drawing an audience into a plot also divert them from their cares? Perhaps the difference can be seen in comparing two examples. The first might be 'Some great Shakespearean scene / Where a ghost and a prince meet and everyone ends in mincemeat': a scene in which there is empathy for characters and a plot with a climax and tragic denouement – the entertainment of narrative. The second might be 'The clown with his pants falling down', a spectacle causing laughter and diversion, though not empathy and engagement. It might divert you but not draw you in.

Musical theatre is almost uniquely equipped both to entertain and to divert through its combination of narrative, song, dance and spectacle. As we suggested in Chapter 3, 'no theatre form is as single-mindedly devoted to producing pleasure, inspiring spectators to tap their feet, sing along, or otherwise be carried away' (Savran, 2004, p. 216). The politics of pleasure in musical theatre arises from its capacity to draw you into a story that can make you laugh or cry, can remind you of real world politics or help you escape from it, and it can offer you the spectacle of a chorus line, moving barricades, or a dream ballet alongside the aural pleasure of solo voices that are determined, vulnerable, hopeful or desperate and choral voices whose volume and textual intricacy is felt viscerally. Curiously, the notion of entertainment in musical theatre hasn't been discussed much at all until very recently.

This historical oversight is in one sense the result of a certain academic elitism. Musical theatre, popular theatre and the commercial industries were less studied than the avant garde for a large part of the twentieth century, and when popular forms were studied they were studied from the perspective of their economic or commercial impact, relying on ideas of mass culture derived from Marxist theories of capitalism. It is only very recently that musical theatre has found its own place in academic studies, and only rarely within that body of work has its function as entertainment been analysed. Music, the culture industry and musical film have a much longer theoretical history – much of which is derived from German intellectual Theodor Adorno's critique of capitalism – so that's where we begin.

Theodor Adorno and the culture industry

As has been reiterated throughout this book, ideas derive from their contexts, so we have to read the ideas Theodor Adorno proposed as deriving from a particular time and place – Germany before, during and after World War II. His critique of capitalism has a particular poignancy when viewed in light of the extraordinary inflation and poverty during the Weimar Republic and the rise of a modernist avant garde in theatre and music. His thinking continues to challenge and unsettle because he suspects popular culture and popular products of having harmful effects. And in many cases when you examine the workings of the contemporary marketplace, he is right.

Theodor Adorno developed theories of contemporary popular culture based on Marx's analysis of capitalism and he used the terms 'the culture industry' and 'mass culture' to demonstrate his understanding that works exist within an industrialized and economic framework. The term 'mass'

of course derives from a Marxist understanding of the people as an undif-
ferentiated 'mass' rather than a group of individuals, and a working-class
group which exists in a binary opposition with the 'elite'.

Adorno argued that the culture industry produced and circulated commodities through the mass media, and through those commodities, the
culture industry manipulated the population. As we saw in Chapter 4, the
amusement products of the culture industry were designed to cause sensations in the recipient, to offer momentary escape from the daily grind of
an industrialized society and to insulate the individual from awareness of
how society could be different. Adorno believed that the result of these
moments of escapism was that any resistance to the capitalist industrial
machine was destroyed and so he argued that the pleasure produced as
a result of escapist entertainments was linked with the continuing help-
lessness of the masses. In this way Adorno identified popular culture as
a reason why people become passive; he argued that the easy pleasures
available through the consumption of popular culture make people docile
and content, no matter how terrible their economic circumstances.

His analysis of popular forms focused on their structures rather than
their contents, which he suggested were repetitive and formulaic; and
many were. Popular song forms such as AABA meant that audiences understood the genre, anticipated the structure and identified the song title or
key theme on first listening. Songs in this format were sold as records, sheet
music and played on the radio in the 1930s and 1940s, a fact that Adorno
interpreted as demonstrating a very high level of *market predictability* which
meant that buyers knew what they were getting and felt secure. The superficial differences between individual songs made them appear different, but
they were all, in fact, just variations on the same theme. Adorno conceptualized this phenomenon as *pseudo-individualization* and the *always-the-
same*. We might think about much contemporary popular music in the
same way. Many rap songs have very similar messages, sounds, timbres
and structures. The differences between them mean that consumers feel
that they need to buy each new song, though Adorno suggested that this
was simply the consequence of the culture industry marketing very similar
products very successfully.

The same argument can be made about musical theatre shows. Over
recent years audiences have been attracted to a whole series of jukebox
musicals and film adaptations. The presentation of the work on the stage
appears to be something different, but, if we follow Adorno's argument
we would agree that producers are simply building on audience familiarity
with the basic materials and generating a new market for something that
is familiar enough to appeal but which appears to be different. As we saw

in Chapter 6, jukebox musicals do this by remarketing a back catalogue as a new show with attached merchandizing opportunities, and very often repackaging that as a film. Adorno suggested that by creating something similar and encouraging the desire to consume it the culture industry cultivates false needs; that is, the industry creates needs so that it can satisfy them and continue to increase its market. True needs, in contrast, are freedom, creativity and genuine happiness. The problem with capitalism, he said, was that it blurred the line between false and true needs altogether.

Another theorist, Walter Benjamin, who was also part of the Frankfurt School, wrote a famous essay 'The Work of Art in the Age of Mechanical Reproduction'. He was addressing the distinction between a unique work of art (an original painting) and a work that is designed for mass reproduction (a postcard of the work of art – or a birthday card design). He argued that the work designed for mass reproduction has a good effect in that it democratizes works of art – making them available to the majority rather than the minority of people – but that as a result the work loses what he called its 'aura'. The work loses its history and context and becomes an everyday object with a new meaning and aesthetic value. Benjamin proposed that objects of popular culture needed greater consideration, especially given that they were available to a much greater proportion of the population.

It is this theoretical framework that underpinned the more recent scholar Richard Dyer's theory of entertainment. Dyer's essay 'Entertainment and Utopia' argues (after Adorno) that entertainment needs are created by capitalism so that the capitalist market can fulfil them. His additional step (after Benjamin) is to propose that by analysing the structure of works of entertainment we can identify the false needs and the structures of society. From his analysis of film musicals he identifies five categories that entertainment provides in film musicals: energy, abundance, intensity, transparency and community. Together these offer a utopian solution to the ills of society.

In *Guys and Dolls* energy is seen particularly in the spectacular song and dance numbers such as those in Havana and at the crap game in the sewer. Abundance can be seen in the numbers of people singing and dancing, as gamblers, in the Hot Box club and in the mission, and in the high stakes games being played. The intensity of emotions is apparent in the two love stories, where love is repeatedly denied and reconfirmed. Transparency refers to the quality of representation; since *Guys and Dolls* is often regarded as an 'integrated musical' transparency relates to the way songs and dances progress the narrative and evoke the relationships. Finally, community is revealed among the gamblers, hot box girls, Salvation Army officers and between each of these groups as, ultimately, they are joined in helping each other and forming marital bonds. So according to Dyer's framework, *Guys*

Guys and Dolls (1950)

Music and lyrics by Frank Loesser

Book by Jo Swerling and Abe Burrows

Based on the characters and plots of short stories by Damon Runyon

Synopsis: The 'Save-A-Soul' Mission is located in downtown New York City where gangsters and gamblers ply their trades. The area is also home to the Hot Box dance hall where Adelaide, the victim of a psychosomatic cold, resulting from her 14-year engagement to Nathan Detroit, works. Sarah the 'mission doll' attracts the attention of the high roller Sky Masterson, who bets Nathan he can take her on a date. To persuade her to go, Sky promises he will bring 12 'genuine sinners' to the mission if Sarah will go on a date with him. At first she refuses, but when it becomes clear that the mission will be closed unless she can improve its success, she agrees. However, while Sarah and Sky are on their date (in Havana) the gamblers use the mission to hold a crap game. Despite Sarah and Sky having declared their love for each other on the date, she is incensed when she discovers that the gamblers have used the mission for their game; she blames Sky, thinking the date was only a ploy to get her out of the way. However, as promised, Sky brings the gamblers to the meeting, by winning their souls in another game. The gamblers attend the meeting and the mission is saved. Ultimately all is forgiven, Adelaide and Sarah decide to 'Marry the man today, and change his ways tomorrow' and perhaps they all live happily ever after.

---

and Dolls functions as entertainment for a capitalist society by providing a utopia that eradicates (for the time of performance) society's needs, but which reveals the lack of these features in society.

Of course, it is not so simple. The community of *Guys and Dolls* is formed of outsiders who break the law, lie and cheat, manipulate and threaten violence – though all in a comical way. The weddings between members of different community groups reveal the development of cross-community interactions – perhaps a precursor of our contemporary multicultural society – but the chances of those marriages lasting beyond the happy ending of the musical are limited given the circumstances and the prejudices that have been revealed during the musical. The energy and abundance, the Technicolor of the film version and the song and dance of the show are also problematic. They glamourize moments of manipulation, gambling addiction and potential violence. Since the 1980s theorists have realized that this type of analysis of plot and structure tells only part of the story about how entertainment functions. New theories have arisen that move the focus away from the structure of the work and onto the ways in which audiences are affected by performances.

Entertainment and Utopia

At the very start of her book *Utopia in Performance* Jill Dolan (2005, p. 2) argues that 'live performance provides a place where people come together, embodied and passionate, to share experiences of meaning making and imagination that can describe or capture fleeting intimations of a better world'. The examples she uses to make her case are not popular or musical; nonetheless, let's apply her ideas to musical theatre performances.

The utopia that Dolan outlines is something that is always in process. It is always slightly out of reach, even if we occasionally sense it in a momentary experience, yet it appears to be as powerfully real as the 'concrete fantasy' of our hopes and dreams (p. 7). Such momentary experiences within performance 'exceed the content of a play or performance' (p. 8), and it is in this sense that we are using the term excess, as something that is beyond what might be anticipated and that lifts us into a moment of illumination that is always ephemeral and evanescent.

A simple example might help. *A Chorus Line* (2013) opens as an audition takes place, dancers rehearsing to a piano in the background. Then suddenly, the director calls, '5, 6, 7, 8' and the brass bursts into sound; for just a moment one's breath is taken away by the extraordinary lift caused by the changed timbre of the orchestra. There have been many other such moments in many performance experiences, but that simple explosion from the 'monochrome' of piano to the 'Technicolor' of orchestra is one of the momentary excesses that stands out as utopian.

Humanity and theatre

Beginning around 1980 new theories were being developed (from Germany) that explored performance as an event or an experience. Erika Fischer-Lichte promoted the 'enchantment' of theatre (this was similar to the ideas of defamiliarization or alienation Brecht had proposed) and espoused the view that 'art exists that one may recover the sensation of life; it exists to make one feel things, to make the stone *stony*' (Shklovsky in Fischer-Lichte, 2008, p. 7). The important step Fischer-Lichte takes in her book *The Transformative Power of Performance* is to think of an event as an experience which causes us to rethink ourselves, our world and our lives.

Like Fischer-Lichte, Jill Dolan (2005) resists the attempt to find images of a better world in the narratives of a show, though they may be present. Instead she focuses on the way audiences respond to performances and the 'utopian performatives' that occur in their reception. Utopias are discovered in moments that lift everyone slightly above the present; they are 'emotionally voluminous, generous, aesthetically striking, and intersubjectively intense' (p. 5). Such moments spring from a 'complex alchemy of form and content, context and location...as process, as never finished gestures' (p. 8). Like Fischer-Lichte, Dolan links the idea of utopian performatives to a Brechtian notion, but in her case it is the notion of Gestus. The moments of insight that occur in the gaps between the narrative and the performance can cause transformations and are thus performative on the spectator. These are the moments she sees as utopian because they have the potential to inspire new understanding and insight. But how does this apply to musical theatre?

Humanity in musical theatre

There are many forms of storytelling that allow audiences to become aware of their own humanity, their vulnerability and their fortune. The two functions of storytelling (according to Jack Zipes in his introduction to Mike Wilson's book *Storytelling and Theatre*) are to communicate relevant values and norms, and to question, change and overthrow those norms. Clearly there is a tension between conservation and transformation, but it is a tension that exists in people's lives. The stories of musical theatre – perhaps because it remains a commercial form of theatre, dependent on popularity for its continued presence – speak about people and their relationships in contemporary settings. A loose generalization suggests a move in the early twentieth century towards stories about aspirational characters from ordinary backgrounds who achieve their goal of marriage and live happily ever after. And as with storytelling, we have to read the 'happy ever after' wedding as allegorical, offering hope of transformation in the same way that journeys through the woods reveal something about transition and moving forward to a new stage of life.

As we saw earlier, even as it subverts several fairy stories, *Into the Woods* relies on our knowledge of them, and a contemporary morality is revealed through the journeying, about honesty, self-reliance and courage. Each time you see a performance of the same show (each time you go back into the woods), you learn something about where you are in your life. So we're suggesting that the heteronormative ending of, for example, *Guys and Dolls* derives from a particular time and place (1950s America) and speaks in a language that will be popular with its audiences. What its narrative mythology reveals, however, is a process of assimilation of diverse communities (the guys and dolls, or the missionaries, the dancers and the gamblers) and their representatives (Sarah and Sky, Adelaide and Nathan) through marriage at a time when immigration was high. Its morality reminds us of the need to be open to other ways of life and not to fear difference, while its mythology encourages us to embrace what frightens us (Sarah engaging with the gamblers and going on the date, the gamblers joining in with the mission meeting, Nathan marrying Adelaide and settling down). Ultimately these characters move forward through difficult times, to embrace transition and transformation as productive, and so encourage audiences to do the same at whatever time of our lives it occurs.

We could read any number of musical theatre narratives in this way, highlighting the mythology and the morality that can be discovered within them. And so the narratives, building on the fairy story analyses of Zipes and Marina Warner, provide examples of life-changing moments or crises, journeys and resolutions. The characters go through these situations and as we empathize with them we rehearse those moments of transformation in preparation for risk-taking in our own lives.

Imago (2013)

Music by Orlando Gough

Lyrics by Stephen Plaice

Production: A community opera developed at Glyndebourne Opera House in the United Kingdom, it involved professional soloists and an amateur chorus and a mixed orchestra of amateurs and professionals

Synopsis: Elizabeth, elderly, bed-bound and isolated in a geriatric ward is given a headset – like wrap-around glasses – so that she can operate an avatar (or Imago) in a technological world (similar to Second Life). The idea is that she will be able to relive her youth and resolve any issues before she dies. The two worlds – real and cyberspace, infect each other so that the avatars, who begin as an outward extension of their creators, gradually take on a seeming independence. The result is that through her avatar, Lisette, Elizabeth is able to reclaim the joy of her youth and dies in a kind of blissfully transcendent experience of youth and love.

Imago, as the programme notes remind us, records a journey we will all take as we leave this life; it's an experience in which none of us is expert but all of us will share. It is the experience of being human, and the opera allows us to rehearse it vicariously. But the work is by no means serious or heavy. Alongside the transcendent and blissful there are playful popular references, electronic sounds and an *a cappella* wedding chorus. The experience of the voices and instruments creates moments of blissful excess through moments of pleasure and pain. Examples include the fun of the *a cappella* wedding, the transcendent music of the death scene and the extraordinary technology of the design that allowed Lisette to appear in several places at once in an excess of presence. These three – humanity, community and excess – and the ways in which musical theatre reminds us of their presence in our lives, are what produce 'affect' in audiences – they produce sensations and emotions that remind us of what it means to be alive. A moment of scenic excess can be seen in Figure 14.1.

Such stories act at a deeper level than the intellect, though. Although the word *empathy* was not coined until later, Aristotle described its effects in his *Poetics*. He explained how feeling pity encourages audiences to recognize what is decent and morally right in society – what is humane. And this awareness allows us to realize what is precious to us. Tragedy is about central and indispensable human attributes, disclosed to us by the pity that draws us toward characters and the fear that makes us recoil from what threatens them. It is the particular and the personal associations we make with the character that engages us, and our feelings of attachment allow us to recognize what is important to us. So when a character with whom we feel empathy is hurt or killed it feels as though a part of us is also hurt. Aristotle used the word *catharsis* in his definition of tragedy (Chapter VI of *Poetics*). He suggested that by experiencing the powerful feelings of

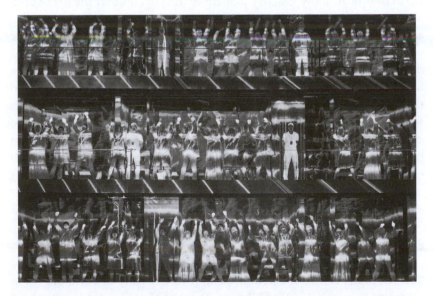

Figure 14.1   The community opera *Imago* performed at Glyndebourne Opera House (2013). Photo: Robert Workman. Courtesy of Glyndebourne Productions Ltd

the characters audience members can purge their own emotions, releasing tensions in their own minds and bodies and achieving a feeling of calm after the event.

For the time of performance audiences can feel for and with another person, experiencing emotions and situations beyond the range of their everyday lives, which allows them to rehearse extreme emotions, and to empathize with unexpected or unknown people. And so we achieve an emotional understanding of the complexity of human experience that we can apply to encounters throughout our lives. One example of a show whose structure enables a significant emotional connection in its audience is Stephen Sondheim and George Furth's *Merrily We Roll Along* (1981) which is played out in reverse. Audiences meet the characters when they are jaded, bitter and disillusioned, but by the end of the show grow to know them as the excited, optimistic young hopefuls of their youth.

In the opening scene – which is at the end of their relationships – Mary is asked what she does, and her reply is: 'I drink.' During the opening number the chorus sings 'How can you get so far off the track? / Why don't you turn around and go back?' Gradually the show enables them to do this, taking the three protagonists back to their meeting on the roof as they sing of their hopes and aspirations. 'Don't you know? / We're the movers and we're the shapers, / we're the names in tomorrow's papers. / Up to us now to show 'em.' For audiences the effect is that the joy of optimistic moments is always tinged with awareness of how the show started and how the relationships will end. So even as the audience feels the youthful optimism of 'Something [...] stirring, shifting ground [...] just begun', they empathize with both the optimism of the now and move beyond the characters' emotions in the awareness of the disintegration they have seen in the course of this show. What the show reveals is the human condition with its cycles of optimism and desperation, hope and cynicism, but most of all, its unexpected transformations and its lost human potential. And yet because of the reverse structure the show ends on a paradoxically optimistic note with an instruction for living – 'hang on to your dreams'.

Empathy

Robert Vischer coined the term *Einfühlung* in Germany in 1873, but it was Theodor Lipps who developed the idea that people understand each others' mental states through a natural instinct based on inner imitation. The term was translated back to English as empathy in 1909 by Edward Tichenor.

Lipps's theory has now been eclipsed by subsequent developments in cognitive neuroscience and the technology of the FMRI (functional magnetic resonance imaging) scanner, but it provides the basis for understanding the interaction of body and mind in empathy that neuroscience has extended. Cognitive theory and music psychology have now provided scientific explanations for the ways audiences embody the experience of living another life while watching a performance.

The basic premise is that humans learn by imitating; first by imitating their mothers, and later by imitating teachers, peers and idols, but a basic feature of skills acquisition is observation and mimicry. Mimicry results from the activation of the mirror-neuron system which humans use to conform to culturally accepted or expected behaviour: children use similar gestures and facial signals to their parents; they dress and behave in accordance with their peer group at school and university; and we learn new patterns of behaviour again in the worlds of work and as we travel. These systems are activated in the theatre too.

Scientists, analysing how this system works, discovered that the brain of a person watching a dancer lit up in almost the same way that the dancer's own brain was activated while dancing. Similarly, the brain of someone listening to a song is activated almost as though they were actually singing. The brain of an audience member at a musical is therefore being activated by observing dance, by the gestures and emotions of acting and singing and by listening to the intellectual communication of narrative and song. Those audience members are not simply using their intelligence to understand the consequences of the events in the plot, but they are recreating the experiences of the characters in their own minds and bodies. Since brain and body are connected, autonomic and somatic responses are triggered and the observer actually experiences the actions and feels the emotions of the performers and can become passionately connected to song, dance and characters. More importantly, 'music has a unique ability to trigger memories, awaken emotions and to intensify our social experiences' (Molnar-Szakacs and Overy quoted in Taylor, 2012, p. 140).

Thus theatre allows audiences to experience another time and place and another mode of being, but musical theatre releases a greater ability to feel the emotions of that time and place and to empathize with situations and characters. It is not surprising, therefore, that musical theatre's uplifting stories, happy endings and vibrant song, dance and spectacle that allow audiences to feel joyful, passionate and emotionally expansive are extremely popular. On the negative side, such events perhaps represent Adorno's nightmare vision of a manipulative sugarcoated popular entertainment. However, the audience's experience of 'Our Time' that occurs at the end of *Merrily We Roll Along* when the optimistic young people first meet, and which takes place at the end of a cynical and dramatic evening, is one of high emotion. The extremes are there – the optimism of youth and the cynicism of age – both embodied in the characters onstage and shared within the audience's listening bodies. This is the human experience of musical theatre, the ability to empathize, to experience high emotions and shattering events and to feel for others.

A community of spectators

One of the unique features of musical theatre, however, is that it is often performed by groups of people collectively, and it is watched/listened to by another group that is *interpellated* by the first (a kind of enforced involvement through witnessing). Victor Turner and Richard Schechner have documented the effect of ritual activities where everyone joins in a performance in a separate place and achieves a feeling of communitas as a result of the liminoid experience of being part of the community event. Attendance at the theatre can be perceived as a ritual event, since we dress differently, join in with other audience members, respond as required by convention (applauding, laughing, sitting silently, etc.), and all this takes place in a special separate place.

Many performances also actively seek to invoke audience response or draw on audience memory through the way the performance is structured, directed or designed. For example, in the original production of *A Chorus Line* (reworked in London in 2013) mirrors are lowered at an angle during the final scenes so that the audience sees itself reflected on the stage. Thus comments about participants in the scene appear to include the audience who also appears on the stage. The audience is both in front of and behind the scene taking place, encircling the performers and thus appearing to be more fully implicated in the narrative. In the 2006 Atlantic Theatre[1] production of *Spring Awakening* seats were sold for audience members to sit on the stage in groups on each side of the action – alongside the members of the company who returned to their seats when not being characters in the action.

In *Merrily We Roll Along* the onstage chorus has a particular role in relating to the audience – it sings together to the audience – one group to another, it moves together as a group and it offers the audience narrative information that these two groups share. So a direct relationship is created between audience and chorus who have different information from the characters, allowing them to share knowledge and experience as time reverses. The chorus keeps reminding the audience of the time frame and the transformations in the characters, warning the audience of how easily optimism and hope dissipate. The message of the musical is shared between chorus and audience even as the cynical catastrophe is enacted by the characters.

The performance of *Imago* by a chorus of 68 youth and amateur volunteers (from teenagers to septuagenarians), and 15 professional singers, 25 student orchestra members alongside 19 professionals of the Aurora orchestra, demonstrated a type of community involvement in the production and performance of a new work that impacted on the audience both through the recognition of individuals on the stage, and in the effect of the massed voices and instruments. People on the stage were 'people like us' and the level of performance as well as the immensity of the forces communicated itself to the audience who gave it a rapturous reception.

Fischer-Lichte proposed the term 'autopoiesis' to describe the feedback loop through which audiences and performers interact. Engaging in this feedback loop can lead to moments of enchantment through which hopeful feelings can emerge. These feelings are constantly developing as newly emerged, unplanned and unpredictable events occur, and it is the heightened awareness or sensitization within theatre, produced by dynamic events and transitions, that stimulates an ever-evolving dynamic sense of being in the world.

But this is not just theory – science has something to add here too. Mirror neurons don't only lead the audience to mirror the stage, but to mirror each other. Audiences are drawn into the emotions of a performance and respond. That sound feeds back into the performance; the roar of an audience's laughter derives from what the performers do, and the performers are affected in turn by the sound of the laughter, and so the performance achieves a new energy. Audiences also mirror each other; many people note that they're more likely to laugh out loud at a live performance where everyone else is laughing than in their own home watching television alone. So the experience of being in a community generates an increased energy in the performance and in the audience as a result of the circularity of mirroring. Clearly this can also go the other way and audiences can become increasingly flat and deflated, but the shared experience is likely to be greater than the individual one. Mirroring might partly explain the enormous energy that is experienced by audiences and performers who leave the theatre buzzing with excitement and on an emotional high.

But there is one more step. Christian Keyser (2010) explained that not only does doing an activity as a group (like singing in a choir or playing in an orchestra) activate the reward areas of the brain and bind the participants together – a process known as entrainment – but that sharing the experience of watching music and dance as a group could activate the same reward areas. Certainly science has now demonstrated that audiences can indeed experience the powerful emotions of musical theatre, and that the dopamine released in the brain as a result not only of the event, but also of the anticipation of this pleasure, can act as a tranquilizer removing or suppressing anxiety.

All these responses are subconscious, and audience members can choose to resist identification, but through this mirroring, audiences do more than understand the events of a plot; they empathetically sense the emotions portrayed and magnified in musical theatre, and they vicariously share these experiences with the performers and with each other. The singing of 'Our Time' provides the audience with the emotional stimulation of the music and the incitement to change the world articulated in the lyrics. These are the moments that allow audiences to experience other times and places, to identify with situations and characters with which they might never otherwise come into contact. Musical theatre thus has a central humanity in its optimistic stories, and the opportunity for community experience, that is amplified by the powerful emotions being expressed and by the way music increases and releases emotional freedom.

But does all this make it entertaining? At the start of this chapter we identified the problem that different people experience different events as entertaining and that this might depend on time, place, historical or geographical context and expectation of the event as much as on the dramatic work or the performance of that work. Instead of defining entertainment we have begun to think about the ways in which musical theatre impacts on its audiences, causing them to feel, to interact and potentially to be transformed. Is this what entertainment means? The experience can be overwhelming because of the excess of signification, because of the outpouring of emotion and because of the levels of sound and spectacle. This is an experience of sound, colour and light that, when it works well, raises the emotions and stimulates passionate responses. The proof is in every Broadway or West End theatre night after night, as audiences rise to their feet in rapturous applause in an excess of approbation and pleasure. When you add this experience of excessive performance to the content of the stories, empathy with characters and experience of community, it is clear why musical theatre stimulates passionate responses. It can be entertaining, popular, moving and memorable. It can also be crass, bland, reductive and simplistic; there are always flops and failures, and we all have different tastes and aesthetic parameters. What we're arguing here, though, is that the potential of musical theatre to reach out to audiences is extraordinary, and it is based on encouraging engagement in human relationships, awareness of community and the blissful loss of self in the experience of excess.

So the next time you think about the populist and commercial form of musical theatre, think too about the scale and complexity of the experience it provides; the awareness of humanity and community and the empathetic utopia that can result from being in the audience. We are all aware of the potential of theatre to transform participants through applied drama, but theatre has a transformative potential that extends way beyond the instrumentalist impacts with which it is most often credited. Theatre audiences can experience what Dolan (2005, p. 2) described as a momentary utopia 'embodied and passionate, [sharing] experiences of meaning making and imagination that can describe or capture fleeting intimations of a better world'. What we've been arguing here is that between empathy with characters and understanding of situations, in the gaps between meaning and interpretation and through the excesses of multiple performances, theatre audiences – and more specifically musical theatre audiences – can experience moments of hope at the theatre, feeling the flow of life and their own potential, that may indeed cause or inspire transformation.

Further reading – theoretical

Dolan, Jill (2005) *Utopia in Performance: Finding Hope at the Theatre* (Ann Arbor: University of Michigan Press).

Dyer, Richard (2008) *Only Entertainment*, second edition (London and New York: Routledge).

Fischer-Lichte, Erika (2008) *The Transformative Power of Performance: A New Aesthetics*, trans. Saskya Iris Jain (London and New York: Routledge).

McConachie, Bruce (2008) *Engaging Audiences: A Cognitive Approach to Spectating in the Theatre* (New York: Palgrave Macmillan).

Witkin, Robert W. (2003) *Adorno on Popular Culture* (London and New York: Routledge).

Further reading – relating to the examples

Dunnett, Roderic (2013) 'Imago, Glyndebourne Opera', *theartsdesk.com* website, 11 March, http://www.theartsdesk.com/opera/imago-glyndebourne-opera, accessed 19 August 2013.

Gordon, Joanne (1990) *Art Isn't Easy: The Theater of Stephen Sondheim* (Carbondale: Southern Illinois University Press).

Riis, Thomas L. (2008) *Frank Loesser* (Yale Broadway Masters) (New Haven: Yale University Press).

Notes

Chapter 2 'A Man Who Can Interpret Could Go Far': Semiotics and Semiology

1. Most song-sheet versions of this song write out the full phrase, following the way in which Elvis performed it.

Chapter 4 'Life Is a Cabaret': Cultural Materialism

1. The problematic use of pidgin English is one of the criticisms of this work in contemporary performances. A discussion of Orientalism and the representation of the 'other' is given in Chapter 5.

Chapter 5 'You've Got to Be Carefully Taught': Orientalism and Musical Theatre

1. We are grateful for the anonymous contributions made by the reviewers of this manuscript on this matter.
2. Sebesta discusses the ways in which Latinos/as are represented in Broadway musicals, and the lack of opportunities that stereotyping leads to for Latino/a performers.

Chapter 6 'I Wanna Be a Producer': Globalization, Capitalism and Consumerism

1. Walmart ($421.89 billion) is bigger than Norway ($414.46 billion) and, were it a country, would be the 25th biggest domestic economy in the world; Ford ($128.95 billion) trumps Morocco ($103.48 billion) and would be 60th; Microsoft ($62.48 billion) rivals Croatia ($60.59 billion) for the 66th place; McDonalds ($24.07 billion) just pips Latvia ($24.05 billion) to rank 92nd. These are just 4 of the 25 companies noted by *Business Insider* as having greater wealth in 2010 than whole countries. See http://www.businessinsider.com/25-corporations-bigger-tan-countries-2011–6?op=1, accessed 2 April 2013.
2. While Russell's experience is valid and speaks of the alienation of the worker, it has occasionally been challenged by other writers who describe the way performers can use their bodily presence to subvert a perceived lack of identity and creativity in performance.
3. One of the things that makes *The Lion King* interesting is the fact that it can be explored from a number of different perspectives. We can view it as a postmodern simulacrum of the savannah, weaving in theories that we discuss in Chapter 7; we can see it as a piece that responds to a late-twentieth-century fascination for world culture, and consider it using Edward Said's Orientalism,

which we discussed in Chapter 5; or we could look at it from any number of post-Marxist perspectives, recognizing it as a truly globalized example of musical theatre. In fact, a real consideration of globalization embraces all of these perspectives.

4. Jessica Sternfeld speculates that it could have been twice that.

Chapter 7 'What's the Buzz?': Meta-narratives and Post-linearity

1. Thirty-five years later, the satirical musical *Jerry Springer: The Opera* had a similar effect when screened by the BBC (see Chapter 12).
2. 'Love Is Like Oxygen' (Sweet), 'Love Is a Many-Splendored Thing' (The Four Aces), 'Up Where We Belong' (Joe Cocker and Jennifer Warnes), 'All You Need Is Love' (The Beatles), 'Lover's Game' (Chris Isaak), 'I Was Made for Lovin' You' (Kiss), 'One More Night' (Phil Collins), 'Pride (In the Name of Love)' (U2), 'Don't Leave Me This Way' (Harold Melvin and the Blue Notes), 'Silly Love Songs' (Paul McCartney and Wings), 'Heroes' (David Bowie), 'I Will Always Love You' (Dolly Parton), 'Your Song' (Elton John).
3. Philip Glass in particular has distanced himself from the term 'minimalism', which may have been coined by Michael Nyman. Glass refers to his music as having repetitive structures.
4. These numbers and symbols were initially aids to memory but became part of the text.

Chapter 8 'Marry the Man Today': Feminism and the Performance of Identity

1. We are grateful to the anonymous reviewer who drew this recording to our attention.
2. http://www.youtube.com/watch?v=YlYZZRMUsCg&list=PLC64453B075E4892 0, accessed 21 June 2013.

Chapter 9 'The Bitch of Living': Youth Cultures, Power and Sexuality

1. http://www.telegraph.co.uk/culture/music/classicalmusic/10588016/ The-history-girls-Canterbury-Cathedrals-first-girls-choir.html, accessed 28 January 2013.
2. All the references to boys' voices in the opera are drawn from an interview with Rachel Cowgill during the programme *About the Boys,* BBC Radio 4, 31 December 2013 (produced by Emma Kingsley).
3. There is an interesting connection here with the hysteria of women in Chapter 8. It is Flora who becomes mad, while Miles is represented as the stronger of the two, and he resists to the death.

Chapter 10 'I Am What I Am': Sexuality and Queer Theory

1. 'Rod on Republicans Not Seeing Avenue Q', YouTube, http://www.youtube. com/watch?v=F6tUV6omRIw, accessed 4 March 2013.

2. Popular music is central to this discourse, and critics have written eloquently about the various social connotations of disco (Dyer, 1992, pp. 151–160), rock (Frith and McRobbie, 1990, pp. 371–389) and the Broadway musical (Miller, 1998; Wolf, 2002).

Chapter 12   'I'm Just a Broadway Baby': Intertextuality in Music and Lyrics

1. We are grateful to an anonymous reviewer for drawing this to our attention.

Chapter 13   'Dreamgirls Will Make You Happy': The Pleasures of Voice and Body

1. We saw in the previous chapter that Roland Barthes described two different sorts of pleasure in relation to written texts: the text of pleasure and the text of bliss or *jouissance*.
2. http://www.youtube.com/watch?v=okTC1i8yKLw, accessed 19 July 2013.
3. http://www.youtube.com/watch?v=7lCd9mY1kIc, accessed 19 July 2013.
4. A concert performance by Jennifer Hudson is at http://www.youtube.com/watch?v=UrZTg-0Ozn0, accessed 19 July 2013, and one by Jennifer Holliday is at http://www.youtube.com/watch?v=OPwPN4xbt4M, accessed 19 July 2013.
5. http://www.youtube.com/watch?v=kJCg3055D7U, accessed 19 July 2013.
6. Only the A section is included in the online recording.

Chapter 14   'Make 'em Laugh': The Politics of Entertainment

1. New York. Directed by Michael Mayer, Choreographed by Bill T. Jones.

Bibliography

Abbate, Carolyn (2001) *In Search of Opera* (Princeton Studies in Opera) (Princeton, NJ, and Woodstock, Oxon: Princeton University Press).

Abbate, Claudia (1993) 'Opera, or, the Envoicing of Women', in Ruth Solie (ed.), *Musicology and Difference: Gender and Sexuality in Music Scholarship* (Berkeley, Los Angeles, and London: University of California Press), 225–258.

Abbate, Claudia and Roger Parker (2012) *A History of Opera: The Last 400 Years* (London and New York: Allen Lane).

Adler, Steven (2004) *On Broadway: Art and Commerce on the Great White Way* (Carbondale: Southern Illinois University Press).

Aristotle (1978) *Poetics* (London: J.M. Dent and Sons).

Arnold, Matthew (1869) *Culture and Anarchy: An Essay in Political and Social Criticism* (London: Smith, Elder).

Aston, Elaine and George Savona (1991) *Theatre as Sign-System: A Semiotics of Text and Performance* (London and New York: Routledge).

Aston, Elaine and Geraldine (Gerry) Harris (2006) 'Feminist Futures and the Possibilities of "We"?' in Elaine Aston and Geraldine Harris (eds), *Feminist Futures?* (Basingstoke and New York: Palgrave Macmillan), 1–16.

Ayers, Rick (2008) '*South Pacific* – Musical Orientalism', *The Huffington Post*, 1 May, http://www.huffingtonpost.com/rick-ayers-/emsouth-pacificem – – musI_b_99550.html, accessed 25 July 2013.

Banfield, Stephen (1994) *Sondheim's Broadway Musicals* (Ann Arbor: University of Michigan Press).

Barry, Peter (2002) *Beginning Theory* (second edition) (Manchester: Manchester University Press).

Barthes, Roland (1975) *The Pleasure of the Text*, trans. Richard Miller (New York: Hill and Wang).

——(1977) *Image, Music, Text*, trans. Stephen Heath (London: Fontana Press).

Baudrillard, Jean (1991) *Simulacra and Simulation*, trans. Sheila Faria Glaser (Ann Arbor: University of Michigan Press).

Baur, Steven, Raymond Knapp and Jacqueline Warwick (eds) (2008) *Musicological Identities: Essays in Honor of Susan McClary* (Hampshire: Ashgate).

Benjamin, Walter (1992) 'The Work of Art in the Age of Mechanical Reproduction', in Hannah Arendt (ed.), *Illuminations* [1955] (London: Fontana Press), 211–245.

Bennett, Susan (1997) *Theatre Audiences* (London: Routledge).

Berson, Misha (2011) *Something's Coming, Something Good: West Side Story and the American Imagination* (Milwaukee, WI: Applause Theatre and Cinema Books).

Block, Geoffrey (2009) *Enchanted Evenings: The Broadway Musical from Show Boat to Sondheim and Lloyd Webber* (second edition) (New York: Oxford University Press).

Booker, Christopher (2004) *The Seven Basic Plots: Why We Tell Stories* (London: Continuum).

Bourdieu, Pierre (1986) 'The Forms of Capital', in J. Richardson (ed.), *Handbook of Theory and Research for the Sociology of Education* (New York: Greenwood), 241–258.

Boyd, Michelle (2010) 'Alto on a Broomstick: Voicing the Witch in the Musical *Wicked*', *American Music* 28(1): 97–118.

Bradley, Ian (ed.) (2001) *The Complete Annotated Gilbert & Sullivan* (paperback edition) (Oxford: Oxford University Press).

Brantley, Ben (2013) 'High Spirits, Higher Heels', *The New York Times*, 4 April, http://theater.nytimes.com/2013/04/05/theater/reviews/kinky-boots-the-harvey-fierstein-cyndi-lauper-musical.html?_r=0, accessed 26 August 2013.

Brett, Philip (2006) *Music and Sexuality in Britten: Selected Essays* (Berkeley and Los Angeles: University of California Press).

Brook, Peter (1968) *The Empty Space* (London: Penguin Books).

Brooker, Peter (ed.) *Modernism/Postmodernism* (London and New York: Longman).

Burston, Jonathan (1997) 'Enter, Stage Right: Neoconservatism, English Canada and the Megamusical', *Soundings* 5: 179–190.

Butler, Judith (1993) *Bodies That Matter: On the Discursive Limits of Sex* (London: Routledge).

——(2010) *Gender Trouble: Feminism and the Subversion of Identity* (second edition) (New York and London: Routledge Classics).

Cahoone, Lawrence (ed.) (2003) *From Modernism to Postmodernism: An Anthology* (second, expanded edition) (Oxford: Blackwell).

Campbell, Neil (ed.) (2004) *American Youth Cultures* (Edinburgh: Edinburgh University Press).

Carlson, Marvin (2001) *The Haunted Stage: The Theatre as Memory Machine* (Ann Arbor: University of Michigan Press).

Carter, Tim (2007) *Oklahoma! The Making of an American Musical* (New Haven and London: Yale University Press).

Case, Sue-Ellen (2008) *Feminism and Theatre* (reissued edition) (Basingstoke and New York: Palgrave Macmillan).

Cavarero, Adriana (2005) *For More than One Voice* (Stanford: Stanford University Press).

Cleave, Maureen (1966) 'How Does a Beatle Live? John Lennon Lives Like This', *The London Evening Standard*, 4 March.

Clément, Catherine (1988) *Opera: Or the Undoing of Women*, trans. Betsy Wing [originally published Paris, 1979] (Minneapolis: University of Minnesota Press).

——(2000) 'Through Voices, History', in Mary Smart (ed.), *Siren Songs: Representation of Gender and Sexuality in Opera* (Princeton: Princeton University Press), 17–28.

Coleman, Bud and Judith Sebesta (2008) *Women in American Musical Theatre: Essays on Composers, Lyricists, Librettists, Arrangers, Choreographers, Designers, Directors, Producers and Performance Artists* (Jefferson, NC: McFarland).

Connor, Steven (2000) *Dumbstruck: A Cultural History of Ventriloquism* (Oxford: Oxford University Press).

—— (2004) *The Cambridge Companion to Postmodernism* (Cambridge: Cambridge University Press).

Cook, Susan C. (2009) 'Pretty Like the Girl: Gender, Race and *Oklahoma!*', *Contemporary Theatre Review* 19(1): 35–47.

Copeland, Roger (2012) 'Visionary Collaborations', Program Note to *Einstein on the Beach* at Brooklyn Academy of Music (Brooklyn: Brooklyn Academy of Music).

Counsell, Colin and Laurie Wolf (2001) *Performance Analysis: An Introductory Coursebook* (London and New York: Routledge).

De Beauvoir, Simone (1972) *The Second Sex* [originally published Paris: Gallimard, 1949] (Harmondsworth: Penguin).

Dean, Winton and John Merrill Knapp (1995) *Handel's Operas 1704–26* (Oxford: Clarendon Press).

Derrida, Jacques (1988) *The Ear of the Other: Otobiography, Transference, Translation: Texts and Discussions with Jacques Derrida*, ed. Christie V. Macdonald, trans. P. Kamuf [1985] (Lincoln, NE: University of Nebraska Press).

—— (1997) *Of Grammatology*, trans. Gayatri Chakravorty Spivak [1967] (Baltimore and London: Johns Hopkins University Press).

—— (2008) *Writing and Difference*, trans. Alan Bass [1967] (London and New York: Routledge).

Dinero, Dan (20120 'A Big Black Lady Stops the Show: Black Women, Performances of Excess and the Power of Saying No', *Studies in Musical Theatre* 6(1): 29–41.

Dolan, Jill (2005) *Utopia in Performance: Finding Hope at the Theatre* (Ann Arbor: University of Michigan Press).

Dorfman, Ariel and Armand Mattelart ([1971] 1991) *How to Read Donald Duck: Imperialist Ideology in the Disney Comic*, trans. David Kunzle (New York: International General).

Dunnett, Roderic (2013) 'Imago, Glyndebourne Opera', *theartsdesk.com*, 11 March, http://www.theartsdesk.com/opera/imago-glyndebourne-opera, accessed 19 August 2013.

Dyer, Richard (1992) *Only Entertainment* (second edition) (London and New York: Routledge).

Eden, David and Meinhard Saremba (2009) *The Cambridge Companion to Gilbert and Sullivan* (Cambridge Companions to Music) (Cambridge: Cambridge University Press).

Elan, Keir (1980) *The Semiotics of Theatre and Drama* (London: Methuen).

Engel, Lehman (1967) *The American Musical Theatre: A Consideration* (New York: Macmillan).

—— (2006) *Words with Music: Creating the Broadway Musical Libretto*, updated and revised by Howard Kissel (New York: Applause Theatre and Cinema Books).

Epstein, Jonathon S. (ed.) (1998) *Youth Culture: Identity in a Postmodern World* (Malden, MA, and Oxford: Blackwell).

Everett, William A. and Paul R. Laird (eds) (2008) *The Cambridge Companion to the Musical* (second edition) (Cambridge: Cambridge University Press).

Fanon, Frantz ([1961] 2004) *The Wretched of the Earth*, trans. Richard Philcox (New York: Grove Press).

Farber, Stephen (1975) 'Bob Fosse's Acid Valentine', *The New York Times*, 3 August: 91.

Fischer-Lichte, Erika (1997) *The Show and the Gaze of Theatre* (Iowa City: University of Iowa Press).

Ford, David (1988) 'Hands across the Sea', *Worcester Evening News*, 13 February.

Foucault, Michel (1985) *The History of Sexuality, Vol. II: The Use of Pleasure*, trans. Robert Hurley (Harmondsworth: Penguin).

—— (1986) 'We "Other Victorians"', in P. Rabinow, *The Foucault Reader* (Harmondsworth: Penguin).

Freshwater, Helen (2009) *Theatre & Audience* (Basingstoke: Palgrave Macmillan).

Friedan, Betty (1992) *The Feminine Mystique* [originally published W.W. Norton, 1963] (London: Penguin).

Frith, Simon and Angela McRobbie (1990) 'Rock and Sexuality', in Simon Frith and Andrew Goodwin (eds), *On Record* (London and New York: Routledge), 371–389.

Garber, Marjorie (1997) *Vested Interests: Cross-Dressing and Cultural Anxiety* (second edition) (New York and London: Routledge).

Garebian, Keith (2011) *The Making of Cabaret* (second edition) (New York: Oxford University Press).

Gerbino, Giuseppe (2002) 'Orientalism in *Madama Butterfly*', in *New York City Opera Project: Madama Butterfly*, http://www.columbia.edu/itc/music/NYCO/butterfly/luther.html, accessed 6 May 2013.

Gilbert, William Schwenk and Arthur Sullivan (1997) *The Complete Plays of Gilbert and Sullivan* (New York: W.W. Norton).

Glass, Philip (1978) 'Notes: Einstein on the Beach', *Performing Arts Journal* 2(3): 63–70.

——(1988) *Opera on the Beach* (London and Boston: Faber & Faber).

Goodhart, Sandor (ed.) (2000) *Reading Stephen Sondheim: A Collection of Critical Essays* (New York: Garland).

Gordon, Joanne (1990) *Art Isn't Easy: The Achievement of Stephen Sondheim* (Carbondale, IL: Southern Illinois University Press).

Greer, Germaine (1971) *The Female Eunuch* [originally published London: MacGibbon and Kee, 1970] (London: Paladin).

Grotowski, Jerzy (1968) *Towards a Poor Theatre* (New York: Simon and Shuster).

Guilbault, Jocelyne (2001) 'World Music', in *The Cambridge Companion to Pop and Rock* (Cambridge: Cambridge University Press).

Hadlock, Heather (2000) 'The Career of Cherubino, or the Trouser Role Grows Up', in Mary Ann Smart (ed.), *Siren Songs* (Princeton and Oxford: Princeton University Press), 67–92.

Hall, Catherine (2000) *Cultures of Empire: Colonizers in Britain and the Empire in the Nineteenth and Twentieth Centuries* (Manchester: Manchester University Press).

Hanisch, Carol (1970) 'The Personal Is Political', in S. Firestone and A. Koedt (eds), *Notes From the Second Year: Women's Liberation: Major Writings of the Radical Feminists* (New York: Radical Feminist).

Hebdige, Dick ([1988] 2002) *Hiding in the Light* (London and New York: Routledge).

Hoberman, J. (1993) *42nd Street* (BFI Film Classics) (London: British Film Institute).

Hoppe, Kirk A. (2005) 'Simulated Safaris: Reading African Landscapes in the US', in Klaus Benesch and Kerstin Schmidt (eds), *Space in America: Theory, History, Culture* (Amsterdam: Rodopi), 179–192.

Horkheimer, Max and Theodor Adorno (2007) *Dialectic of Enlightenment*, trans. Edmund Jephcott (Palo Alto, CA: Stanford University Press).

Howard, Patricia (1985) *The Turn of the Screw* (Cambridge Opera Handbooks) (Cambridge: Cambridge University Press).

Hunter, Mary (2008) *Mozart's Operas: A Companion* (New Haven and London: Yale University Press).

Hurd, R. Wesley (1998) 'Postmodernism', http://msc.gutenberg.edu/2001/02/postmodernism/, accessed 29 July 2013.

Isherwood, Charles (2007) 'From the Corner Bodega, the Music of Everyday Life', *The New York Times*, 9 February.

Jameson, Fredric (1991) *Postmodernism, or, the Cultural Logic of Late Capitalism* (Durham, NC: Duke University Press)

Jardine, Lisa (1999) 'Growing Up with Greer', *The Observer*, 7 March, http://www.guardian.co.uk/books/1999/mar/07/society, accessed 3 June 2013.

Jenkins, Chadwick (2002) 'The Original Story: John Luther Long and David Belasco', *New York City Opera Project: Madama Butterfly*, http://www.columbia.edu/itc/music/NYCO/butterfly/luther.html, accessed 6 May 2013.

Joe, Jeongwon (2013) 'The *Acousmêtre* on Stage and Screen: The Power of the Bodiless Voice', in Dominic Symonds and Pamela Karantonis (eds), *The Legacy of Opera: Reading Music Theatre as Experience and Performance* (Amsterdam: Rodopi).

Jones, John Bush (2003) *Our Musicals, Ourselves: A Social History of the American Musical Theatre* (Lebanon, NH: Brandeis University Press).

Karantonis, Pamela (2007) 'Takarazuka Is Burning: Music Theatre and the Performance of Sexual and Gender Identities in Modern Japan', *Studies in Musical Theatre* 1(2): 153–166.

Kerman, Joseph (1956) *Opera as Drama* (New York: Vintage Books).

Kerr, Walter (1975), ' "Chicago" Comes On Like Doomsday', *The New York Times*, 8 June: 109.

Keysers, Christian (2010) 'From Mirror Neurons to Kinaesthetic Empathy', Keynote Presentation, *Kinaesthetic Empathy: Concepts and Contexts*, Manchester University, 22–23 April.

Kidd, Kenneth B. (2004) 'Disney of Orlando's Animal Kingdom', in Sidney I. Dobrin and Kenneth B. Kidd (eds), *Wild Things: Children's Culture and Ecocriticism* (Detroit: Wayne State University Press), 267–288.

Kinder, Marsha (2002) 'Moulin Rouge', *Film Quarterly* 55(3): 52–59.

King, Thomas Alan (2008) *The Gendering of Men, 1600–1750: Queer Articulations, Volume 2* (London: University of Wisconsin Press).

Kinkade, Patrick T. and Michael A. Katovich (1992) 'Toward a Sociology of Cult Films: Reading *Rocky Horror*', *The Sociological Quarterly* 33(2): 191–209.

Kirle, Bruce (2005) *Unfinished Show Business: Broadway Musicals as Works-in Progress* (Carbondale: Southern Illinois University Press).

Klein, Christina (2003) *Cold War Orientalism: Asia in the Middlebrow Imagination* (Berkeley: University of California Press).

Knapp, Raymond (2005) *The American Musical and the Formation of National Identity* (Princeton: Princeton University Press).

Knapp, Raymond, Mitchell Morris and Stacy Wolf (eds) (2011) *The Oxford Handbook of the American Musical* (Oxford and New York: Oxford University Press).

Koestenbaum, Wayne (1993) *The Queen's Throat: Opera, Homosexuality, and the Mystery of Desire* (New York: Da Capo Press).

Kracauer, Siegfried ([1927] 1975) 'The Mass Ornament', *New German Critique* 5: 67–76.

——([1931] 1992) 'Girls and Crisis', trans. Courtney Federle, *Qui Parle* 5(2): 51–52.

Kristeva, Julia (1984) *Revolution in Poetic Language,* trans. Margaret Waller [1974] (New York: Columbia University Press).

Kroenert, Tim (2010) 'Imelda Marcos the Musical', *Eureka Street* 20(7): 29–30.

Lacan, Jacques (1977) *Écrits: A Selection*, trans. Alan Sheridan (London: Tavistock).

Lahr, John (1996) *Light Fantastic: Adventures in Theatre* (New York: Dial Press).

——(2002) *Show and Tell: New Yorker Profiles* (Berkeley and Los Angeles: University of California Press).

Laird, Paul (2011) *Wicked: A Musical Biography* (Lanham, MD, Toronto, Plymouth, UK: Scarecrow Press)

Langley, Carol (2006) 'Borrowed Voice: The Art of Lip-Synching in Sydney Drag', *Australasian Drama Studies* 48: 5–17

Lee, Charles (2008) *Cameron Mackintosh and the McDonaldization of Musical Theatre Marketing* (PhD Thesis) (London: University of London).

Lehmann, Hans-Thies (2006) *Postdramatic Theatre* (New York and Abingdon: Routledge).

Leve, James (2009) *Kander and Ebb* (New Haven: Yale University Press).

Lewis, Jon (2004) 'The Body's in the Trunk: (Re-)presenting Generation X', in Neil Campbell (ed.), *American Youth Cultures* (Edinburgh: Edinburgh University Press), 182–208.

Lincoln, Siân (2013) ' "You Don't Own Me!": *Dirty Dancing* as Teenage Rite-of-Passage Film', in Yannis Tzioumakis and Siân Lincoln (eds), *The Time of Our Lives: Dirty Dancing and Popular Culture* (Detroit: Wayne State University Press), 167–182.

Lovensheimer, Jim (2010) *South Pacific: Paradise Rewritten* (New York: Oxford University Press).

Lundskaer Nielson, Miranda (2008) *Directors and the New Musical Drama: British and American Musical Theatre in the 1980s and 1990s* (New York: Palgrave Macmillan).

Lyotard, Jean-François ([1979] 1984) *The Postmodern Condition: A Report on Knowledge*, trans. Geoff Bennington and Brian Massumi (Minneapolis: University of Minnesota Press).

Magee, Gary B. and Andrew S. Thompson (2010) *Empire and Globalisation: Networks of People, Goods and Capital in the British World, c. 1850–1914* (Cambridge: Cambridge University Press).

Marks, Peter (2013) ' "Book of Mormon" Restores Faith in Musicals', *The Washington Post*, 12 July, http://www.washingtonpost.com/entertainment/theater_dance/book-of-mormon-restores-faith-in-musicals/2013/07/11/f965037a-ea68–11e2–818e-aa29e855f3ab_story.html, accessed 26 August 2013.

Marx, Karl (1904) *A Contribution to the Critique of Political Economy*, trans. N.I. Stone (Chicago: Charles H. Kerr).

——(1975) *Collected Works, Volume VI* (Moscow).

——(2008) *The Communist Manifesto*, trans. Samuel Moore (London: Pluto Press).

——(2009) *Das Kapital: The Critique of Political Economy* (Washington, DC: Regnery).

Mast, Gerald (1987) *Can't Help Singin'. The American Musical on Stage and Screen* (Woodstock, NY: Overlook Press).

McClary, Susan (1991) *Feminine Endings: Music, Gender and Sexuality* (Minneapolis: University of Minnesota Press).

McConachie, Bruce A. (1994) 'The "Oriental" Musicals of Rodgers and Hammerstein and the US War in Southeast Asia', *Theater Journal* 46(3) (October): 385–398.

McGinley, Phyllis and Nathaniel Benchley (1959) 'Loafing: Two Points of View', *Life*, 28 December.

McMillin, Scott (2006) *The Musical as Drama* (Princeton: Princeton University Press).

McQuillan, Martin (ed.) (2000) *The Narrative Reader* (Abingdon and New York: Routledge).

McRobbie, Angela (2009) *The Aftermath of Feminism: Gender, Culture and Social Change* (London: Sage).

Middleton, Richard (1990) *Studying Popular Music* (Milton Keynes: Open University Press).

Miller, D.A. (1998) *Place for Us: Essay on the Broadway Musical* (Cambridge, MA: Harvard University Press).

Mills, Sara (2003) *Michel Foucault* (London and New York: Routledge).

Mordden, Ethan (1983) *Broadway Babies: The People Who Made the American Musical* (Oxford and New York: Oxford University Press).

——(2003) *One More Kiss: The Broadway Musical in the 1970s* (Basingstoke and New York: Palgrave Macmillan).

Morris, Mitchell and Raymond Knapp (2011) 'Singing', in Raymond Knapp, Mitchell Morris and Stacy Wolf (eds), *The Oxford Handbook of The American Musical* (Oxford and New York: Oxford University Press), 320–334.

Most, Andrea (2000) ' "You've Got to Be Carefully Taught"': The Politics of Race in Rodgers and Hammerstein's South Pacific', *Theater Journal* 52(3) (October): 307–337.

Munford, Rebecca (2007) ' "Wake Up and Smell the Lipgloss": Gender, Generation and the (A)politics of Girl Power', in Stacy Gillis, Gillian Howie and Rebecca Munford (eds), *Third Wave Feminism: A Critical Exploration* (second edition) (Basingstoke: Palgrave Macmillan), 266–282.

Nayak, Anoop and Mary Jane Kehily (2008) *Gender, Youth and Culture: Young Masculinities and Femininities* (Basingstoke: Palgrave Macmillan).

Nelson, Steve (1995) 'Broadway and the Beast: Disney Comes to Times Square', *TDR* 39(2) (T146): 71–85.

Noonan, Ellen (2011) *The Strange Career of Porgy and Bess: Race, Culture, and America's Most Famous Opera* (Chapel Hill: University of North Carolina Press).

O'Flaherty, Mark C. (2013) '*Einstein on the Beach*, 1976–2013', *Civilian: Global Intelligence, Style and Culture*, 9 January, http://civilianglobal.com/arts/review-philip-glass-einstein-on-the-beach-amsterdam-2013/, accessed 29 July 2013.

Pavis, Patrice (1982) *Languages of the Stage: Essays in the Semiology of the Theatre*, trans. various (New York: Performing Arts Journal).

—— (ed.) (1996) *The Intercultural Performance Reader* (London and New York: Routledge).

Peck, Ellen Marie (2009) ' "Ah, Sweet Mystery": Rediscovering Three Female Lyricists of the Early Twentieth-Century American Musical Theater', *Contemporary Theatre Review* 19(1): 48–60.

Poizat, Michel (1992) *The Angel's Cry: Beyond the Pleasure Principle in Opera*, trans. Arthur Denner (Ithaca and London: Cornell University Press).

Potter, John (ed.) (2000) *The Cambridge Companion to Singing* (Cambridge: Cambridge University Press).

——(2006) *Vocal Authority: Singing Style and Ideology* (paperback edition) (Cambridge: Cambridge University Press).

Powils-Okano, Kimiyo (1986) *Puccinis Madama Butterfly* (Bonn: Verlag für systematische Musikwissenschaft).

Rebellato, Dan (2009) *Theatre & Globalization* (Basingstoke: Palgrave Macmillan).

Rice, Tim and Andrew Lloyd Webber (1970) *Jesus Christ Superstar: The Authorised Version* (London: Pan Books).

Ritzer, George (2011) *The McDonaldization of Society* (Thousand Oaks: Pine Forge Press).

Rodgers, Richard and Oscar Hammerstein II (n.d.) *Six Plays by Rodgers and Hammerstein* (New York: Modern Library).

Rooney, David (2007) 'Tunes Offer Fresh New Voice with a Latin Beat', *Variety*, 12 February: 52–54.

Rosselli, John (2000) 'Song into Theatre: The Beginnings of Opera', in John Potter (ed.), *The Cambridge Companion to Singing* (Cambridge: Cambridge University Press), 83–95.

Rossi, Roberto (1998) 'Times Square and Potsdamer Platz: Packaging Development as Tourism', *TDR* 42(1) (T157): 43–48.

Russell, Susan (2006) 'The Performance of Discipline on Broadway', *Studies in Musical Theatre* 1(1): 97–108.

Rutherford, Susan (2013) *Verdi, Opera, Women* (Cambridge: Cambridge University Press).

Said, Edward (1978) *Orientalism* (London: Routledge and Kegan Paul).

Sandell, J. (2010) 'Transnational Ways of Seeing: Sexual and National Belonging in *Hedwig and the Angry Inch*', *Gender, Place and Culture* 17(2): 231–247.

Sandoval Sanchez, Alberto (1994) '*West Side Story*: A Puerto Rican Reading of "America"', *Jump Cut: A Review of Contemporary Media* 39: 59–66.

Sater, Steven and Duncan Sheik (2007) *Spring Awakening: A New Musical* (New York: Theatre Communications Group).

Saunders, Robert J. (1987) 'American Gothic and the Division of Labor', *Art Education*, May: 6–11.

Savage, Jon (2007) *Teenage: The Creation of Youth 1875–1945* (London: Chatto and Windus).

Savran, David (2004) 'Towards a Historiography of the Popular', *Theatre Survey* 45(2): 211–217.

——(2009) *Highbrow/Lowdown: Theater, Jazz, and the Making of the New Middle Class* (Ann Arbor: University of Michigan Press).

—— (2012) 'Outsourcing Broadway', paper presented at 'Song, Stage and Screen VII: The Musical's Global Conquest' conference, University of Groningen, The Netherlands, 4 July.

Schechner, Richard (2006) *Performance Studies: An Introduction* (second edition) (Abingdon and New York: Routledge).

Scott, Derek B. (1997) 'Orientalism and Musical Style', *Critical Musicology: A Transdisciplinary Online Journal*, http://www.leeds.ac.uk/music/Info/critmus/articles/1997/02/01.html, accessed 2 May 13.

Sebesta, Judith (2007) 'Just "Another Puerto Rican with a Knife"? Racism and Reception on the "Great White Way"', *Studies in Musical Theatre* 1(2): 183–197.

—— (2013) 'Angry Dance: Postmodern Innovation, Masculinities and Gender Subversion', in Dominic Symonds and Millie Taylor (eds), *Gestures of Music Theater: The Performativity of Song and Dance* (Oxford and New York: Oxford University Press), 146–160.

Seeley, J.R. (2010) *The Expansion of England: Two Courses of Lectures* (Cambridge: Cambridge University Press).

Seldes, Gilbert (1957) *The Seven Lively Arts* (New York: Sagamore Press).

Seymour, Claire (2007) *The Operas of Benjamin Britten: Expression and Evasion* (Woodbridge, Suffolk: Boydell Press).

Smart, Mary Ann (ed.) (2000) *Siren Songs: Representations of Gender and Sexuality in Opera* (Princeton and Oxford: Princeton University Press).

States, Bert O. (1995) 'The Actor's Presence: Three Phenomenal Modes', in Philip Zarrilli (ed.), *Acting (Re)Considered* (London and New York: Routledge), 22–42.

Sternfeld, Jessica (2006) *The Megamusical* (Profiles in Popular Music) (Bloomington, IN: Indiana University Press).

Storey, John (2006) *Cultural Theory and Popular Culture: A Reader* (third edition) (Harlow: Pearson Education).

Strauss, E. (2012) 'How Madonna Defines the Third Wave', *Jezebel.com*, 28 February.

Sussman, Mark (1998) 'New York's Facelift', *TDR* 42(1) (T157): 34–42.

Swayne, Stephen (2005) *How Sondheim Found His Sound* (Ann Arbor: University of Michigan Press).

Symonds, Dominic (2007) 'The Resistible Rise of Jerry Springer: How an Opera Revived the Polemical Stage', in Chris Westgate (ed.), *Brecht, Broadway and United States Theater* (Newcastle: Cambridge Scholars), 146–165.

Symonds, Dominic and Millie Taylor (eds) (2014) *Gestures of Music Theater: The Performativity of Song and Dance* (New York: Oxford University Press).

Taylor, Dianna (ed.) (2011) *Michel Foucault: Key Concepts* (Durham: Acumen).

Taylor, Millie (2010) 'Experiencing Live Musical Theatre Performance: *La Cage aux Folles* and *Priscilla, Queen of the Desert*', *Popular Entertainment Studies* 1(1): 44–58.

—— (2011) *Musical Theatre, Realism and Entertainment* (Ashgate Interdisciplinary Studies in Opera) (Farnham and Burlington, VT: Ashgate).

Thielman, Sam (2007) 'It's Mr Rogers' Barrio in Song', *Newsday*, 9 February: B7.

Thorncroft, Antony (1988) 'Carried Away by the Cash', *Financial Times*, 6 February.

Till, Nicholas (ed.) (2012) *The Cambridge Companion to Opera Studies* (Cambridge: Cambridge University Press).

Titrington Craft, Elizabeth (2011) ' "Is This What It Takes Just to Make It to Broadway?!": Marketing *In the Heights* in the Twenty-First Century', *Studies in Musical Theatre* 5 (1): 49–70.

Tzioumakis, Yannis and Sian Lincoln (eds) (2013) *The Time of Our Lives: Dirty Dancing and Popular Culture* (Detroit, MI: Wayne State University Press).

Wagner, Richard (1993) *The Art-Work of the Future and Other Works*, trans. W. Ashton Ellis (Lincoln, NE, and London: University of Nebraska Press).

—— (1995) *Opera and Drama*, trans. W. Ashton Ellis (Lincoln, NE, and London: University of Nebraska Press).

Warner, Marina (1995) *From the Beast to the Blond* (London: Vintage).

Wedekind, Frank (2009) *Spring Awakening*, trans. Edward Bond [1980] (London: Methuen Drama).

Wells, Elizabeth (2010) *West Side Story: Cultural Perspectives on an American Musical* (Lanham, MD, Toronto, Plymouth, UK: Scarecrow Press)

Whalen, Lauren (2013) 'Review: Anything Goes (Broadway in Chicago)', *Chicago Theater Beat*, http://chicagotheaterbeat.com/2013/04/27/review-anything-goes-broadway-in-chicago/#review, accessed 26 August 2013.

Wickstrom, Maurya (1999) 'Commodities, Mimesis and The Lion King: Retail Theatre for the 1990s', *Theatre Journal* 51 (3): 285–298.

——(2005) '*The Lion King*, Mimesis, and Disney's Magical Capitalism', in Mike Budd and Max H. Kirsch (eds), *Rethinking Disney: Private Control, Public Dimensions* (Middletown, CT: Wesleyan University Press), 99–121.

Wickware, Francis Sill (1948) 'Report on Kinsey', *Life*, 2 August.

Willett, John (1978) *Brecht on Theatre: The Development of an Aesthetic* (new edition) (London: Methuen).

—— (ed.) (1993) *Brecht on Theatre: The Development of an Aesthetic* (London: Methuen).

Williams, Patrick and Laura Chrisman (1994) *Colonial Discourse and Post-Colonial Theory: A Reader* (New York: Columbia University Press).

Williams, Raymond (1987) *Culture and Society: Coleridge to Orwell* (London: Hogarth Press).

——(2001) *The Long Revolution* (Letchworth: Broadview Press).

Wilson, Michael (2006) *Storytelling and Theatre: Contemporary Storytellers and Their Art* (Basingstoke: Palgrave Macmillan).

Wilson, Robert (2012) *Program Note to Einstein on the Beach at Brooklyn Academy of Music* (Brooklyn: Brooklyn Academy of Music).

Wilson-Kovacs, Dana (2001) 'The Fabric of Love', in Backett-Milburn and Linda McKie (eds), *Constructing Gendered Bodies* (Basingstoke: Palgrave Macmillan).

Wolf, Stacy (2002) *A Problem Like Maria: Gender and Sexuality in the American Musical* (Ann Arbor: University of Michigan Press).

—— (2008) 'Defying Gravity: Queer Conventions in the Musical *Wicked*', *Theatre Journal* 60: 1–21.

—— (2011) *Changed for Good: A Feminist History of the Broadway Musical* (Oxford and New York: Oxford University Press).

Woll, Allen (1989) *Black Musical Theatre: From Coontown to Dreamgirls* (New York: Da Capo Press).

Wollman, Elizabeth L. (2006) *The Theatre Will Rock: A History of the Rock Musical: From Hair to Hedwig* (Ann Arbor: University of Michigan Press).

—— (2012) *Hard Times: The Adult Musical in 1970s New York City* (Oxford: Oxford University Press).

Zadan, Craig (1994) *Sondheim & Co.* (second edition) (New York: Da Capo Press).

Zipes, Jack (1991) *Fairy Tales and the Art of Subversion* (New York: Routledge).

Žižek, Slavoj (1997) *The Plague of Fantasies* (London and New York: Verso).

Zuccarini, Carlo (2014) 'The (Un)Pleasure of Song: On the Enjoyment of Listening to Opera', in Dominic Symonds and Millie Taylor (eds), *Gestures of Music Theater: The Performativity of Song and Dance* (New York: Oxford University Press), 22–36.

Index

Note: Page numbers in semibold refer to text boxes.